LOVE'S SILENT GIFT

LOVE'S SILENT GIFT

LEONORA PRUNER

BETHANY HOUSE PUBLISHERS

MINNEAPOLIS, MINNESOTA 55438

A Division of Bethany Fellowship, Inc.

The author wishes to express appreciation to George Gallup, Jr. and William Proctor for extensive research into people's near-death experiences which was published in "Adventures in Immortality" by McGraw-Hill.

Published by Bethany House Publishers
A Division of Bethany Fellowship, Inc.
6820 Auto Club Road, Minneapolis, Minnesota 55438

Printed in the United States of America

Library of Congress Cataloging-in-Publication Data

Pruner, Leonora, 1931-
   Love's silent gift.

   I. Title.
PS3566.R83L7 1987   813'.54   87-15767
ISBN 0-87123-928-0 (pbk.)

To my children and their spouses,
whose love and encouragement were essential.

Mark and Trish,
Andy and Deborah.

LEONORA PRUNER was born in Iowa and moved to California at the age of twelve. She received degrees from John Muir College, Westmont College and an MBA from Pepperdine. Her writings include articles for *World Vision Magazine*, *Presbyterian Life*, and *Athletes in Action* and short stories. She lives in Santa Barbara, California, and has a grown son and daughter.

One

*I*f you look ahead, girls, *that* one is owned by Lord Omsbridge. The one with the ugly gargoyles," announced Lady Patty Morton with a flutter of her hand.

As Angelea gazed obediently at the designated London residence, the pretty dark-haired young lady beside her in the open carriage dug her elbow sharply into Angelea's ribs.

"Is he someone important, Aunt Patty?" she inquired, stoically bearing the discomfort without flinching.

"Oh, he is quite the scandal of Society. He is known as 'the Blue Devil'!"

Angelea giggled. "What a funny name."

"He has ruined countless men and women without the least scruple. They say he is totally without conscience. But he is immensely wealthy, and the old king likes him, because of his father I should imagine, and so he must be received." She finished with a sigh and shake of her head. "There, on the corner, is Admiral Byng's house. He is a very gallant gentleman, though often away at sea."

The stately old conveyance rumbled around the large fenced park centering the square. The trees cast inviting pools of shade in the warm July sunlight.

"This is such a lovely select place, I think it a terrible shame that those horrid things should be the first one sees when coming this way," Lady Patty added, gesturing back toward the gargoyles. "And, of course, no one comes from the other side, for then one should pass through Mayfair, which no one does. Money and influence can achieve most any end, even the presence of gargoyles in the square."

"Oh, girls, there he is now!" she exclaimed, suddenly flustered.

Angelea and her friend twisted around to see a smart blue cabriolette draw up before the leering gargoyles. The driver handed the reins to his groom in blue livery, and stepped down from the high seat with surprising ease. As he approached the door, it swung open and Angelea could make out a dim form inside.

Although she could not see details at this distance, she was certain his dark blue coat was of the best cut and material. From his straight posture, she knew he must be unbearably arrogant. Undoubtedly, beneath his white wig, his hair was jet black and his face swarthy. Very likely a silvered scar marred one cheek, a reminder of a duel when he killed his man.

The door closed, and the girls turned back to face the two women.

Angelea tucked a stray golden curl under her chip hat, trimmed with a fashionable mass of pink ribbons. "Why would no one pass through Mayfair?" she asked, widening her brown eyes innocently.

Lady Patty smiled and patted Angelea's knee affectionately. "Because Mayfair is populated by thieves and cutthroats. Girls"—her tone became severe—"never go there. It would certainly cost you your virtue, and possibly your life."

"Do attend your aunt, Angelea," added Lady Anne Byngstone as if aware her daughter was already considering a means to investigate the forbidden area. "London is not like Surrey. There are delightful events to attend, but you may not roam as freely as at home."

"That is so true!" exclaimed Helen Mason, at Angelea's side. A vigorous nod of her head set her glossy black curls to bouncing. "You remember Miss Mamesom, she was presented when we were, the one with all those pearls?"

Angelea nodded.

"She was accosted but a fortnight past when returning from Richmond. It was only the timely arrival of several men of the ton that saved her."

"Oh, Anne," moaned Lady Patty, "I do so regret that your presence was required in Surrey after Angelea's presentation. She made an excellent impression. His Majesty even inquired after her identity, and the Prince, young George, smiled. Such a shame she could not be here for these last six weeks. They have been quite the gayest in years."

Angelea heartily agreed with her aunt. She well knew the "emergency" at home had been a ploy to remove her from most of the season's activities. On overhearing her parents discussing their intention to permit her only the last three weeks for her first season, she had burst in upon them. "I agree, she is yet too young," Lady Anne was saying when Angelea interrupted, imploring them to relent. To her amazement, for the first time in memory, they steadfastly refused her tearful pleas.

She had chafed and wailed over this outrageous treatment to Simmons, her governess, who merely endorsed her parents' decision. They were trying to spare her the pain of exposure to heartless fortune hunters, she told Angelea. Presumably, in another year she would be better equipped to handle them. Helen was fortunate not to have such overprotective parents. Or was it because her fortune was less attractive?

"You will see what I mean at the Barringtons' ball tonight," Aunt Patty assured her. "The best of society will be there, with a few others, of course. One cannot escape them altogether, more's the pity. But it shall be an event where you will meet many gentlemen of the finest families."

After dinner, Angelea and Helen escaped to the shade of an oak tree in Aunt Patty's garden for a private chat until the Mason's carriage should call for her.

"I missed you so sorely!" Helen exclaimed, embracing Angelea. "I had no one to talk to, and there has been so much to tell!"

"I read your letters again and again. How I longed to be here with you!" Angelea sighed wistfully. "Is Tommy still tiresome?"

"Oh yes. He tries to give the impression that you are virtually promised to him already."

"Surely he realized Papa would not approve for all the time we've known each other. Nor would I accept him. I should like someone more exciting, whom I do not know quite so well. And who is not so foolish."

"Who knows the ways of the ton, who is both masterful and tender," agreed Helen.

"Exactly. Now, what was special about the house with the gargoyles?" asked Angelea.

"That is where *he* lives."

"He? Lord Oxbridge?"

"*Omsbridge*. He is wealthy beyond belief, not yet married, though ever so many have tried to fix his attention. They say he has no real affection, and is a known rake, quite *evil*!"

"Evil? And you are interested in him?"

"Oh yes!" Helen clasped her hands, her dark eyes shining. "As you know, it only takes the right woman to settle a man down. I danced with him once, and he is perfection."

"And what does your mother say?"

Helen's enthusiasm vanished. "That we must on no account associate with him. I was only able to dance with him that once because she was diverted from my side for a few minutes. Such a great scold she gave me afterwards! But it was a small price to pay for that glorious dance. He's had ever so many mistresses and it's even said he killed a man in a duel some years ago, although no one really knows.''

"I daresay his charm is due to his evil reputation," Angelea observed primly. "And I should love to meet him," she finished with a giggle. "Is he also handsome?"

"Not very, a little. Quite ordinary beside his friend Sir Deuxbury. Now there is a man with the profile of a Greek god! Can you imagine Miss Mamesom's good fortune? The men who rescued her were led by Sir Deuxbury. He pledged her to secrecy, but I teased it out of her. He doesn't want it known that he is a daring swordsman, but she said he and his friends fought off the criminals fiercely."

"And was Lord—Lord Omsbridge with them?"

"No. He has been at his home in Sussex these three weeks. I feared he would not return before the Season ended, and I should not see him until next year. But he is back, as you saw!"

"You will point him out to me tonight?"

"Oh yes. I am sure you will find him as attractive as I do. However, I suppose we must look for husbands elsewhere, someone quite unexceptional and boring."

"You know, of course, that my wretched parents have decided I am not to marry this year. They claim I am too young and innocent and that they only have regard for my happiness. Parents can make the most odious, unfair decisions sound so virtuous! And it's only because Papa was very old and Mama in her third season when they met."

"Your mother in her *third* season!" exclaimed Helen. "But she is beautiful!"

"Papa was not the first to offer for her. She refused all the others, being of high principles. I shan't let a few principles stand in my way."

"Nor I," Helen agreed. "I am eager to manage my own household, to drive in my own carriage, and order the dresses I choose."

"But, Helen, dearest," Angelea objected, struck with an unpleasant thought, "what if our husbands do not live near each other? We may be together but very rarely!"

"We shall contrive," Helen assured her. "We always do."

Two

*O*msbridge must have an heir, mused Lord Omsbridge as he mounted the Barringtons' steps, lit by flaming torches. Still pondering his problem, and barely aware of the bowing lackies to whom he gave his cloak and tricorn, he paused to adjust the thin black solitaire ribbon tied at his throat and shake the French lace out from the sleeve of his royal blue satin coat.

The demands of Omsbridge were not to be regarded lightly. His ancestors had protected and embellished that particular hill in Sussex since King Henry V rewarded Edmund Westover's great valor at Agincourt with a knighthood and the hand of the young widow of the Earl of Omsbridge along with his holdings. Personal considerations were always set aside to assure the continuation and improvement of the Hall and its lands. Even Louis XV's rumored invasion posed a lesser threat to the estate than the lack of an heir. Pitt's proposed militia would take care of the French, but only Lord Omsbridge could produce an heir.

His haughty manner on entering the crowded ballroom gave not the slightest hint of his unhappy inner turmoil. He scarcely heeded either his own words or those of the persons he addressed in passing from one acquaintance to another. The familiar atmosphere of fashionable people absorbed in pursuing pleasure emphasized the depressing mood haunting him since leaving Sussex.

His mood was brought about by a brief consultation on the previous day with Eldridge, his businessman, before leaving Omsbridge. Having finally discharged the last of the deceased lord's heavy obligations, Eldridge had said, "Your skill with cards and understanding of wise

11

investments have brought the estate from the edge of disaster to a fairly safe position. If we continue as we have done, in time it will even be in a sound position, for the first time in thirty years. Now, it is time, milord, that you settled on a lady of good family and concentrated on producing an heir."

Lord Omsbridge had tried to dismiss this with a wave of his hand. "In good time, my dear Eldridge, in good time."

The spare little man leaned his elbows on the cleared space before him and peered earnestly at his master over the clutter of papers and books covering his desk. "So you have long declared." A worried frown creased his forehead. "To put it bluntly, you are not becoming more youthful as the days pass. Should you become involved in a fatal accident while racketing around, Omsbridge would go to"—his voice had quavered as he finished—"to Frederick."

"Who is barely this side of Bedlam and certainly incapable of producing an heir," Lord Omsbridge had finished for him.

"Precisely." Eldridge pulled on the long nose dominating his freckled face. "You have been on the town these ten years, milord, and you have scattered your oats far and wide."

Omsbridge smiled tolerantly. "Neatly put for one who never fails to speak his mind."

"The reason you stated you liked my services," Eldridge reminded him.

"Oh yes, I do recall some such foolish remark." Eldridge had come to his attention while they were Oxford undergraduates. The loyal servitor possessed generous gifts of intelligence and uncommon understanding. When the former servitor, inherited from his father, sickened and died, Omsbridge knew of none better to bring his father's confused affairs into order than the poor scholar from Lincoln. It proved a wise choice.

"Believe me, Eldridge, I am entirely in agreement with you. However, I have yet to meet a lady, any female, who does not shortly prove tiresome." *And untrustworthy*, he added to himself. "If she is blessed with a fair face, her mind is small. If she has intelligence, she resembles the offspring of a mare. I have no desire to propagate either stupidity or ugliness in a world where both are in lamentable abundance already."

Eldridge bobbed his grizzle wigged head in understanding. "You have known a number of ladies, er, rather well. Is there not one whom you can, er, respect?"

"None!" was the prompt response.

"I see." Eldridge had picked up a quill and brushed the feather across his palm several times. "Then, you may have to settle for less. May I speak plainly?"

"I can think of no way to prevent it."

"Very well, milord. I visited your Cousin Frederick last week. And, well, I could not sleep for several nights afterwards. It would be disastrous should your estates fall into his hands. Hundreds of years of careful, of—of *sacrificial* management would be wasted by an incompetent . . ." Tears had filled his eyes.

Cyprian sighed. Eldridge was right. But to have an heir, he must be married. An estimable peer came into his view, well regarded by society. Descended from one of Charles II's notorious affairs, he was living proof that bloodlines were of prime importance, even if unblessed by the church.

He knew of no woman of good family who in her soul was not a materialistic schemer, faithful only to her own desires, and wholly undependable. Having indulged in numerous affairs, he had ample reason to fear being a cuckolded husband and an object of malicious gossip.

The sins of Omsbridge flashed across his mind and with it the image of the strange fanatic he saw at the weathered Paxwell Cross on his way to London. He had paused to listen, curious about what attracted the shabby crowd.

Although the man wore a plain cravat, not a clergyman's squared tabs, his manner evidenced that he considered himself a preacher of sorts. Fervently, in a loud, clear voice, the thin man in black proclaimed, "Your sins are an affront against the Almighty God." He pointed a boney index finger upward. "He will not long countenance such behavior. Repent! Repent!" Authoritatively he jabbed his finger at someone in the audience with each "repent."

For one jarring moment he pointed directly at Omsbridge, evoking shuddering chill. He was almost tempted to join the jeering group that began pelting the man with rocks, but such action was beneath his dignity. Enough to let others do it for him. If Rev. Pettigrew ever dared speak in such a manner in the parish church, it would cost him the preferment. Omsbridge sought to banish the condemning image from his memory with a sharp shake of his head. Probably that foolish man labeled any pleasure as a sin. The glittering throng tonight would likely be castigated as—

"Cyprian, my dear!" A plump lady arrayed in puce and an abundance of bouncing ruffles patted his arm to gain his attention.

"Aunt Matilda! Forgive my rudeness. I was, er, thinking."

"I understand, my dear. Such an effort! Come, I want you to meet your Cousin Agatha. I promised her mother I would sponsor her this season. And, of course, it would not be complete without meeting you."

Obediently, Cyprian followed his aunt and suffered through her introduction to a well-formed girl of proper and pleasing manner. For his aunt's sake, he danced with the girl but was utterly bored by her silly chatter. She would not do.

Critically, he assessed every female in sight, along with his extensive recollections of those absent. Bloodlines, physical appearance, intelligence, temperament, and dependability. None passed on all counts. None was fit to wear the Omsbridge sapphires.

Only a week ago Eldridge had displayed the sparkling necklace in its velvet case on his return from the jewelers. The piece dated back to the days of Queen Elizabeth. At that time the first Viscount of Omsbridge had presented the jewels to his young bride as a gift of love. Ever since then, Lady Omsbridge was known for beauty and virtue—save for Cyprian's recently deceased mother. He winced and blocked her mocking memory from his mind. He had sent the jewels to be cleaned in an effort to remove her stains.

His lady must be different. It was imperative that she restore virtue and dignity to his house. However, he could see she was not present in this assemblage.

Seeing Sir Anthony Deuxbury, Cyprian delayed the problem for another day with a shrug. Over his friend's shoulder he noticed two strange women, the center of attention for several men of the ton. In fact, Anthony was leaving this interesting group. Mildly curious, Cyprian raised his quizzing glass to better examine the ladies.

The older was obviously the mother or guardian of the younger. The latter held his gaze. *Exquisite, fragile, dainty, charming* led a multitude of adjectives flooding his mind. As an animated porcelain figurine, she fluttered her pink lace fan and smiled sweetly at those about her. She embodied purity and radiated a—he groped for an adequate expression—splendor. Purity and splendor.

The words suddenly triggered an overwhelming yearning for that long-forgotten moment in the new Jesuit church in Lucerne. Briefly he had felt a healing Presence restore his shattered life in the purity and splendor of that place. The transitory emotion dissipated over the ensuing months of his Grand Tour. He craved that experience again. Perhaps, embodied in a person such as this lovely creature, it would not vanish.

Whoever this enchanting child might be, Tony would certainly know all the important information. He must have her.

With the air of a connoisseur, Tony stepped back and studied the assemblage while brushing an imagined speck from his lemon-yellow satin sleeve and smoothing the ruffle of lace around his left wrist. Not bad for the end of the Season. In fact, above the ordinary in tone and style. No reason for him to be ashamed to be seen here. At least it solved the problem of what to do with the evening after that meeting with Pitt was set back a day.

Then, there was the morrow. Much as he needed a new suit before retiring to Stonehead, it would not do to be seen in Bond Street until certain bills were settled. Cursed nuisance, these merchants. They seemed to sense when his pockets were to let, and then rushed to present their demands. Never when he was plump. Then all they presented were their newest fabrics at prices he would be a fool to ignore. Life was such a confusing tangle!

And there was Pitt. That bravest of men extricating his country from a disastrous situation while beset with enemies on all sides. Serving him secretly provided Tony with the greatest excitement he had known, although the irregular early hours it demanded greatly interfered with his comforts.

By the end of the week, all this would be behind him. He permitted himself a brief mental glimpse of a certain azure lake encircled with thick, stately woods, its cool waters shimmering beneath a blue sky dotted with pristine fluffs of clouds. A deep spot protected from the falls at the upper end by an outcropping of granite would yield a bounty of succulent fish. Beside that still pool far to the north, or in that panelled room overlooking the west terrace, he could sit alone with no prying eyes or ears and be himself. And in his private workshop down in Wiltshire, the delights of tooling and creating with wood awaited him. Such a relief when the Season ended! Resolutely he slammed memory's door. If Minorca had fallen to the French, he might not see his beloved Stonehead for many weeks.

He glanced back at the newest sensation and composed his painted features in happy approval. What winning ways she had, this new toy for society. She provided a delightful diversion from national worries. Imagine old Byngstone siring this choice morsel. Sly fox he was, setting the whole town on its ear by introducing her at the end of the Season. She did not possess the sensational attractions of the Gunning sisters, but her sparkle, charm, and fortune would soon bring most bachelors to her feet.

Then out of the corner of his eye, he saw a familiar figure and turned his head to assure himself he was not mistaken. "Cyprian!" he exclaimed, his feet almost tripping over themselves in his eagerness to join his friend. "Dear boy, I'd no idea you were back in town!"

"Um, what? Oh, Tony, did you say something?"

With a chuckle and pat on his shoulder, Tony commented, "I perceive an air of thoughtful speculation. What devious plans are boilin' in your mind?"

An engaging smile transformed Cyprian's skillfully painted face as he answered, "No devious plans, Tony. I was thinking of sapphires."

"Sapphires?" Tony glanced at his friend's jewels, his own, and then surveyed the persons nearest them. "Pearls, rubies, diamonds, a rather fine emerald on Uxton's finger, but no sapphires."

"Yes, one wonders why he doesn't sell it. They say he's about all done up."

"Justice for one so devoid of scruples or honor."

"The sapphires I have in mind are in a box in a safe on a hill."

"In a box in a safe on a hill," echoed Tony, his brain quickly sifting various possibilities. "A riddle if ever I heard one," he said with glee as he rapidly reviewed the possibilities. "I love riddles. Aha! Tell me if I've got it. I've surely got it." Tony hummed a brief snatch of tune. "The hill. Omsbridge Hall stands on a hill, very commandingly. A safe is where valuables are kept, and sapphires are certainly valuable. And the Omsbridge sapphires are famous." His eyes widened in horror. "Dear boy, don't tell me you've taken it into your head to hang them around some female's neck and choke yourself in the bonds of matrimony!" His left fist smote his breast dramatically. "No! It cannot be! Tell me I err! Please, it must not be true!"

Cyprian laughed.

Tony shielded his eyes with his right hand and averted his face. "I am desolate! I shall go into deepest mourning! That you, the noblest of the free, should fall into the toils of woman! Alas, alack, what tragedy!"

"Bravo, Tony. Drury Lane can boast nothing to compare with you!"

"Yes, I did that rather well, didn't I?" Tony responded with a grin.

Taking his arm, Cyprian led Tony into the adjoining room. "I am touched by your deep grief, but please, a little less public. As yet I've not announced my intentions, and I'd as soon wait awhile before all the town is told." He paused, then inquired, "Aren't you in the least curious as to whose neck I've decided to grace with the sapphires?"

"Languishing, perishing with curiosity," Tony answered promptly.

"And grief, don't forget the grief."

"A shadow will hover over my heart the rest of my life."

"Come"—Cyprian nodded toward a refreshment table—"a cup of punch will brighten your outlook."

"How shallow you think me!" Tony protested, leading the way to the glass bowl presided over by a sober man in claret livery. With impish delight, he snatched up a filled cup and raised it with a grand flourish.

"To the beauteous neck, slender, graceful, white as alabaster, soft, and rounded—"

"To the neck," Cyprian interrupted gravely, and drained his cup.

Tony drank his, then, eager to be the first to know the details, lowered his voice to say, "And now, dear boy, the identity of the possessor of this fabled neck. Will you entrust me with this knowledge?"

"I would do so gladly if I knew it."

Startled, Tony looked at his companion blankly. "Have you decided to hand the famous necklace around *any* neck, or one in particular?"

Cyprian chuckled. "No. I am not so desperate as to choose just any female. One in particular. The name in question I do not know, but I believe you do. If not, you can easily ascertain it for me, as you are always well versed in the news of the town."

"True, I am. But, dear boy, am I to understand you have not been *introduced* to this lady?"

"I have not. You have a privilege not yet granted to me."

"I know her, and you do not?" Tony's astonishment was rapidly replaced with a frown of concentration.

Cyprian watched him closely, a smile teasing the corners of his mouth.

"Another puzzle, and so soon. Really, dear boy, you are most kind to me tonight. Now, let me stir my brain. Who in town would you not know that I would? A female, that we know." Tony's nimble mind recalled Cyprian's expression earlier. "When I first saw you, you were bemused with a pleasant thought. This could be someone whom you have seen this very night, perhaps?"

Cyprian nodded encouragingly.

Tony looked back through the door into the ballroom; then understanding lit his face. "It could be none other than the lovely Miss Byngstone! Angelea Byngstone. She would add sparkle to any gem, no matter how humble. And those are not humble gems. Now, why did I not see that at once? She is perfect for the sapphires. Perfect. I can see her with them. A truly beautiful neck."

"Angelea," Cyprian said as if savoring each syllable. "Who is she?"

"Why, Sir Matthew Byngstone's daughter, you know. But you don't know. She came to town only two weeks past, while you were down at Omsbridge. What a stir you missed! Put the ton on its ear, she did. Imagine, presenting so lovely a daughter at the end of the Season! Must be touched in the head."

"Sir Matthew is many things, but touched in the head he is not. So the silk heiress has come of age . . . beautifully."

Caught by his friend's mood, Tony said, "By Jove, that would be a sight—you two at the Hall! I can see her in your gardens, at your banquet table, in the grand salon. She'd charm your ancestors right off the walls." Abruptly Tony remembered others with similar dreams seeking Sir Matthew's approval. The well-known repercussions of those requests moved Tony to touch his friend's arm and add kindly, "But it cannot be. You'd best set your sights on another neck, my friend."

"Is she promised?"

"No. A good many tried right after her presentation." Tony reeled off a half dozen names belonging to leading families. "Old Byngstone's refused them all."

"Are his reasons known?" Cyprian asked quietly.

"Widely. He will not permit any man to pay addresses to his precious daughter who is known to be . . . whose reputation is . . . in the least reprehensible."

"Mine would not pass his scrutiny?"

"Not even on a foggy day could—And anyway"—Tony took a lighter tone, sensing his friend's quest was serious—"she really would not suit you. Despite her fine looks, she is a country child, ignorant in the ways of our society. You would soon tire of her."

"I wonder. Perhaps fresh innocence is what I really desire."

"Innocence is a passing quality, Cyprian. No matter how carefully she is protected, she cannot remain innocent for long. And what then? It is really beside the point. Sir Matthew will not let you within talking distance."

"He does not hesitate to do business with the likes of me, does he? Or is he as nice as his scruples there?"

"He does business with anyone. His scruples are kept for his precious daughter. She is his only child, you know."

"I had forgotten. We shall do business, a great deal of it. In this case, I perceive I must set about charming the father rather than the lady in question, a far less pleasant task. Thank you for the warning. You will yet have occasion to wish me happy with Angelea at my side.

"And now, shall we visit the gaming tables?"

"By all means, dear boy. I am curious to see if this new interest has affected your usual luck. 'Tis said gaming and love often quarrel."

"Who said?" Cyprian asked with a chuckle.

"I said. My own observation."

"May I lure you into a game tonight? I vow you always were more adventurous than I, yet never will you play."

Tony shrugged. "My tastes run to other areas. But I enjoy watching you and the Fates spar."

Leisurely they moved toward the heavy wine velvet curtain shielding the gaming room from the noise of the ball.

Three

he light of many candles flashed from gold fittings. Occasionally a sharp laugh or cry of success punctuated the murmur of voices. Streamers of blue smoke lay above the white heads of men and women totally caught up in the games before them. Footmen in claret livery moved about silently, bearing silver trays of drinks and refreshments. Music from the ball provided a muted background, lending the scene a faraway, unreal atmosphere.

At a table near the entrance, a young man, sporting a purple satin coat sprinkled with large bouquets of red and yellow appliqued flowers, played his last card. Trying not to look too smug, he scooped up his winnings. His opponent, an older gentleman in a green coat, lavishly trimmed with gold and lace, rose smiling jovially, gave the victor a congratulatory pat and sauntered off to watch the play some tables distant.

With a self-conscious flourish, the younger man dropped his gains into his pockets already heavy with gold, then snapped his fingers. A footman appeared promptly at his side with a tray of punch cups. He took two, turned his back on the rest of the room and faced the door, ready for a fresh partner. Tonight's unprecedented run of luck put a flush in his cheeks and a thirst in his throat. In the manner of an expert, he raised his glass cup and examined the sparkling color of the punch. A sip revealed a perfect blend of lime, lemon, orange, and rum, worthy of a winner's discriminating palate.

Well-being cuddled him securely, a sensation lacking for months. Enjoying the new experience, he tipped his chair back on two slender legs, and reviewed his recent triumphs. True, old Hampson did have a reputation for being a poor player who usually lost, but that was not said of Merriweather, whose pockets he had emptied first, nor of Wolf, whose gold now mingled with the others' in his coat pocket. This evening the cards fell into his hands with incredible regularity. Finally, he could enjoy his night of luck. A few more successes and he would ask old Byngstone for Angelea's hand.

Six months ago he had won a sizable sum and a matched pair of grays, the envy of the town, until he lost them a fortnight later. He erred in quitting too soon on that last winning streak. This time he would ride it to the full extent. Tonight was magical. The universe's scales, tipped against him all his life, were now realigned. Lady Luck, the fascinating phantom he had pursued so long, was smiling on him.

If only a person really plump in the pocket would come his way, he could gain a fortune many times over. Those loudly lamenting the dissipation of his mother's estate would be forced to hold their tongues. He would restore it, no, improve it beyond its former splendor.

As if his inner desires were commands, the wine velvet curtains parted and two men entered—haughty, consciously poised in faultlessly tailored, expensive garb. Their faces were painted and patched in the latest style, and their white bag wigs precisely curled in the highest fashion. Well known to all, they walked the earth proudly, as if lords of the universe.

Deuxbury, the taller and more slender, had a narrow face and thin nose. His manner, as he leaned to whisper in his friend's ear, was disgustingly effeminate. Why anyone tolerated that pretty-boy was a mystery.

Omsbridge was of a heavier frame and slightly shorter. Even his paint did not conceal the coarseness of his features, most noticeably his firm jawline. In response to Deuxbury, he raised his gold quizzing glass with a languid ease and grace, prompting a twinge of jealousy in the gambler. Hard as he tried, the young man could not develop the elegant, fluid movement. Omsbridge surveyed the room methodically. When his gaze centered on Lady Luck's newest protégé, the young man nearly choked with joy. The biggest game of all, the infamous Blue Devil was to be his victim! His fortune was soon to be made.

With a careful attempt at nonchalance, he curved his lips into a smile, nodded politely to the two fops and drained his second cup. He glanced idly at the nearest table where a game was still in progress, and ruffled the deck of cards with his left thumb. "Send them here, divine goddess of Fortune," he prayed under his breath. He heard a low murmur as the two approached over the thick carpet, but he did not look up until Deuxbury spoke.

" 'Evening, Becket. I hear you're to be congratulated on an astonishing run of luck and skill. I encountered no less than half a dozen who admitted to having their pockets lightened tonight because of him, Cyprian."

"Only three. Won't you sit down?" Becket motioned to a footman, who responded quickly, placing three cups on the table. "Haven't seen you around lately, Omsbridge."

"I was in Sussex for a few weeks tending to things."

"You're in time to witness my Angelea's return to society."

Omsbridge's eyebrows flew upwards.

Becket corrected hastily, "Not mine, really. You see, Byngstone bought a corner of my mother's estate some years back and built him a country place. I've known Angelea since she was . . . quite young. Pretty, ain't she?"

"Very," Omsbridge agreed.

Confidently Becket suggested, "Care to play a few hands? A pleasant way to pass the time, don't you think?"

"The most pleasant," Omsbridge nodded, then looked askance at Deuxbury.

"No, no, not me, dear boy," the fool answered with a nervous flutter, for a fool he did appear to Becket. "I've no nerve for that sort of thing, you know. I'll just watch you two, and take my, er, enjoyment vicariously."

They cut for deal. Becket's confidence soared higher when he turned a king to Omsbridge's four. The first hand went easily to Becket. To lure his opponent into greater betting, he deliberately gave away the next two hands with careful mistakes, not obvious to anyone else. He feigned a mild concern and a rash air.

The stakes rose and he won. With great skill he manipulated the hands so that he lost a few and again masked his boundless confidence as the stakes increased markedly. But this time he was shocked to see his queen topped by an ace, and Omsbridge pulled in the winnings.

Certain this was a setback of the mildest sort, he plunged heavily on the next hand and lost again. He drew back to playing more carefully and won several hands. The winnings were small, to be sure, but Becket felt he was again in harmony with the delightful Lady Luck. Overconfidence tripped him into careless playing, and his bountiful deity would not tolerate carelessness. He bolstered his confidence with another glass of punch. The hands continued falling, first to one, then the other. Becket kept his pile of gold replenished as a symbol of inevitable success.

An hour later Becket was startled to realize he held the last handful of earlier winnings. Cautiously he felt in the seams of his pockets for coins he might have missed or a possible tear. It could not all be gone. He picked up his hand and studied the cards. They were not high, but three were eights. All evening he had won with eights.

With an air of confidence Becket shoved his pile into the center of the table.

Omsbridge counted it, pushed in an equal amount, and added half again.

"You will take my draft?" Becket asked, motioning to a footman.

Lord Omsbridge's cold, piercing gray eyes stared into his as if he was assessing his opponent's integrity.

Becket hoped his paint concealed the rush of blood to his face under the penetrating search. The man had no right to look at him that way, he thought angrily.

"Yes. I am confident it will be honored."

The footman brought pen, ink, and paper. The draft was quickly written. The hand was played, and Becket saw jacks take precedence over his lucky eights.

"The fickleness of Mistress Fortune," Omsbridge commented, collecting his winnings.

"Wait, another hand. You must give me a chance to win back a portion."

"Must I?" the proud peer asked. "And what would you stake? It is against my policy to accept more than one draft from an opponent in an evening. The hour is late—rather, early. We impose on our hosts." He nodded to the thin group watching their play.

"Only one more." Becket grasped Lord Omsbridge's arm as he rose. "A cut. Merely a cut of the cards."

"And what would you risk on the cut of the cards?"

"My property in Surrey. It is a large tract with a fine house."

Omsbridge looked surprised. "Is it not entailed?"

"No. It came from my mother. The entailed estates went to my older brother." He flushed, recalling his father's relief that, as he was the younger son, his reckless gambling would not ruin the family inheritance.

"What is its value? I must raise a just wager. It would be more than we have played for this night, I should think."

"Oh, considerably. It was last valued at 50,000." He did not add that since the valuation he had sold off a small parcel to settle a recent debt of honor. That detail was unimportant since he would win the cut.

To Becket's relief, Deuxbury murmured an agreement of his estimate. It would be as when he won the first cut. However, this time he would gain a fortune solely on his nerve. But Omsbridge seemed reluctant to make the bet.

With a frown, Omsbridge said, "I never place my land in jeopardy. I have misgivings over this wager."

Becket was in agony of apprehension lest the wager be refused. With a sneer he said, "I had not thought such a minor sum would cause you a problem." Could it be that the Omsbridge fortune was not as large as rumored? No matter, the bet must be placed, for he, Becket, would prevail.

"I will take your draft," he offered magnanimously.

Omsbridge motioned for more paper. Then he studied the blank sheet, obviously in a state of indecision.

Deuxbury leaned over to whisper in Omsbridge's ear.

Not knowing whether this was to encourage or discourage the bet, Becket became even more anxious. With jerky movements he daubed at the moisture on his brow.

"You are sure, Tony?" Omsbridge asked his friend.

Deuxbury nodded.

"Surely the famous Omsbridge nerve is not failing you," Becket goaded.

Steely eyes met Becket's. "I do not like to play for a man's inheritance."

"That is *my* choice."

"So it is."

Again Deuxbury whispered advice, shaking his head.

Omsbridge answered, "You may be right, Tony, but . . ." He picked up the pen and hastily wrote his note.

Relieved, Becket commented, "I suppose it is unwise of me. You have the devil's own luck." Sharply he watched the pen's progress.

"It is never wise to bet against the devil," Omsbridge reminded him. "He always wins."

Becket took a fresh sheet of paper and wrote out his deed with a flourish. His heart beat rapidly as he thought of redeeming Omsbridge's note on the morrow. These few onlookers tonight would spread the word before the dawn and his sagging credit would be elevated to the clouds. No longer would he be laughed at, the butt of jokes. And then, he could speak to Sir Matthew for Angelea and be approved. And she would smile in her slow, special way, and tell him she had loved him for years, since they were but children.

"Shall we let Allen do the honors of shuffling?" Omsbridge proposed.

"Of course. A good man."

Richard Allen stepped to the table immediately and, without comment, picked up the deck. Quickly, efficiently, his fat, stubby fingers ruffled and shuffled the cards—four, five times. He left them in the center of the table, a neat stack, the edges precisely even.

Omsbridge nodded and turned over his right hand, a gesture of invitation to Becket.

Running the tip of his tongue over his lips, Becket stretched out his right arm with a graceful twist, brushed his fingertips across his thumb, and rested his hand on the stack. He caressed it briefly, then cut thin.

A great breath seemed sucked in around him as he turned the queen of diamonds. His wayward deity had returned to his side!

Omsbridge's face betrayed no emotion. He too rested his hand momentarily on the deck before cutting deeply. He paused a brief moment to look hard into Becket's eyes before showing his cut.

The ace of spades.

Four

ony sauntered idly down Ivy Lane toward St. Paul's, his gait deliberately slow and uneven, his attention seemingly intrigued by anything of the slightest note. He bowed and doffed his apricot tricorn to each female he encountered, regardless of her station, and even paused to eye one or two of the more attractive ones after they had passed by. Having displayed with great care to all the world that he was a man of fashion, intent on nothing, assuredly *not* in the least hurry, he turned in under the sign of the Kings' Head.

Inside, his glance darted from one to another of the gentlemen enjoying the paper or a pipe over a plate of food. About to continue his search elsewhere, his eye was caught by the setting down of a paper in the far corner. He ambled in a zigzag manner, pausing to greet various friends before dropping into a shadowed seat opposite Omsbridge. "My dear boy," he exclaimed, "I have worn myself to a frazzle looking for you!"

Cyprian pulled out his watch and studied its face in the light of the single taper on the table. "Why, it's barely two. I'd no idea you'd be astir so early."

"Lucky for you I decided to leave for Stonehead tomorrow and dropped by Lloyds to see my broker. The place is abuzz with the news."

"The news? Tony, have a cup of coffee. Better, join me with a plate of this excellent stew and calm yourself. I cannot follow you in your agitation."

"*I'm* agitated! *You* are the one who should be!"

Cyprian beckoned to a waiter and ordered a dinner for Tony.

"No, really, Cyprian, you know I can't bear to face so much food at this hour."

"Nonsense. At the rate you've been racketing around at early hours, you need to fortify your failing strength. Tony, if you waste away and die from a lack of nourishment, half the tailors in town will go bankrupt."

"At least the good ones would," Tony agreed with a grin.

"There, you see, and where would I be when I needed something to cover myself? At the mercy of the incompetents. And you know I cannot abide incompetents! I'll not hear a word of your news until you have eaten heartily."

Tony leaned across the oak table and grasped his friend's arm. "Cyprian, you don't understand. The scandal is . . . is . . . it may well be the *ruin* of you!"

"Really? Here? I think not. When I venture beyond these walls to the tumult of the street, perhaps then. Relax, Tony. We will find some way to muddle through whatever it is—after you have eaten."

Resigned to the delay, Tony turned his attention to the plate of stew.

"Aha!" exclaimed Cyprian softly, "behold, his slovenliness, the most self-important Johnson has arrived."

"Who?" Setting down his fork, Tony twisted around to face the entrance, and raised his quizzing glass. Locating the object of Cyprian's attention, he studied the portly person making his way to a table near the fire. The rumpled coat and messy cravat so offended him that Tony dropped his glass and returned to his dinner with an impatient shake of his head. "Have nothing to do with him, dear boy. I have it on good authority that the Earl of Chesterfield was foolish enough to say something favorable about that scribbler—not too surprising, when you think about it."

"You mean the earl?"

Tony nodded. "It's hard for me to understand how a man with a natural feel for style and elegance can still be totally without sense otherwise. Confounding!"

"It was a mistake to speak favorably of that gentleman?" Cyprian persisted gently.

"Definitely. Don't do it. Never. Nothing good one can say about him, anyway. Just look at him! He's been hounding the earl ever since with some ridiculous project of his. Can you imagine, a dictionary! Why would he think anyone, least of all the *earl*, would want a stuffy old dictionary nobody'd ever look at dedicated to him? It passes belief! Take my word for it, have nothing to do with that man. He'll bring no credit to you and he'll make life miserable hanging on to your sleeves."

"I'll keep your advice in mind if ever I'm tempted to speak to or of him."

Tony sipped a glass of port and leaned back contentedly.

"And now, what brought you in search of me, my friend? Did Byng succeed at Minorca, or have the French invaded?" Cyprian asked.

"Neither, that I know of. The cursed thing is, that the action's all over, you know. Happened days ago. We're just sitting here waiting to find out the result, unable to do anything."

Cyprian shrugged. "There's no way to move news more quickly from the Mediterranean than a ship can take it."

"Someday there must be a better way. This waiting is terrible. A signal of some kind should be arranged, like when we light bonfires. News travels rapidly then."

"True. But I hardly think the French would approve our sending a signal of victory across their land."

"I suppose not. But, it might not be a victory. In fact, it'd be a wonder if Byng could pull it off with the few ships they let him take to do the job. It was a scandal!"

"If you have no word on Minorca or a French invasion, what was the news you heard?"

"Why, the scandal, of course! If you've set your eye on the lovely Mistress Byngstone, you must not be tinged with the merest hint of scandal. In fact, I'd say this puts her beyond your reach. And so unnecessary—"

"What do you mean?" Cyprian interrupted sharply.

"Why, Becket went to the Field of Nine Steps and blew his brains out." Then he added upon reflection, "Shouldn't have made a very large hole."

Cyprian's stunned expression satisfied Tony he was the first to impart the news. "Somehow we've got to clear you of any involvement," he said anxiously. "I mean, half the town knows you cleaned him out and won his place in Surrey. They'll put this down to despair."

"Very likely."

"I warned you if you won the cut you might lose Mistress Byngstone, but you went ahead."

"And last night he claimed the friendship of a long-time neighbor."

"He and Miss Byngstone were playmates. Naturally you noticed he indicated she was virtually in his pocket, calling her 'my Angelea.' There were already entries in the betting books on whether he would make his suit plain before she left town or after he had her to himself down in Surrey. The odds were mostly against him. Byngstone will want a better position for his daughter than what Becket can, er, could offer."

"The Byngstones are returning to their country seat soon?"

"In a fortnight or so."

"You're remarkably well informed, Tony."

"My dear boy, there is little in this town I don't know. For instance, the one most likely to blacken your name, or anyone else's in the fair young woman's ear, is Uxton."

"Uxton! But of course. We are always in contention."

"Everyone knows he lost his head as badly as Becket and suffered at your hands as well as several others. He has no skill at all with cards, but he keeps playing. Mistress Byngstone is the only matrimonial diamond large enough to meet his needs. His campaign was begun a week since."

"It would be so. Since our days at Oxford, Uxton and I have been in contention. Our fathers were closer than brothers. Contrary to their expectations, we seem to possess an inborn antagonism. Now he actually hates me, wouldn't you say?"

"With vigor. Trust him not in the *smallest* matter. I know, a black armband. You must wear one."

"Why?"

"You can let it be told how you regret Becket's death. Send a big wreath."

"And lead the mourners?"

"Yes!" Tony nodded, pleased that Cyprian understood the problem so quickly.

"No. I will not." Cyprian's tone was low, unemotional, and final.

Tony gaped at him, horrified. "But, my dear boy, you must. It is essential that Sir Byngstone and his lovely daughter know you had no part in Becket's death!"

"I will not pretend to mourn the death of an idiot. I should rather rejoice. The world is better off without such fools. Should I make a display of grief I do not feel? I had no part in his decision to kill himself. It would appear that I regretted my part, that in some way I felt responsible, even that I *am* responsible. Devil I may be. Hypocrite I am not. No. I will not mourn Becket.

"However, Tony, you have gone to the heart of my problem. I must woo the father with great care. He will not want a devil in his family. If I am to repair my reputation, it will take considerable effort on my part. In fact, I believe that you and Eldridge will rejoice over the transformation. Already I have—"

"Omsbridge and Deuxbury! What luck!" Two fashionable young men approached the table. "Pay up, Fox, my buck," demanded a dandy sporting an oversized corsage on his lapel. His plump, broad-faced companion cheerfully placed a note in the extended palm. Both drew up chairs and sat down.

"Heard the news about Becket and set out to find you. It wouldn't be a celebration without you two. After all, you brought it about. I knew I should find you here. Fox thought you'd be at the Brown Bear, but I know that ain't in your style."

"Please excuse my slowness, my dear Aylesford, but to what celebration do you refer?" Cyprian inquired.

"What did we bring about?" Tony asked apprehensively.

"You rid the streets of Becket's nasty tongue. For that you deserve a medal!"

Tony jumped. "Oh no, Aylesford, no, no. You credit us with far too much. Much too much. Oh my, yes. Under the circumstances you must make your presentation to the deceased. He did it to himself, you know."

"Perhaps." Aylesford considered this, then shook his head. "No, he'd never have done such a considerate thing on his own. It was your assistance at Barringtons' last night that did the trick. But for that, already twice today I should have been subjected to his vile tongue. I swear, he took delight lying in wait to sharpen his wits at my charge! Never have I hated anyone so enthusiastically!

"I am giving a supper tonight for a few of our dear friends. And later"—he leaned over the table eagerly—"there's a new watch over by the Strand. I saw him last night, a dottering old fool afraid of the lumps in the dark, hardly able to cry out the hours. It'd be great sport to spook him a bit. Why, I wager we can have him a quivering jelly afraid to move within an hour. And then, there's all sorts of fun to be had. Join us at the Cat and Crown at nine."

"Would love to, old friend," Cyprian replied, "but I've given my word to Lady Wilt to wait on her this evening. She had some new fellow called Reynolds do her portrait, and is having a private showing. She earnestly covets my opinion of its excellence, so she said, and, in a weak moment, I promised not to disappoint her. My word's been given."

Aylesford shook his head. "Bound to be a tedious affair. She won't invite anyone else of interest, you may be sure. Tell her you're ill and come racketting with us."

"Without doubt you are right, but it is essential I be there."

Heaving a disappointed sigh, Aylesford turned to Tony. "And you, Deuxbury? You will come, won't you?"

"I may join you for supper. The Cat and Crown serves an excellent table. But such activity afterwards would upset my digestion. If I engage in any physical effort following a meal, my whole constitution rebuffs me for days. Believe me, I have learned the hard lessons of living in charity with my stomach, regardless of the delights tempting me."

Aylesford laughed, with Fox echoing him. "So all your physical activities are to be accomplished before breakfast," quipped Fox in a deep voice with broad country accents, "since the rest of the day falls after some meal."

"I eat breakfast in bed, before rising," Tony assured him solemnly, "and so avoid that temptation."

Aylesford doubled with laughter. "I'll order a cover laid for you at the Cat and Crown, at the head of our table. Do not fail us, dear Deuxbury. You shall be the light of the night."

After the pair left, Tony raised one brow and queried, "Lady Wilt's showing is part of your wooing?"

"She reviewed her guest list with me but an hour since. Byngstone's not on it but Richardson is . . ."

"And they are bosom friends," Tony murmured with approval.

"My most exemplary behavior will be reported. It will be so outstanding he cannot fail to comment."

"And you will not make any attempt to meet the delightful lady before you leave town."

"Precisely. She will meet me at her home in Surrey, and there she and her family shall see only my best side. All evil rumors will be smothered under a quantity of good works. God himself will smile His approval on this devil. As I was about to tell you, my reformation is begun. I have already declined a race to Bath at an attractive wager I could not fail to win. No more will I play deeply at the gaming tables.

"Perhaps I should have stopped short of emptying Becket's pockets, but when you assured me the property he wagered ran alongside Byngstone's, the temptation was irresistible. The manor will be invaluable in winning the lady's favor—and her heart. Becket's stupidity has thrown a rub in my way, but I will yet turn it to good use."

"I shall eagerly await the news of your happy nuptials."

"No effort will be spared to prevent your disappointment. And I shall inform you when the matter is settled.

"Will you be residing at Stonehead this summer?"

Tony frowned as his uneasiness returned. "I fear my stay there will be brief."

"More machination with Pitt? You know, old friend, you may call on me anytime for such as I may do."

"Thank you. Quite possibly I will have several occasions to make passing visits through Omsbridge in the coming months. Matters with France will not be resolved quickly."

Five

*Y*es, milord." Edmund Feldman straightened as he closed the door. With the click of the latch, his air of humility vanished. Taking a deep breath, he set about restoring order to his domain. Briskly he moved across the blue and ivory Chinese rug, taking pleasure in its luxurious, soft depths. He picked up a bright blue satin coat thrown across a deep armchair. With practiced skill he slipped it onto a hanger, smoothing out a few wrinkles and flicking away a piece of lint picked up from the wool upholstery. Of late, it seemed his lordship was favoring the more somber colors in his wardrobe, a preference Feldman had been encouraging unsuccessfully these many years.

As he hung the garment carefully in the ornately carved oak wardrobe and began picking up scattered small clothes and stocks to give to the laundress, he was thinking of the definite stamp the recently deceased lady had left on her son. Like her, his lordship was impatient of conventions, interested in people only as they served his immediate desires, self-sufficient, independent of everyone and everything.

Feldman was grateful his lordship's father also passed on to his successor the virtues of love of land, a powerful sense of honor, and the obligation to care for his household. So long as the man possessed these three, Feldman could forgive any other inconsequential failings of his master. It was fortunate for everyone that the deceased lord did not imbue his son with his disastrous indifference to business and addiction to alcohol.

With a deft hand, Feldman swept grains of powder from the gold-lacquered dressing table and restored lids to their paint pots. His lordship

31

may be indifferent to people in general, but not to him. He knew Feldman held his interests first, and trusted Feldman's judgment in all matters relating to his dress. It was a matter of pride that, whether on the Continent, in the country, or here in town, his lordship never encountered a person better turned out than himself, nor a situation for which he was improperly dressed. Feldman smiled, remembering the many sharp disagreements they had over which coat was the most suitable or over a style his lordship was taken with but Feldman held to be beneath his dignity.

However, his lordship was changing. This fortnight he had involved himself more in business than idle pleasure, although why the silk trade was selected mystified Feldman. He deplored the taint of trade being associated with his master, but, otherwise, it was a definite improvement. No longer lost in glum preoccupation, as on his return from Sussex, his lordship's alert interest in everything reminded Feldman of those glorious days before the shocking exposure of Lady Omsbridge's infidelity. Edmund thought the joys of that period would never again grace his master's life. But now he hoped to be shown in error. It was not the silk trade that was rejuvenating his lordship, but something, nay *someone* other. From his heart, Feldman earnestly called for heaven's blessings on the unknown person.

He arranged the pots efficiently in the prescribed order, laid the feather in front of them, and placed the silver brushes and mirror in their velvet-lined drawer. He united the blue brocade slippers and set them beside the deep overstuffed chair. Intently he scanned the luxurious room. All was in its proper place. Not a wrinkle marred the gold tapestry bed covering.

Methodically Feldman pulled the thickly fringed gold curtains against the coming night and checked the supply of firewood. It was low. He must instruct Jimmy Boy to remedy that promptly. If his lordship returned early and decided to spend the night before this fire, or any of the fifteen or so others in the house, there must not be any possibility of his taking a chill for lack of logs.

Pausing before the gilt-edged mirror, Feldman straightened his old-fashioned cravat. More comfortable than the modern stock, it was modestly and precisely tied, appropriate to his being an expert in gentlemen's attire. He turned to examine the fit of the back of his new bottle green coat critically. It was a discard of his lordship's from several years before, when he selected blue as his personal color. Recently Edmund had it altered to fit his slighter frame and the cut changed to one of a more current style. The tailor had done excellent work. The cloth lay smoothly across his shoulders with just enough ease to permit Feldman to do his work in comfort. In a few months time, he would also have remade the dark brown coat his lordship gave him.

He fingered the dark wood buttons with a twinge of regret. The original brass ones looked much better, especially the large ones holding the deep cuffs at his elbows. But they were too ostentatious. It was well and good for fools like Brindlebottom to ape their betters in elaborate dress, but all the world knew them for what they were.

Since his lordship spent the day working in his library with men of business, there were no muddy boots to shine or breeches to be cleaned of spots or clinging horsehair. Indeed, Feldman could anticipate several hours below with Mrs. Banks in the kitchen, or elsewhere.

He was grateful she was not a prim, sour woman like that self-righteous Croft. Mrs. Croft may call it Christianity, but Feldman had a higher regard for Mrs. Banks' understanding of the blessedness of giving than of Mrs. Croft's tight-laced morality. And such a waste that was. He remembered her as Mary the upstairs maid, a sweet, pretty thing she was then. Feldman shook his head. *Marriage and widowhood do spoil people sometimes,* he thought.

Feldman carefully removed his treasured watch to check it against the flowered French china clock on the mantel. He wound it slowly before replacing it in the tiny pocket of his dun vest. As he arranged the chain to drape to the best advantage, he recalled his lordship presenting him with the valuable watch shortly after the old lord's death. "It is appropriate that you should have my father's prized watch, considering all your years of faithful service to our family," he had said. Then, detaching a gold fob from his own chain, he placed it in Feldman's palm. "And this is for the years of faithful service I know you will give me." Nothing further was said during the intervening years, but each time he touched the watch and fob, Feldman felt the honor and trust of that moment.

And he was faithful, whether in European inns, or the elegant surroundings of Sussex or London. During those dark days at Oxford, when he despaired of his lordship's sanity, never had he failed to maintain his master's appearance in the highest style. Many times Feldman went beyond his duties to protect his master from the consequences of folly committed while drunk or in a rage.

Even in Lucerne, when he daily feared the young man would take his own life, he watched over him loyally. Then came a sudden turning after a rainy afternoon visit to the beautiful, modern baroque Jesuit church. Feldman didn't hold with popery, but his master evidently found release there from the furies pursuing him. He never explained his new tranquillity of spirit, but it persisted through much of the remainder of his Tour. Would it could be regained.

No one knew his lordship so well as Feldman, nor loved him more. Their bond was developed in adversity and strengthened with respect. Not one of the many secret, lucrative offers he received from time to time seriously tempted him to leave his master for another. Feldman could not visualize himself in any other place, taking orders from a person inferior to his lordship.

As with his father, mother, and grandfather, Feldman served the family all his life, beginning as a youth in the scullery. He did well, saving the various generous gifts of appreciation presented to him. Now, any time he chose to give in to the increasing aches here and there in his wiry body, he could live comfortably in the cottage where he was born at Omsbridge. Sweet little Hetty, his dear niece, would do for him. Even should she marry that headstrong groom, Percy, she would care for him with love and a cheerful song on her lips. Percy was a good enough lad, respectful as he ought to be, save for his temper. He could well rise to be the head groom what with the natural way he had in handling spirited horseflesh.

Feldman smiled, thinking of Hetty: robust, honest, not too bright, but the joy of his life. Mrs. Banks may think *she* was his light and joy. That fallacy suited him, for she was a fine cook, and often slipped him choice dishes. He repaid her in full with soulful glances, whispered words and lighthearted kisses in the dim halls of the kitchen. Tonight, with his lordship out most likely 'til dawn, they could spend a companionable evening together in her tidy room to their mutual enjoyment.

Feldman smoothed his brown wig, pleased with the youthful appearance it gave his unlined face. Last week when he shaved his head, he was reminded of his age by the scarcity of dark gray hair among the white clippings. This fact he wished to share with no one.

Having approved of his appearance, Edmund Feldman left his master's room humming softly, walking with a confident, swinging stride. He assumed an air of propriety as he passed the pleasant Italian oil paintings newly acquired from the Earl of Breckenhill's collection through his master's gambling skill. This was indeed the best of all worlds, living in a household ruled by a man of good taste and wealth.

Even when his lordship married, as he must do soon to continue the family line, their relationship would not change, for the new mistress would have nothing to do with him. On the other hand, she might have a maid or two to add pleasant variety to his world. Perhaps, if a suitable lady had engaged his lordship's attention, a likely reason for his laudable change, this addition might not be far distant.

A nodding footman caused Feldman to interrupt his humming for a reprimanding scowl as he drew near the back stairs. Really, Dagon should run a better household, in keeping with his lordship's rank. But, that was no concern of his. On the whole, Dagon probably did rather well with the poor quality of help available in town these days. It was inferior to that in Sussex.

He descended the narrow steps speculating on the tasty dish Mrs. Banks had prepared. Perhaps a tender bit of lamb with the spicy sauce his lordship mentioned when he came up after supper to change. He hoped there would also be a slice or two of her moist, fresh bread. What more could he desire? Even gentlemen at a fancy ball would not have more satisfying pleasures than those Feldman anticipated.

Six

ngelea looked idly at the long purple clusters of wisteria blooms hanging near her window. The hungry humming of bees rose and fell as they moved among the flowers. How boring it was at The Willows this warm August morning. While awaiting Simmons' return to help her out of her new dress, Angelea leaned her elbows on the windowsill, dreamily recalling the balls in Town, and routs, and shopping, and handsome men of fashion, and jewels and—A movement near their gate at the distant road interrupted her reverie.

Snatching up her spyglass, she focused it and saw a man riding up their drive at a deliberate pace. Angelea frowned, trying to determine his identity. He was not one of the men in the neighborhood. Her heart skipped a beat. Maybe he was someone she had met in London, seeking her father's permission to address her. She knew several hopefuls were rejected. How vexing not to see his features. He was wigged. His suit of a dull blue color was appropriate to the country. And he wore heavy riding boots. Although his pace was slow, his air did not seem to be hesitant, merely leisurely. Whoever he was, his sensible air indicated he was not one of the silly fops she met in town.

In following a curve, he faced her briefly. Seeing his features clearly, she gasped in astonishment. This was the evil Lord Omsbridge whom her dear friend, Helen Mason, had pointed out to her on his arrival at the Barringtons' ball. His haughty demeanor and elegance of dress had been most attractive to Angelea. To her disappointment, she did not meet him that night. Her determination to win his notice received a significant setback when the suave Lord Uxton informed her that Lord

Omsbridge had goaded poor Tommy Becket into a reckless wager. Uxton inferred Omsbridge was as guilty of Tommy's death as if he had fired the gun himself.

True, Angelea mourned the loss of her longtime friend, Tommy. However, she felt he was foolish to gamble for such high stakes. And, it was past understanding why he should kill himself. Rather go to sea and gain a fortune as her father did.

She set aside the spyglass thoughtfully. The idea of a known rake, a really evil person, coming to her home piqued her curiosity. Certainly neither her father nor her mother would permit her to meet him, so she must invent something quickly. A glance in her mirror showed her newly hemmed gown was sufficiently becoming to encounter this stranger. If she escaped down the back stairs before Simmons returned, she could . . .

Action followed her thoughts as she ran into the hall.

Cyprian rode slowly past a small artificial lake surrounding a new miniature Grecian temple on a patch of turf. Willows drooped tastefully beside chestnuts along its far edge. A persistent woodpecker drummed on a hollow bough not far distant. Set on a knoll ahead, in an expanse of velvety green lawns, was his goal—a gracious brick manor in the new Georgian style. Keeping his pace barely above a walk, his passage up the sweeping drive consumed considerable time. Deliberately he scanned the structure and the terraces of bright flowerbeds flanking it, liking what he saw.

While yet several yards down the drive, he was diverted to see a barking dog round the far corner pursued by a laughing golden-haired miss. Slight tension on the reins brought Blue Star to a halt as he watched the chase. How appropriate that the object of his visit should come to meet him.

Her pink petticoats billowed as she stooped to catch her pet, who danced beyond her reach toward Cyprian's standing gray. "Freckles! You imp!" she scolded the brown and white spaniel as she came to a stop a few feet away from Cyprian. She looked up, frankly studying him. Freckles barked and leaped against her, leaving streaks of dirt on her petticoats. "Down!" she commanded. For a long moment her dark brown eyes met Cyprian's black ones.

Memory had served him poorly. She was far more charming and beautiful. And free of powder, her ringlets shone as gold. Again her purity and splendor touched a deep yearning. Through her he could regain the peace he experienced in Lucerne.

"I don't know you, I think," she commented.

"Cyprian Westover, at your service." He doffed his dark blue tricorn with a flourish and bowed.

"Oh!" She watched him dismount, her red lips slightly parted, her widened eyes shining.

He casually looped the reins around his arm, saying, "I apprehend you are Miss Byngstone. I saw you in town, at the Barringtons'. It was my loss we were not formally introduced then."

"We don't stand on ceremony here in the country," she assured him quickly. She turned her inspection to the ground, ignoring Freckles' frantic yaps for attention. "I don't suppose I should regard you as a friend even though you are our near neighbor."

"Because of the honorable Becket?"

"It was monstrous of you to deprive him of his inheritance."

"Lest you labor under a misapprehension, I did not suggest the wager, but rather tried to dissuade him. He was insistent, to the point of abuse, forcing me to accept."

"But he was foxed!"

"Is Sir Matthew in residence?" Cyprian asked coolly, turning the conversation into more neutral channels.

"Yes. But he is out in the stables or someplace. Would you like to wait in the drawing room? He shouldn't be too long."

"That will be quite agreeable."

"I expect you want to talk about the marsh."

"The marsh?" he asked as they strolled toward the front steps.

"That's what we call the damp place by the creek bordering our two properties. It is always a problem. Down, Freckles! You're such a nuisance, spoiling my new gown!"

"A new gown?" Cyprian exclaimed in surprise.

She dropped her chin slightly and gave him a sidelong look.

The smile quivering at the corners of her mouth went straight to his heart.

"I saw you coming, and it would not do for me to meet you in my old rags. And, if I waited until you were received, I never should get a good look at you. Your evil reputation preceded you."

"I collect that if my reputation had been of the ordinary sort, you might not have taken such trouble."

"True. I must not miss viewing the Blue Devil closely."

"I regret you associate that unfavorable title with me."

"It's quite exciting! Tommy, Mr. Becket, said you were called that because you made everyone blue deviled." She paused, giving him another tingling sidelong look. "He was not quite correct, I think."

"Angelea! Angelea!" called a gray-robed woman from the far end of the terrace.

"Oh, fudge!" Angelea exclaimed. "Now Simmons shall give me a great scold."

"Which you deserve, ruining your new dress."

"It's not ruined, quite. They can clean it up. She will tax me for talking with you alone. I am hemmed in in the most odious manner just because she is forever afraid I shall be considered fast. You will be staying to dinner?"

"That depends on your father."

"Angelea!" Simmons was bearing down upon them rapidly.

"He'll ask you." Angelea skipped toward the gray person explaining that Freckles was a naughty dog running away from her and forcing the chase into the front.

Bewitched by her mannerisms and open naturalness, Cyprian watched her go. The risks at the gaming table and the subsequent inconveniences suffered in his changed lifestyle would be amply repaid when he achieved his prize.

Seven

Sir Matthew arrived shortly and greeted his unexpected visitor cordially. While Lord Omsbridge drank the glass of wine offered for his refreshment, Sir Matthew chatted amiably about the countryside. Although the smile never left his round, florid countenance, he shrewdly appraised his new neighbor.

He was quite gratified to learn that Lord Omsbridge was interested in drainage, a subject the late senior Becket refused to consider. Since the Hillview property belonged to Becket's wife and would pass to his younger son, that gentleman had refused to spend anything on its improvement. "Many's the time I heard him say, 'Tommy will gamble it away all too soon,' " Sir Matthew confided to his guest. "And so he did, more's the pity. But, then again, maybe not, if you care for it properly. Land is a sacred trust."

"I quite agree," Omsbridge responded.

"I beg of you, stay to dinner. Afterwards we may ride out and survey that troublesome tract together."

The august peer accepted the invitation with polite restraint. Contrary to his wild reputation, upon being presented to Sir Matthew's wife and daughter, the man conducted himself most properly.

To Sir Matthew's annoyance, Omsbridge owned to having met Miss Byngstone on his arrival in front of the house, and thanked her for her kind welcome. He must speak severely to Simmons about letting her charge run around unattended.

Sir Matthew felt proud of his good lady as she graciously presided at the foot of the table. On her right Angelea sat, unusually subdued, wearing a becoming light green muslin gown with a lawn fichu modestly tucked into her bodice. The mild concern Sir Matthew felt on exposing his daughter to a reputed rake was set aside over the first course. Although his lordship directed a few remarks to the ladies, he seemed far more interested in conversing with Sir Matthew regarding estate management.

"I was given to understand you spent some years in India," Omsbridge commented as the game pie was being served. "How do you think our tensions with France will affect the trade there?"

Sir Matthew readily responded with a discourse on the conditions of trade with that foreign land. His visitor was so attentive, he elaborated on his intimate knowledge of the situation throughout the serving of a sweet. It was a pleasure to talk with someone whose questions revealed an informed interest in India and the silk trade, instead of the abysmal blank ignorance he usually faced.

On the way to the marsh, Sir Matthew continued revising his earlier opinion of Lord Omsbridge. He regretted that this fine, sensible man was saddled with a notorious reputation. Had he been as the gossips said, he would not have ignored Angelea in favor of practical drainage matters. Nor would he call on a neighbor wearing a plain coat obviously cut at least two years earlier.

"You surprised me, milord," Sir Matthew said as they returned from their survey. "I was of a mind that you would gamble Hillview away or sell it. I did not expect you to take this interest in it, nor to invest in its maintenance."

"As you said, land is a special trust, a valuable asset. I never endanger it with a whim of Fate. However, I might have been wiser to sell it. From what I have learned, the property needs a great deal of care. The tenants' houses are in a tumbledown state and the farm seems run in the manner of the fifteenth century. Since the retainers loyal to the Beckets left last month, everything suffers from neglect. Even the bailiff departed. Would you recommend some of the local people to work for me?"

Finding himself in sympathy with Omsbridge, Sir Matthew readily offered advice and aid. He also extended an invitation to return at will, and Lord Omsbridge reciprocated, suggesting Sir Matthew join him for a friendly game of whist the following evening.

Later, Sir Matthew was brought to account by his lady for taking up so quickly with an evil man who plainly had his eye on their innocent daughter. "You have introduced a man into our household whom even his *friends* name as the 'Blue Devil'!" she concluded.

"Well, he's no such a thing!" he declared as they dressed for tea.

"The man is our new neighbor. He has a true interest in the land. If I deal with him regarding our common interest, it will not concern our daughter in the least way. We did not mention her name once. I would guess, if he's so notorious as you say, that Angelea's quiet manner at dinner would quench any interest he might have."

"It was unusual. And for that reason I am quite concerned," Lady Byngstone said stubbornly.

"Nonsense. She's probably just not feeling quite the thing."

The following evening of whist confirmed Sir Matthew's opinion. The company was good, including Squire Simpson, whose land adjoined the far side of Hillview, and a house guest, a dandy from town, Sir Anthony Deuxbury. No one drank more than was seemly, although the wine was very good. The cards fell so evenhandedly and the stakes were so slight that Sir Matthew returned home feeling in great charity with the world and two pounds richer than when he departed.

It was but six weeks later that Lady Byngstone and her close friend, Mrs. Lydia Mason from Near Muchworth, were strolling along the south terrace of the Willows enjoying a bit of gossip among the beds of asters, dahlias, and delphiniums. They relived the events in London, comparing their daughters' experiences with their own presentations. Lydia Mason reported the varied escapades and illnesses of her three younger children. Having exhausted the family news, they turned to wider affairs.

"My dear Anne, I was scandalized to hear you must tolerate that horrid Blue Devil as a *neighbor*!" Lydia exclaimed as they turned down a path through the rose garden, now showing a few late blossoms. "I heard he won Becket's home in a most unsavory manner, but I did think he would have the decency to sell it and not inflict his presence on the poor boy's bereaved friends. You aren't going to *receive* him, are you?"

"I have already been obliged to receive him," Lady Byngstone replied, opening her fan and using it vigorously to move the warm air and scatter annoying insects as they turned onto the path skirting the lake.

"Oh, my dear! Is he insufferably proud as they say?"

"No. In fact, Lydia, I can reasonably find no cause for complaint. His manners are proper and pleasant. Despite my concerns, he shows no marked partiality for Angelea."

"Anne! You allowed him to come in contact with your daughter?"

"With reluctance, and only in my presence. He is polite and no more attentive than is proper. He and Sir Matthew are draining the marsh. Consequently they have much business to discuss. Lord Omsbridge has come several times to confer with Sir Matthew, and usually remains for dinner or tea. Over these past weeks, I should say we have come to know him quite well."

The women settled on a marble bench offering a pretty view of the lake and the Greek temple.

"I am astounded! Are you saying his reputation is false?" Lydia asked, arranging her primrose skirts. "You know, all those terrible things we heard about . . . about . . . Quite, er, unscrupulous, so they say."

"I know, Lydia. I was prepared to dislike him. However, I must say I have seen nothing of that here. On the contrary, he has conducted his affairs in an exemplary manner."

"His affairs! My dear, does he keep a woman at Hillview?"

"No, no. Sir Matthew says that John Whitley, the new bailiff at Hillview, whom Sir Matthew recommended, was ordered to make all the tenants' homes tight against the weather and even to repair fireplaces and ovens as needed. He was specifically instructed to hire village men for the work. Many were idle, you know. Sir Matthew says that they were talking about going to town in search of employment. Lord Omsbridge even provided whitewash for the tenants' use! You know, no one has ever undertaken such a project here. Some of the gentry are alarmed lest they may be expected to follow his costly example.

"And, Sir Matthew says the Hillview farm is fast becoming the most modern in the district. Furthermore, improvements along the latest lines are being made in the house and gardens. It has become a matter of the greatest interest to everyone. Becket, you know, did nothing since he acquired control of the property through his wife. And his son actually plundered it."

"You sound as if you approve of this Blue Devil."

Lady Anne brushed a fly from her lilac sleeve before replying. "Lydia, I do not know why he was given that name. In our district, he is viewed more as a saint than a devil. His projects have put new life into the village. Rev. Pennywaithe says he sees a new spirit in the people directly attributable to what Omsbridge is doing at Hillview."

"Are you telling me this leopard is changing his spots?"

"Perhaps the spots never existed."

"Or, he may be playing a part for his own ends," Lydia observed sagely. "We have not met, but those who know him say that, although he deals honestly at the card table, he lacks principles in other matters."

"I sent him an invitation to our Michaelmas ball. You may meet him then, if he is in the neighborhood."

"You invited him to your ball! And this year Angelea will be receiving with you?"

"True. Several times she has met him while out riding with her groom. She reported he greeted her quite civilly, inquired about us, and perhaps commented on the weather." Lady Anne chuckled, recalling Angelea's tone on relating the last inconsequential incident. "Frankly, Lydia, she seemed miffed by his restraint. You know the romantic fancies girls have. He's even replaced the vicar as the most attractive man in our parish. You will be bringing Helen, won't you? Angelea would be very unhappy should you leave her behind."

"To say nothing of the storm Helen would raise. This event of yours is the highlight of the year. You plan it so well." Lydia cast a sideglance at Lady Anne. "So, you believe him harmless."

"No, I have no reason to exclude him. And, if I did, I should be taken to task by most of the families in the area. They are all agog to meet him. Especially those with marriageable daughters."

"Really! Your Angelea is by far the prettiest and the best match here. How would you view him as a son-in-law? You have considered that possibility, I dare. . . ."

Lady Anne frowned as she gazed at the far shore. "Yes. I grant you, it is not a match of my seeking. Angelea is a country child. I want her to find a husband as considerate as her father. For all that we have seen, I am not sure he would treat her so. However, Sir Matthew is convinced he is a man among men, one with an uncommon sense of responsibility to his property."

"Well, my dear, I shall bring Helen, of course. But, if the Blue Devil is present, I shall keep a sharp eye on him."

The moment the Hillview groom handed Cyprian the Byngstone invitation in the Omsbridge library, his lordship began planning his appearance. All the families of quality would be present; therefore consideration was given to every detail for creating the perfect impression.

Cyprian and Feldman rode into the Hillview stable yard at noon the day of the ball. The blue coach would follow within an hour or so. As usual, Feldman expressed dismay over the inadequacies of the house and the untrained staff. While Cyprian discussed business with Whitley, Feldman improvised what he needed in this ill-equipped country manor.

As the final touch to his dress, Omsbridge deftly placed a discreet patch below and slightly forward of his left ear and examined the result in the dressing table mirror. He rose and stood before the long mirror to view his full image. Wide white lace frothed at his neck and wrists, falling onto his light blue satin coat, heavily laced with silver. A large sapphire glinted from his finger and one was tucked in his powdered bag wig. From the top of his head to the diamond buckles on his high-heeled shoes, he displayed fashionable elegance. Yes, his toilet was complete.

According to his plan, Cyprian arrived last. This provided a better entrance and shortened the boring evening. He maintained an absolutely correct manner as he bowed over Lady Byngstone's hand and that of her daughter. With care he focused his charm on each person he encountered, regardless of station, well aware that any favorable gossip would enhance his reputation. Although he was tempted to join those seeking a breath of cool air by stepping through the tall windows onto the terrace, he refrained, knowing he would rouse immediate speculation with regard to a companion. Resolutely, he participated in every dance, deliberately selecting the plainer girls for some, and refrained from the least flirtation. He made himself agreeable to protective mamas, and was pleased at his ability to turn a wary greeting into an approving smile. And, he avoided the gaming room.

As Cyprian went through the steps of a country dance he particularly disliked, he thought, "Tony, old friend, you should see this devil now. You would be in whoops!" The one pleasure he permitted himself was a minuet with Angelea.

Laughter brought an enchanting sparkle to her eyes as they executed the stately figures. "You have bewitched those who spoke evil of you," she said. "All is forgiven. No longer are you painted in such black colors."

"But my color is blue."

"I am certain you do not mistake my meaning, milord."

"Odd, is it not, the power of a reputation? And what of yourself?"

"I think that 'Blue Devil' is a misnomer for you."

"Perhaps. It is not a misnomer to call you a 'Blue Angel.' "

Angelea's blush tinged her paint. "Thank you, sir. I think my shade is a bit paler than yours."

"Delicate, like a robin's egg. Very becoming." For a moment his eyes rested on her comely white neck rising from a curving bodice. The sapphire necklace would indeed be lovely there.

The delightful dance, all too brief, generously compensated him for an otherwise trying evening.

Eight

Save for a few shrubs broken by an unwary guest's feet, the ravages of the Michaelmas ball were repaired by the following afternoon when Cyprian again rode slowly up the Willows' drive. He suppressed his regret at not being greeted with a swirl of pink petticoats and a barking dog. He was further disappointed in being received by Lady Byngstone alone, who graciously served him a dish of Bohea tea.

After expressing his pleasure over the previous evening, and sharing a little proper gossip concerning those he met, Lord Omsbridge inquired after Sir Matthew. That gentleman was overseeing some unexpected difficulty with the new drain on their side of the marsh. A groom led Cyprian to meet him.

Investigating the problem necessitated Lord Omsbridge dismounting and muddying his boots in the marsh. Finally, an adequate solution was determined. After the two men combined their directions with the muscles of the laborers in making the drain function, Sir Matthew accepted Cyprian's invitation to refreshment at the newly decorated Hillview.

Stopping at the library, his lordship poured two glasses of brandy, and having rested a bit, led his guest on a tour of the salons and dining room. Their footsteps sounded hollow in the meagerly furnished rooms. Cyprian explained the walls were bare because he had not decided which paintings would replace those removed by the former owner. He further lamented his lack of taste in selecting curtains and rugs.

"Perhaps, milord, a sister or a cousin could assist you," Sir Matthew suggested.

"My dear sister resides several days' journey from here and is busy with her four children. I think they still number four. It has been awhile and I may have yet another niece or nephew," Cyprian responded. "I am totally without feminine guidance."

"Perhaps, milord, you have reached a time in life when you might well consider taking a wife to oversee these details for you. At one time I thought I should enjoy living alone all my life. Then I realized the benefits in having a wise woman at my side. I have not regretted my decision."

Pleased at this turn of thought, Cyprian adopted an air of solemn earnestness, saying, "You must not let a breath of this go beyond these walls, Sir Matthew, but I have indeed come to that conclusion." Leading his guest onto the side terrace, he continued, "I enjoy the freedom of being a bachelor. But, of late, it has paled. There is much attraction in seeing your household well ordered by your gracious lady and enriched with the presence of your beautiful daughter. My friends in town would be shocked to learn I am seriously entertaining marriage."

Sir Matthew nodded. "For many years I cut wide swath in India. Then, on a visit here, I met my dear wife. All the glory of the past faded as a dream. Indeed, it was nothing. She has made me very comfortable. In fact, my friend, I know nothing to equal the contentment the right woman can give a man."

"Do you really think so? I did not realize you were of a similar disposition. Perhaps you will understand when I say I truly wish to alter my manner of life," Cyprian said sincerely.

"The key is finding a woman who engages your affection. I know most peers marry for other reasons, but it is not impossible to find a woman of good family and fortune whom one can love. My Anne is granddaughter to an earl. True, her fortune was quite modest, but mine is adequate for us both. We are most happy."

"So I have observed. As you said, most of my acquaintances marry for other reasons. In fact, yours is the first home I have known based upon a love match." Cyprian paused, then continued, his voice lowered as if imparting a confidence. "After many seasons in town, I thought my affections could not become engaged. But they have."

"Oh? I hope the lady responds." Sir Matthew waved to the freshly trimmed side gardens below them. "You have provided a most pleasant view for her here."

"I confess, I ordered the changes in the gardens with her in mind. However, we would spend little time here. The grounds of Omsbridge are several times as large as these. My family has lived there since the days of Henry V. The Downs roll off to the north, and the Oms below winds its way to the channel a short distance away. She has never seen it. I have not yet asked her hand."

"I am sure, milord, she will be honored to receive you favorably."

"Do you? In spite of my reputation as the Blue Devil?"

Startled, Sir Matthew paused, then laughed. " 'Pon my soul! I'd forgotten that. What a hum! Why, you're no devil at all. On the contrary, I've never had so congenial a neighbor, nor one with such a fine appreciation for the land."

Earnestly Cyprian said, "I am happy to hear you say so, sir. You raise my hopes, for I should like to pay my addresses to your charming daughter, and," he added humbly, "with your permission, to ask her hand."

"My little puss? Well, now!" Sir Matthew looked his host up and down, then surveyed the gardens again, rocking back and forth from heel to toe. He tugged thoughtfully on his lower lip.

Regarding him closely, Cyprian's fingers clenched and opened spasmodically. Months of planning and investment hung on the rotund silk merchant's reply.

"Well, now!" Sir Matthew met Cyprian's steady gaze with a nod. "Our greatest concern is her happiness. You've the reputation of a rake, but not a fortune hunter. I think a man who cares for the land as you do cannot be so evil as they say. If you take this trouble over property won at a hand of cards, I'd give a lot to see Omsbridge. It must be a fair place indeed!"

"It is, Sir Matthew. I would be pleased to show it to you and your wife. It would be an even greater pleasure to install your daughter as its mistress."

"Angelea, the mistress of a great estate. Well now. I expect she could do it. Yes, I'd say it would be an honor to have you in the family. However, I'll not speak for her. Lady Byngstone and I agreed not to force on her a man of our choosing, but rather permit her to select whomever she wishes, providing, of course, he meets with our approval. If she accepts you, milord, we will welcome you into our family."

Cyprian smiled with relief. "I could not ask a kinder response. Thank you, sir. I must ride to Omsbridge to finish some business I interrupted to attend your delightful ball. On my return, I shall endeavor to make myself agreeable to your daughter."

Lady Byngstone received the news of Lord Omsbridge's desire to marry their daughter with conflicting emotions. Naturally she was pleased Angelea had attracted such a wealthy suitor of noble rank. However, being more familiar with the ways of the ton than her husband, serious doubts intruded into her mind. When she expressed these reservations to him, he laughed and dismissed them.

"That's all rumor, and little else. I daresay I once led a wilder life than he has, and you've had little to complain of since we were wed."

She touched his cheek lovingly. "Oh, but you are a prince among men. There are no others like you."

"And that, my love, is pure flattery."

"Not so. Nonetheless, he is known as a heartless, selfish rake. All we see is a perfect gentleman, nearly too good to be true. Perhaps he *is* too good to be true."

A week later Cyprian saw the lovely Angelea in a habit of emerald green riding with her groom. This was the day to bring his careful planning to fruition. By adopting a circuitous route, he met her as if coming from the opposite direction. They exchanged bows and pleasantries. Then, since they were only slightly over a mile from Hillview, he suggested she might like to see the grounds and the newly redecorated manor.

"I should love to! Everyone in the district is talking about the transformation you are making." As they rode to the house, she enthused over the improvements bringing out the potentials in the grounds.

Inside, her disappointment over the sparse furnishings was plain. "Will you leave it thus?" she asked anxiously as he led her through the echoing drawing room onto the side terrace overlooking the gardens.

"No. I have a number of paintings, rugs, and furnishings to bring here from Omsbridge and one or two other residences. But I must leave their selection to someone else. I have no head for that."

"What a delightful challenge to fill these rooms with beautiful things. The outside is lovely. The interior must be as fine."

"Would you recommend the Chinese style?" he inquired with a smile.

"That is all the thing now." Leaning backwards over the stone rail, she surveyed the lines of the building. Her slender, graceful pose speeded his pulse. "Perhaps a room or two, if your taste runs in the modern mode. But, in general, no. There is a man named Chippendale who made a few of our things in a most pleasing style. I think you would like his work—dark woods, delicate lines, but not fragile, with bright upholstery. In blues, for the Blue Devil."

Her teasing glance darted straight to his heart.

"You might try a few pieces of gilt rococo in the large drawing room," she continued. "I don't know. There are so many possibilities. You mentioned bringing things here from your other places. I suppose it depends largely on what you wished to part with for this place and how you intend to use it." She frowned and turned to face him fully, her back on her groom at the far end of the terrace. "Will you furnish this place with odds and ends and spend little time here?"

"Omsbridge demands most of my time. And I have a place in Lincolnshire as well that requires my attention on occasion."

"And that house on Berkeley Square during the Season."

"You have seen that?"

"Oh yes. Aunt Patty pointed it out on a drive. 'And *that* one is owned by Lord Omsbridge. The one with the ugly gargoyles—' " Angelea broke off, blushing.

"They are ugly. I believe they were designed to frighten evil spirits away. The interior is much nicer. In fact, once inside, you can forget the gargoyles protecting you."

"Do you have many old things there?"

"Both old and new. Some things have been in the family for many generations. I have purchased a few."

"And won a few?" she asked mischievously.

He looked at her soberly. "I have won a great many things, by honest means only."

"How can people call you a devil? You are quite the opposite."

"I am pleased to hear you say so. Perhaps it is easier losing to a devil than a mere mortal."

"Mortal you may be, but not 'mere.' 'Exceptional' is more suitable," she said, her smile adding a glow to her countenance.

Ignoring the compliment, Lord Omsbridge continued in a serious tone. "Miss Byngstone, would you enjoy overseeing the furnishing of this house?"

"Me? I—I know very little about such matters." Her cheeks flushed bright red, she clasped her hands nervously, and looked at the stone paving. "I would like to please you, but—"

"Please, I meant no alarm. Any number of people would be available to advise. If you preferred, they could take full charge of it. What I am suggesting . . . what I am asking . . . Will you be the mistress of Hillview, and of Omsbridge, and of the house of Berkeley Square? Miss Byngstone, will you honor me by becoming my wife?"

She looked up quickly, her eyes wide, her face paling. "Your wife?" She swayed unsteadily.

Cyprian offered his arm and she clutched it to regain her balance. Confident of her response, he waited patiently while she scanned the vista as if seeing it for the first time.

With sparkling eyes, she faced him and took a deep breath. "Do you really mean it?"

He answered soberly, "I really mean it."

"Yes, oh yes!" she exclaimed, throwing her arms around him and offering her lips for a kiss.

Cyprian obliged quickly, acutely aware of her groom taking hesitant steps in their direction. Surprisingly, her stiff, puckered lips pricked feelings long dulled by soft excesses. Yes, her purity would heal the pain he hid and fulfill his yearning for peace and wholeness. With her he could turn aside the preacher's accusing finger.

"But what will Father say?" she asked as their lips parted.

"I think I may bring him around," he responded, placing a gentle kiss in her palm. "I will escort you home and meet with Sir Matthew immediately, if he is available."

Angelea stared up at Cyprian and whispered, "He will agree. He must. Oh, I know he will."

Cyprian felt as if he was plunging into the depths of her soft, gold-flecked eyes. Dizzily he recalled Tony's recent warning, *Cyprian, you are the sort of fellow to fall for a pair of innocent eyes and be utterly lost.*

Nine

Stiffly erect, lips tightly pursed, Simmons sat at the far end of the Willows' drawing room, apparently engrossed in a leather-bound book of sermons. In a window recess, Cyprian spoke softly to Angelea, elaborating on his plans for their marriage trip through Italy. She stared at her handkerchief, pleating it nervously in her lap.

Being allowed extensive periods of intimate conversation with a man gave her at once a sense of maturity and alarm. Since her experience was limited to her father and the unfortunate Becket, she never knew quite what to expect from this man she was to marry. Although charming and romantic, he remained an enigma.

"I know you will enjoy visiting with my friends in Tivoli and seeing the antiquities being found near Rosina."

"Yes, milord," she agreed, apalled at meeting strangers in foreign places.

When he did not continue, she looked up anxiously, and was relieved to see him smiling.

He took her hand and pressed it affectionately. "You may call me Cyprian, my dear."

"Cyprian! Are, are you quite sure?"

"My Christian name," he apologized. "My good friends, and you, may use it in preference to 'milord.' I trust you do not have a dislike of it."

"Oh no!" She glanced over her shoulder toward Simmons, then spoke barely above a whisper. "Would you—would you please tell me what it means?"

"What it *means*? My dear child, in my family husbands and wives customarily use each other's given names when speaking privately. I was under the impression the same prevailed in your family."

"It does," she agreed in haste, her cheeks a flaming red. "But, you see, the name 'John' means 'beloved.' What does 'Cyprian' mean?"

"I understand. I beg your pardon for disappointing you, but I don't know. It's an old family name. Many generations ago someone had an unfortunate religious turn and named the eldest son Cyprian."

"*Religious* turn?"

"Yes. There once was a man," he began, "I believe he was the bishop of Carthage. Although of a leading family, he or his faith proved troublesome. He was beheaded, and therefore became a saint, like Thomas a Becket. All this was in the distant past, the first or second century. My ancestor read some of his letters or heard about him. At any rate, he was sufficiently impressed to adopt the name for his heir. 'Cyprianus' was the original name. Fortunately, it was shortened to 'Cyprian.' "

"Oh." Once again she felt awed by his family's lengthy history, even more impressive than her mother's.

"The young man became a leader of men, courageous, and virtuous beyond belief. Subsequent generations used the name, hoping their sons would become as singular as he."

"Is this always the name of the eldest son?"

"Oh, no! We're not so stiff as that. Usually the eldest son is named for his grandfather, sometimes for an uncle. My elder brother died at an early age . . . five, I was told. I was but two at the time. I was named for one of my father's cousins, whom he greatly admired. Those bearing this name have been held in high affection, a position I covet."

A hint of wistfulness in his tone prompted her to respond, "I see many fine qualities in you. And, I hold you in high affection."

"Do you, my dear? When you know me better . . . But tell me, why were you curious about the meaning of my name?"

"You will not laugh?" she asked anxiously with a sidelong glance.

"I assure you, I will not laugh," he answered solemnly.

"The other night Mother and Father were talking about—about someone. I think they forgot I was in the room working on my stitchery. At least Father forgot about me. And he said, 'Oh, she's just a cyprian. But I'll grant you a very pretty one.' Mother shushed him and looked my way. I made no sign of hearing them, but the conversation turned to the weather and crops.

"Later I asked Simmons what 'cyprian' meant. She pursed her lips like she'd eaten something quite sour and read me a lecture on young ladies learning not to ask improper questions and rather concentrating on running a household. She said if I applied myself to housewifery and the social attainments, I should not have room in my head for—You promised!" She interrupted her account, indignant at his obvious difficulty in maintaining his countenance.

"My dear, I am not laughing at you, but at your Simmons. What a foolish woman trying to stifle your very active curiosity. No wonder you ran away to meet me that day. What a dragon she must be!"

"Oh, she is!" Angelea agreed warmly. "Now, will you tell me what Father meant?"

Cyprian raised his eyebrows and cleared his throat in a manner similar to her father's when he was uncomfortable about something her mother said. "Well, the term 'cyprian' as used by your father goes back to Greek mythology. Are you familiar with Aphrodite?"

"The beautiful goddess of love, is she not?" Angelea asked eagerly, pleased her perusal of dusty legends might be useful.

"She was said to be the mother of Eros and she was reputed to have been born in a cave on Cyprus. One of the centers of her cult was in Cyprus."

Angelea broke in eagerly, her tongue and thoughts running ahead together. "So 'cyprian' refers to a pretty woman who worships the goddess of love. I see. One of those, er, petticoats everyone knows about but doesn't mention. How strange. A saint and a . . . a whore"—she spoke the word gingerly with an audacious glance at Cyprian—"both with the same name," she finished in a rush.

He laughed and patted her hand. "And to complete the irony, the saint's name probably came from the, er, goddess of love, as she was hundreds of years older than he."

"Do you suppose he was ever like her, loving and warm? The saints always seem so dull, so sober and, and . . ."

"Grim?"

"Very," she nodded.

"Perhaps he was, before he was elevated to being a bishop. Have no fears, my dear, I possess not the slightest bent in that direction." He frowned briefly, as if an unpleasant memory crossed his mind. Firmly he declared, "Ours is to be a life of excitement and happiness."

Angelea paused at the tall window overlooking the neatly trimmed hedges forming an intricate design in the Simpson's gardens. Such a relief to be free of people for a quiet moment. Mornings she was engaged in shopping and fittings enough to fulfill her wildest dreams. The afternoons and evenings were occupied with calls, dinners, suppers, concerts, and balls. She fingered the thickly fringed green curtain beside her. Tentatively she drew it about her, musing that it so nearly matched her gown as to make an appropriate cloak to wear with it.

Much as she had anticipated this dazzling array of social delights, they fatigued her beyond measure. Perhaps when she was escorted by her husband instead of being pushed about by her mother and aunt, then she could respond with more enthusiasm. As Lady Omsbridge, she must be able to go these rounds without betraying her exhaustion.

Lord Omsbridge, Cyprian, as she tried to think of him these past months, was most attentive. His tender concern for her pleasure and comfort aroused delightful fancies of their future life. And yet . . .

Idly she twirled a golden curl about her right index finger. In this private moment, she admitted her most wearing burden was anxiety over her coming role as a wife. In observing her parents' life more closely, she caught mysterious looks between them. Papa's touch on Mama's arm could bring a flush to her cheeks and a smiling glance. Would she and Cyprian share something special like that? And what did it mean? A great deal more seemed involved in marriage beyond running a household and attending social activities.

"I tell you, Maria, you've nothing for concern!"

Startled by this assertion, Angelea peeped around the curtain. Two strange women approached the fireplace at the far end of the empty salon. Not wanting to be drawn into their conversation, she shrank against the green curtain.

"He may be about to marry that country mouse," the speaker continued as they settled in the highbacked chairs before the blaze, "but you are more in his style."

The soft reply was unintelligible.

"Nonsense. Amuse yourself with James for a while, until the wedding trip is over, or a few months more. I am confident our dear Devil is only concerned with gaining an heir for his precious Omsbridge. Mark my words, when he gets a son, he will be back on the Town."

A hard knot formed in Angelea's stomach. Her dizzy gaze began to darken, and she grasped the window handle to keep from collapsing.

The relentless speaker added, "Bear in mind that no relationship is lasting with him. He is generous, a delightful lover, as I well know, but he soon tires and moves on to someone else. He will tire of that country child. Then you will surely draw his attention. Just keep your heart whole, for it will not last. Nothing does."

Finally her feet responded to her panic. Angelea sped on tiptoe through the nearby door, across the hall, and into the drawing room. She faced countless people babbling streams of words at each other. As quickly as possible she pushed through them to her mother.

"My dear, you look so pale!" Lady Anne exclaimed. "Is something wrong?"

"Oh, Mama, I have the headache, and am so tired. Would it disappoint you terribly if we went home?"

"Of course not, my dear." With dispatch, Lady Anne bid their adieus and summoned their carriage.

As they jolted over the rough London cobblestones, she said, "I hold myself responsible, for I have driven you excessively with fitting and parties. It is a wonder you survived the rush of activities so well." She sighed. "It's just that this is a special Season for us. I do so want everything to be perfect. After your marriage we will not have each other's company freely."

Suddenly Lady Anne took Angelea's hand and held them tightly. "You were a precious gift to me, to us, your papa and me. We did everything in our power to protect you from evil and provide for your happiness. I have thrilled to your growth into beautiful womanhood." She reached out to cup Angelea's cheek in her palm. "We were going to name you Charlotte, for my mother, you know. But when I saw you, you were so sweet I called you 'My little angel.' And, truly, you have been a blessing to us. I shall miss you deeply, my dear. But, I am confident you will enjoy managing your own establishment even as I do."

Angelea forced a smile, but the unknown woman's assessment of her future husband's character had thrown her expectations into disarray.

$\mathcal{T}en$

$\mathcal{M}$ ary Croft straightened a vase of fresh roses and checked once more that all was in order in the master's room. As countless times these past hours when near a window facing east, she paused to look for a carriage.

The avenue, curving through the bright green swells of the Downs, was marked by tall, old beeches and oaks, splendid in autumn gold and red. Winding walks below the Hall led past flower beds of asters and petunias into the park, artfully contrived to look natural in the modern mode, and skirted a placid blue lake, streaked silver by the afternoon sun. Graceful willows trailed into its waters. Beyond the gentle rise of south lawn and grove of chestnuts and ash trees, she could barely see the outer rim of the new fountain. It put her to the blush having that indecent statue of a naked woman standing there poorly screened by jets of water. Old Moses' cracked tenor-singing drifted upward from the front terrace where he was trimming the hedges and mingled with Jeff's bright whistling from the side rose garden.

About to turn away, a faint movement and flash of reflected light caught Mary's eye. She sucked in her breath and leaned forward, her hand on the sill, waiting until the miniature horse-drawn conveyance came into view. At last, the master was coming! Whirling about, she ran into the hall.

"Sally!" she called to a young maid at the far end, "tell Fothering his lordship is coming! They're about to cross the bridge."

"Aye, Muss Croft, dracly minute. Everthing be mucked-out, I bluv." She paused at the head of the back stairs to say over her shoulder, "Be

57

her an abuseful 'ooman, Muss Croft?"

"We'll soon know," Mrs. Croft answered coolly. "Be quick now."

What would the new mistress be like? Mrs. Croft entered the newly decorated room adjoining the master's and took in the pink velvet hangings, lace canopy, fringed bed curtains and the new chair by Adams in flowered tapestry. She must be fair and frivolous. At least he saw her that way. She fingered the rich drapery. Nothing was too good for his lady. He certainly behaved as a man besotted these past months, fussing over this room and even the whole house. Hopefully her strong character would guide the master from his sinful, wasting ways.

A quick glance assured her the door was shut against a sudden intrusion. Moving to the side of the bed, she knelt and raised folded hands to her chin. Only God could make this woman be right for her master. Her poor master's mother did nothing to inspire him in resisting fleshly temptations. Her wanton example merely encouraged his base nature. Mrs. Croft was determined the Almighty would not be ignorant of the important role the new mistress could play in reforming the master.

With a smile, she recalled the sturdy child she occasionally minded for the old nurse. A bright, eager, happy boy he was. And then the spindly, awkward lad learning to love the grand land that would one day be his. All the staff hoped the idealistic young master would redress his alcoholic father's neglect.

Never would she forget his disillusionment. Then she was Mary, the upstairs maid, depended upon for the work old Miss Dove, the housekeeper, forgot or was too tired to do. Mary was in the upper hall that day, carrying fresh linen to the yellow guest room for that horrid man, when the young master bounded up the front stairs. Startled, she dropped the sheets. No one expected him down from Oxford for several weeks. Joyfully he waved to her, then knocked on his mother's door. Before Mary could forestall him, he entered this very room.

Then it was hung with green brocades and cluttered with expensive trinkets. She heard a few sharp exclamations, and that woman's thoughtless laughter. Mary had barely recovered when she heard his steps. Over her shoulder she had an unforgettable glimpse of the young master's ashen face, grimacing in grief as he rushed to his room.

Whenever Mary Croft heard gossip of his sinful affairs, she remembered that moment and begged God's mercy. Surely he was driven into his wild ways by that evil harlot, that late Lady Omsbridge. Surely his transformation could be achieved through a truly good woman. The new mistress *must* be that woman.

Having made her wishes known at the throne of grace, Mrs. Croft went to the new gold-framed mirror. With a sense of satisfaction, she adjusted her plain white cap and smoothed her demure gray petticoats. The preparations for her dear master's return with his bride were complete. Nothing physically or spiritually was left to chance.

Slowly the carriage rolled through intermittent showers of leaves loosened by windy gusts from the golden archway spanning the drive. Inwardly, Angelea tried to ignore her rising nervousness and listen to Cyprian's comments. But, despite her efforts, she understood little as he pointed out places here and there.

During their four months' wedding trip in Italy and Spain, her new husband had revealed himself as considerate, loving, and firmly in charge. He guided her through the sites he enjoyed on his Grand Tour following his studies at Oxford, and frequently surprised her with lovely gifts.

She may not share his enthusiasm for ancient marbles in Rosina, but now she understood it better. The earnest Swiss engineer, Karl Weber, assisted her by explaining the importance of what he was doing. He and Cyprian showed a deep appreciation for each other. Cyprian found the tunnels and excavations an exciting contact with people living centuries past. She found them dark, frightening, and ghostly. Climbing worn stairs, clambering over the old hewn stones of Virgil's tomb near Naples was fatiguing to her. And who was Virgil, anyway, but a long dead poet who wrote in a foreign language?

Rome was better, for they attended parties in spacious villas. In Tivoli she was even pleased by the lovely Franchesca's attempts to attract Cyprian's interest, for he ignored them.

Spain was more to her taste. There they traveled through the beautiful countryside unencumbered by ruins awaiting their investigation. People of social distinction entertained them, and they were presented to Ferdinand VI and Queen Barbara through the good offices of Ambassador Keene.

The one distressing event involved "the man in brown." Angelea saw him only three times. First he was their inept waiter in a little ship where they paused for refreshment outside Madrid. He upset a glass of wine on their table. Fortunately their clothes were not stained, but the wine flowed over the table and onto the floor, spattering Cyprian's boots. The waiter wiped them off pouring forth a stream of Spanish apologies.

A night or two later, Angelea awoke hearing low voices in the next room. Frightened at finding Cyprian absent, she arose, and peered anxiously through the large ornate keyhole in their door. She saw the waiter, now wearing a plain brown suit, standing in their sitting room, earnestly talking with Cyprian, who was frowning intently. Puzzled, she returned to bed resolved to ask him what it meant. However, she fell asleep. In the morning, he made no comment about the visitor, and Angelea felt too awkward about spying through the keyhole to venture an inquiry.

The next day, as they were entering their traveling coach, several bystanders screamed. A dark object fell from above, and the man in brown sprawled on his back but a few feet distant. Glancing upward, she saw a movement on the balcony above him. Instantly Cyprian moved to shield her from the grotesque sight, assisted her to her seat, and bade the coachman drive on as if nothing untoward had occurred.

When she asked who the man was, Cyprian shrugged. "I suppose he was some local person who drank more than he should."

"But he was our waiter a few days ago," she had persisted.

"Really, my dear? I did not notice."

"But—"

"My dear"—he took her hand caressingly—"put this unfortunate from your mind. He is of no consequence to us."

With a troubling flash of insight, Angelea became aware that she was locked out of a part of Cyprian's life. An important door slammed in her face.

Now, nearing their journey's end, Angelea realized she was no longer the prime object of her husband's attention. He talked incessantly about Omsbridge's history and its people. It was time she assumed her position as the mistress of his establishment, a task of frightening proportions.

Suddenly Cyprian rapped sharply on the carriage roof. It stopped. The footman opened the door and lowered the steps. Cyprian jumped down, turned, and offered Angelea his hand. Carefully she placed her feet on the tiny steps and paused a moment to glance over their wooded surroundings. "Are we to walk the rest of the way?"

He laughed, lifting her down. "No. I doubt you could walk so far in those shoes." As he tucked her hand into the crook of his arm, he explained, "It is still well over two miles, for the road snakes and twists down this hill and up the other to the Hall. I nearly always pause here when I come home . . . I like the view." He led her to the edge of the road and pointed through the trees. "There, do you see it?"

Angelea stretched on her tiptoes to see where he was pointing, but the branches blocked her sight.

Cyprian laughed again and rolled a stone into place for her to stand upon. When she was securely positioned with his hands on her waist steadying her, she could see across a small vale to an aged stone structure dominating the scene.

It sat as a crown, rising at least four stories, with an additional one or two in the turreted corners. The front, mellowed by old stone and ivy, extended farther from wing to wing than any building she could remember. A large gothic window, appropriate for a cathedral, dominated the east end. Graceful trees framed the majestic structure, blurring its severe lines. Gentle slopes fell away from it in a series of terraced gardens. Sunlight danced on scattered pools of water.

Awestruck, she stared at the imposing mass. How could she hope to be its mistress! She always imagined Omsbridge Hall as larger than her father's home. But reality far exceeded her grandest dreams.

Cyprian spoke softly in her ear. "Isn't it beautiful? Time has been kind, don't you agree? There's an archers' walk behind that battlemented top. The view from there over the Downs to the sea is magnificent. I want to show it to you soon, and all my special places. Dearest, I know you will come to love the Hall and the land as much as I do. As do all who live here."

Anxious to please her new husband, Angelea replied, "Yes, I am confident you are right." Then as her emotions overcame her, she exclaimed, "But it is so huge! I shall be lost!"

"No, no, my dearest. You shall be found." He swung her down from the stone. "It is the perfect setting for you, my treasure, and for our family."

Angelea tried not to flinch as he said that too familiar word "family." He was all she longed for in a man—tender, kind, determined, enthusiastic, adoring. But, his obsession with a large family of sons frightened her. Truly, as the women at the Simpsons' said, he married to gain an heir. What if she could not bear children? What if, as her mother, she bore only one daughter? Would he cast her off if she failed him in this?

And, as an experienced man of the world, how could she interest him for long? What would happen when he tired of her? Could she prevent that?

The last portion of their journey was covered at a slow pace. Cyprian eagerly pulled her from one side of the carriage to the other, pointing out the trees he climbed as a boy, the streams he fished, and his favorite secret niches.

The carriage halted, and once again the steps were lowered. When Cyprian handed her down, Angelea looked up to see the thick oaken door studded with iron bolts swing open on gigantic hinges. It appeared as a cavern about to devour her. Clinging tightly to Cyprian's arm, she climbed the broad stone stairs leading to that terrifying, yawning door.

Cyprian patted her hand reassuringly, commenting, "I believe they are all here to welcome us, my dear. No doubt they've had a watch trained on the bridge all day."

At that moment, a black and white kitten scampered across the stairs, turned a summersault as it captured a yellow leaf with its paw, then leaped sideways on its toes, and ran away. A peal of spontaneous laughter freed Angelea from the grip of fear.

An awesomely dignified man of indeterminate age, wearing the Omsbridge livery of dark blue and silver, stepped forward to the top of the stairs and bowed. "Welcome, milord, milady."

"Ah, Fothering," Cyprian responded warmly, "how good to see you. How good it is to be home!"

As the carriage had approached, the servants lined up by seniority in the entry hall, their tongues competing for prominence and speculating about the new lady. Mrs. Croft descended the stairs thinking them foolish. But, what else could be expected when, for generations, the staff came from nearby villages with little outside contact? Most bore a hint in eye, chin, or nose that Omsbridge blood flowed in their veins. She herself suspected that her grandmother owed half her heritage to the first Lord Omsbridge. "The sins of the father will be visited unto the third and fourth generation," she recalled. She was the third generation. An immediate reply popped helpfully into her mind. "I will show mercy to thousands of those who love me." Surely that counteracted the sins of her great-grandfather.

She silenced the chattering maids with stern looks, leaving verbal reprimands to Fothering. In the expectant hush, they heard the rattles of the carriage and clomping horses' hooves. Fothering's hand was raised in silent signal to the footman holding the front door. A few seconds after the sounds ceased, Fothering's hand fell to his side and the great door swung open.

The silence was broken by a tinkling cascade of laughter. Mary Croft's heart sank at the frivolous sound.

Fothering stepped outside to extend formal greetings on behalf of the household. Lord Omsbridge appeared on the threshold with his lady on his arm.

Mrs. Croft glided forward to drop her deepest curtsey. She bowed her head, hiding her disappointment, and composed her features respectfully. This golden-haired child did not live up to her hopes. But surely God would not pass over her many requests. If He selected this woman to be the mistress, Mary Croft would ease her way.

Eleven

Angelea twisted to look over her shoulder into the mirror, scrutinizing the fit of her new sapphire riding dress. The bright color topped by a perky white feather in her small tricorn provided the right effect. The door opened behind her, and she saw the reflection of Cyprian's pleased expression. Confidently she greeted him with a kiss, then tucked her hand under his arm. It was a glorious morning for their ride at Omsbridge. Angelea was determined nothing should mar it as they walked through the long, confusing passages populated by an army of strange servants.

In the stable yard, her stunned attention was caught by the glossy bay mare being led out after Cyprian's stallion, Blue Star. The horse of her dreams was alive, even to the white blaze down her face and four matched stockings on her dainty feet.

"I hoped she would please you, my dear," Cyprian said as Angelea left his side.

Clapping her hands in delight, Angelea walked around the animal, exclaiming, "She is beautiful!" Gently she stroked the white blaze, murmuring, "You are my own, my special pet. Freckles shall be envious when he arrives."

"Let's see how she goes," Cyprian suggested, cupping his hands to help her mount. "Give her the reins, Percy." He stepped back, hands on his hips.

Angelea rode several turns about the yard, thrilled with the mare's even stride and power. "Such beautiful manners!" she declared. "Her pace is smooth. Oh, what a marvel she is!" Suddenly she called, "See if you can catch me!"

She turned the mare down the drive, slapping her hind quarters smartly. The mare sprang into a gallop. In response to only a slight nudge from Angelea, she left the smooth drive to cross the meadow below the terraces. Effortlessly, she skimmed over a low wall. They covered a considerable distance before Angelea heard Blue Star's pounding hooves behind her. Rather than be overtaken, she reined to a halt under a tree and dismounted.

Undaunted by Cyprian's thunderous expression as he joined her, she said gaily, "Ah ha! We beat you here! What a shame I did not wager on her speed."

He leapt from his horse, grasped her shoulders and shook her fiercely. "Never again! Don't ever ride like that again!"

Shocked into silence, Angelea staggered when he released her, throwing her hand against the tree trunk to keep from falling. Then indignation obliterated other emotions. "How dare you treat me this way!"

Rapidly Cyprian strode away from her, then back, his color high, his lips pressed tightly together. Stopping in front of her, he declared, "It was foolhardy of you to race an untried horse over strange terrain." He took a deep shuddering breath. "She might have balked at the wall."

"Then I should have ended in an undignified heap, as I have done before," she answered, chin raised defiantly.

"Or broken your neck, and I should have lost you."

His concern softened her, but she suppressed the urge to rush to his arms, begging pardon for her impetuous behavior.

"Now that you know she has speed," he added in a more moderate tone, "I trust you will not need to test her again."

"But what a waste that should be!"

"And if she stepped in a hole and broke her leg, how would you feel?"

"Devastated! I've longed for this very horse all my life! Oh, Cyprian, I am sorry!" She ran to the shelter of his arms.

"My father died in just such a gallop not far from here," he said, holding her tightly. "I feared I would hold your lifeless body as I did his."

"Forgive me?" She looked up anxiously.

His burning kiss made an eloquent reply. As he tossed her into the side-saddle, he instructed sternly, "Save for an emergency, you may only run her where neither of you may be injured. I will show you a safe place."

The level area designated by Cyprian seemed far too tame to Angelea, but she had to admit the wisdom of not risking her new pet on rough country unnecessarily. She kept her reservations to herself. On occasion, just for exercise, she intended giving the mare her head.

"What do you choose to call her?" Cyprian asked as they approached the Hall.

"Starlight," Angelea answered promptly. "As a child I named my dream horse Starlight. Beautiful Starlight. My beautiful Starlight. Oh, how can I thank you? You are too generous!" When he lifted her down, she slid into his arms to give him an enthusiastic kiss, to the delight of the grooms.

Anxiously Tony watched Cyprian pace silently around the triangular chest standing in the center of the entry hall. Although he feigned interest in the cobalt blue vase standing on the oaken side table, Tony followed his friend's reactions intently from the corner of his eyes.

Angelea stared at the piece, then tentatively touched the painted garland of fruit, flowers, and wild life decorating its door. She studied the miniatures interspersed among the fruit, pictures of herself, Cyprian, the gothic temple in the garden, and five different aspects of Omsbridge Hall.

Tony felt a rush of pleasure as he heard her exclaim in an awed whisper, "Who did this beautiful work? Vanbrugh?"

Laughing, Cyprian caught her in a light hug with his right arm. "You see, Tony?" he exclaimed. "My dearest, you validate my opinion precisely. I doubt not this is Tony's own handiwork. He insists he is the merest dabbler. I regard his work highly."

Tony turned from the vase to the newlyweds with a depreciating gesture. "The quality is poor, the work of an amateur."

Cyprian placed his hand on Tony's shoulder. "We shall cherish this masterpiece. You must have done the pictures of Omsbridge while here on holiday."

Gratified, Tony flushed and apologized, "Yes, at odd moments, here and there. If you notice, the flowers, fruit, birds, and that squirrel are seen here. Of course, I've sketched you times out of mind, but your portrait, dear lady, I did from memory. I fear it does not reflect your beauty accurately."

"But this is the image living in my mirror!"

"Barely your likeness. I am grateful it does not offend you. Note the design on the top." He pointed to the inlaid geometric pattern composed of several kinds of wood. "I used pieces collected from here. Inside, you will find several drawers which, I trust, will make the cabinet of some small use."

"Angelea, did you ever know such a man?" Cyprian commented as they explored the velvet-lined drawers. "He has entrusted us with a treasure and then devalues it. A corner in our sitting room would be appropriate, don't you think?"

"Oh yes. You will be with us in spirit even while you are at Stonehead or London."

"I am pleased you like my inept efforts," Tony said, delighted with their reaction to his work. "Whatever faults it has are all mine, for no other hand touched it during its construction. Now, please show me this fountain you've added. Did you truly copy it from those in Rome?"

"Yes. Angelea's arrival gave me the motive to do it, although I've long had the idea and the statue."

The three friends strolled arm-in-arm to the southeast corner of the Hall where the midday sun transformed jets of water into a thin, shimmering veil about a marble maiden half-clad in drapery.

"Behold Cyprian's first love, his Aphrodite!" Angelea announced. "She captivated him in Florence on his Grand Tour."

"Is she not perfection?" Cyprian asked. "You see why Angelea is the only woman I have found to compare."

"And you hid her all this time?" Tony exclaimed.

"Of course," Cyprian responded. "I know your love of beauty too well, dear friend. You would have me surrender her to you."

"Ah yes. Had I seen her in a crate—I know a perfect setting for her at Stonehead. But now, in your fountain, I may only express admiration."

"Besides being beautiful," Angelea commented, "she links us with ancient Greece, which fascinates Cyprian. Like the piece of marble fingers he found near Rosina and keeps on his desk."

"I call it his touchstone," Tony said with a smile. "He is forever rubbing it when he considers a problem, or wishes to think deeply about a subject. As if he gains wisdom from the past."

"Now, before we go in to dinner, you must approve my darling," Angelea said, leading the way to the stables.

Henry, the head groom, led Starlight out for inspection. Tony ran his hand over her back and patted her flanks in appreciation. He nodded and gave his unqualified approval.

"And you should see how she goes!" Angelea exclaimed enthusiastically. "Like the wind. Even Blue Star has a hard time catching her."

Tony's skin prickled at the sudden tension he sensed between the couple. Angelea's sparkling eyes seemed to challenge Cyprian's frown and raised chin.

"Like her mistress, hard to control," Cyprian said stiffly. "I fear for your lovely neck."

"She is as surefooted as an antelope," Angelea declared, flashing a winsome smile. "And you know, I feel so free, so excited when we are out for a gallop."

"Yes, my dear, I know. Well, Tony, we must not keep Mrs. Worth's dinner waiting."

"No indeed," Angelea agreed. "She prepared your favorite pheasant a la orange and other delicacies. They deserve our full attention."

Tony found the meal equalled any at Stonehead or in town. Truly he was as comfortable here as at home.

As the chocolate tart was served, Angelea commented, "Tony, your skill in making that beautiful chest is amazing. You must enjoy creating such things."

"Ah yes, dear lady. Working with fine woods, fashioning furniture pleasing to the eye and useful in the pursuits of life, is one of the joys of my life," he answered, smiling at her. "Even a greater joy than a perfect meal, such as we have just eaten. Stonehead is crowded with my creations. Some I entrust to my dearest friends."

"Our chest is as fine as one by Mr. Adams or Mr. Chippendale. Have you thought to sell any?"

Shocked by her suggestion, Tony appealed to his old friend. "Cyprian, you understand, it would be scandalous for a man in my position to become an artisan, even an architect, or a painter. Much as I would enjoy it, I am a man of fashion. I am obliged to live like one." He sighed heavily for emphasis. "Such is my cross in life. Boredom reaches out to engulf me constantly."

"But not here," Cyprian countered. "Come, admit it, you do not find us boring."

Assuming an attitude of worried earnestness, Tony stretched his left hand toward Angelea, pleading, "Dear lady, do not betray me to a living soul. I must hide my failings from my acquaintances."

Anxiously Angelea glanced at Cyprian. Seemingly reassured by his low chuckle, she answered with a nervous giggle, "I pledge my solemn word."

"Very well. I own I am never bored here while we are unencumbered with the presence of others. Cyprian permits me to draw, paint, sketch, carve, and muck about, never betraying my foolishness to the world. If your lips are truly sealed, I would be most happy for you to visit Stonehead with him. I am never bored there, either, doing all manner of silly things."

Cyprian added, "You see, my dearest, Tony spent years convincing everyone his sole interest is pursuing the latest mode."

"How do your people say it? I have no 'heart for the land.' It is very respectable for a man in my position to exhaust himself in overseeing lands and improving agriculture. However, not being so gifted, I am reduced to practicing my weakness in secret."

Cyprian laughed. "And, my friend, you possess another disreputable talent—playacting. What a waste that you are of noble birth! The theatre would profit immensely if you could tread the boards."

Tony struck a think pose. "Is that truly your opinion?"

"Truly."

With a deep sigh and shake of his head, Tony said, "Angelea, I fear you chose your husband poorly. He says the most outrageous things about those he claims as friends. Never believe a word he says about me."

"Not even that you are honorable and honest?" Cyprian asked.

Tony covered his pleasure with a flip of his hand. "That least of all. I use every skill I possess to prevent anyone from forming such an opinion."

Cyprian let Blue Star's reins go slack, permitting him to graze. He glanced at Tony's tense profile. His friend was staring at the gray fog bank hovering over the surface of the Channel as if he could see the French coast beyond. "And now, Tony, what is on your mind?"

"My mind? Whatever do you mean?" Tony relaxed and twisted in his saddle to face Cyprian, his eyebrows raised. "Oh, I am remiss. You should know that the Spanish information you brought is valuable. What a pity De la Rubio died. An able man, hard to replace. I sent the packet on to Pitt as soon as I checked it."

Cyprian exclaimed in surprise. "Really? How?"

"While we ride above the Oms, my coachman is meeting a traveler at the Dancing Skillet. Is that what you meant?"

"Old friend, you have been on the figit since you arrived. Much as I appreciate your excellent chest, I do not think that it or the Spanish papers are the prime reason for calling on us so promptly."

"I suppose it is somewhat soon as you are still newly wed. I hope you are not offended. You are right, of course. As you face the chest, you will notice a square of mahogony on the left side. It is the only bit of wood not from Omsbridge. Press it and a hidden compartment will open on the right side, suitable for keeping secret documents."

"I wonder why I should possess secret documents! I perceive you are including me in a plan."

"Alas, you know me too well. I hope others do not read me as easily."

Cyprian narrowed his eyes thoughtfully. He recognized an undercurrent of excitement in his friend, certain prelude to a rash scheme. "Tony, you are remarkably pleased. I expected to find you in the dismals after word of the signing of the treaty of Versailles. Surely this means France is intent on war with us by denying us the support of our old ally, Austria."

"No, no. Don't you see? War with France has been inevitable. The Peace of Paris is but a charade. With Frederick we have a common interest, namely the strength of Prussia. If he is strong enough, he will protect Hanover for us. With our subsidy and cavalry, he will be able to handle Russia and Austria. They are united against him by hate, but hate is not trustworthy. It sometimes clouds judgment. Frederick fights for survival. I have no doubt which will win.

"Frederick will free us to defeat France in the Colonies. This treaty shows Louis for the fool he is. He views Europe as the main struggle. The best of his armies and generals with the bulk of his money will go to the struggle near at hand."

Tony shook his head. "Europe is tiny compared to the Colonies and their wealth. I am grateful I was sent to the Colonies before the Continent on my Tour. To see the immensity of the land and sense the people's spirit is—is—I cannot explain it. Afterward the Continent seemed very old and tired. Our future is in the Colonies. See if I am not right."

"And you are right, old friend, because that is what Pitt thinks."

"You must not say so," Tony said quickly. "I trust you with my thoughts as no one else. It is imperative that all the world thinks I am a silly fop without a serious thought in my head. People say the most amazing things around me because they think I have not the least understanding in the matter. It is of great value."

Cyprian laughed. "Have no fear. I will not betray you to anyone, not even my beloved Angelea."

Tony looked horrified. "Especially not her. I have no confidence in the discretion of a beautiful woman. If she knew, I should not sleep well."

"Your secrets are safe. I will entrust them to no one."

"You must not, for, you see, this is an adventure of great proportions. I believe Pitt has it in mind to seize *Canada*! Do you see what this means?"

Cyprian frowned. "How can this be done?"

"With the Colonials. Our move last December to make the provincial troops equal with the regular British army has infused new life into the Colonials. Mark my words, they will be of great value to us under their Colonel Bradstreet."

"You cannot seriously consider that those poorly trained colonials can be the equal of our regulars!"

"They are better trained than you think, and they have a personal stake in the land they are fighting for and on. For years the French treated them badly, stirring up the Indians to make savage attacks on the frontier settlers. They will fight with a will and a knowledge our men do not possess.

"Our navy will keep Louis busy here. You watch. In the coming months, we will have France by the ear. We will strike here and there along the coast. Those Frenchies will not know where to expect us, so they will deploy their forces widely. We will know where they are and go elsewhere. Pitt is a genius. Even the ship's captains will not know until they are at sea, for they sail under sealed orders, so no enemy spy will be the wiser.

"Don't you see, dear boy, if Frederick should fail and we lose Hanover, only King George will feel very badly. But, if we gain Canada, the West Indies, and India, even he would be reconciled to the loss. We could even trade for Hanover."

These grand plans, involving distant lands he had never seen, passed Cyprian's comprehension. "Why do we need Canada?"

"It is rich beyond imagining. But also, it would protect the Colonies to the north and unite them with Hudson's Bay. England would then control the accessible land along the coast, save for Spanish Florida. The opportunities are . . ." He flung his arms wide.

"Limitless?" Cyprian queried skeptically.

Tony chuckled. "Nothing is limitless. But this is close. Look at the ring you are wearing, the one I gave you."

Cyprian examined the nugget set in silver. "You called it a turquoise, from some place with a Spanish name."

"Santa Fe. It is crude compared to a sapphire. But, since it is the color of heaven, the natives revere it. And its strange markings make it uniquely interesting. It is like the land beyond. Incredible!"

"Old friend, at times I think you would like to return there."

"I would. Indeed I would. But my responsibilities here prevent it. Had I none, I should not have returned."

"Not even to your Stonehead?"

"Stonehead *is* my responsibility." For a few moments he stared again at the fog bank. "I am about to embark on an adventure of great import for England."

"Ah. London's political scene has begun to pall?"

"Pitt has commissioned me to obtain certain information. I go beyond the fog to France. Tomorrow night I meet certain smugglers in a nearby cove and cross over."

Cyprian felt a shiver along his spine. "You will be a spy? And work with smugglers? Must you do this? Old friend, I should very much regret it if the French caught you."

"No more than I," Tony replied.

"You are part of my life. I cannot view this lightly."

Tony laughed. "Thank you, dear boy. But, you must not sound so ominous. It is really very easy. Have no fear. My tongue will not betray me. As you know, my grandparents were Huguenots, so both my governess and the cook were born in France. I grew up in a French atmosphere. *Es verdad*?"

"That is Spanish." Anxiety sharpened his tone.

"True. I speak that too, *nict wahr*?"

"German."

"I know that," Tony said impatiently. Then, with a chuckle and a shrug, he asked, "You doubt me? I just need to hear it. Say something. Anything will do. In French, of course."

"N'importe."

"Ici on parle francaise."

"Grace a Dieu," Cyprian responded fervently.

"Yes, I thank God. But it is important. I shall return successful."

"How will you return?"

"With your permission, I shall come here, to that cave we used to explore, pretending to be smugglers or pirates—the mermaid's cave. When I go up to town, everyone will think I was with you, as I often am."

"And if someone comes looking for you?"

"Tell them I went to see another friend in . . . in Chichester, and will return in a few days. After all, I must not trespass too long on your hospitality, your being newly married."

Cyprian frowned, unable to define his growing uneasiness. "*Mon ami*, all I have is yours. I am happy to assist you in any way. But . . . there is danger here. Not only the spying, but the smugglers. They are a desperate lot. They kill easily. Are you able to deal with them?"

"They know I am on an important government mission, so important I will be blind to their activities. If a coast guard intercepts us, I shall arrange special treatment for them. The French will think I am working with the smugglers, arranging another shipment, as I will do." Tony's eyes took on the light Cyprian recognized as the prelude to a harebrained proposal. "It will be rather like shooting London Bridge. Remember?"

Cyprian shuddered at the memory. Tony's delight in challenging death in the drenching spray of the Thames was not to his taste. He preferred risking a fortune in a throw of dice or the turn of a card.

"Flirting with danger adds a dash of spice to life, you know."

Cyprian shook his head. "Please see that the spice is not so strong it makes *my* eyes water." Then he asked with a gleam of humor, "Surely you have not lost your belief that God is English! Will He not defend our shores without these dangerous missions?"

Tony laughed. "Old Dalrymple would say something like that. Doubtless, God is the best of all Englishmen. But to assume He will raise up a mighty storm every time we are attacked, borders upon, er, the sin of presumption. We are obliged to do our part, and He will do His. Rather like a partnership, I should imagine."

"Perhaps so."

"Never fear, dear boy. I always contrive to survive."

Taking up the reins, Cyprian turned Blue Star toward the Hall. "We must tell Angelea something to explain your presence in absence. If anyone inquires about your comings and goings, she must not betray you in ignorance."

"Yes, I should feel it acutely. I could tell her I've taken to drinking the sea waters at Brighthelmston for my diseased glands under the care of that Doctor, er, whatever is his name?"

"Dr. Russell."

"Of course. Dr. Russell. I don't suppose that village will ever amount to anything. But I might give him some consequence. Nash, you know, has ruined Bath. He made it so rigidly proper and healthy. Proper, health, virtue. No vices allowed. Now, I ask you, how long will the ton keep that as its watering place? I should think he's contributed materially to the success of Wells, or even little Brighthelmston."

"Angelea will not believe you wish to spend any significant time there drinking its bitter water and dipping in the sea. Nor will she believe your glands are diseased. She considers you extremely healthy."

"I suppose you are right. Pretty dull stuff." Tony thought a moment. Then a smile brightened his face. "Ah ha! She is a romantic woman. Let us say I am meeting with a lady for whom I have a grand passion."

"A lady who lives in France?"

"But of course. Because of the hostilities between our two countries, I must cross in the dark of the moon. If our attachment becomes known, my beautiful lady's life will be forfeit and mine will be endangered."

Cyprian considered his bride's reaction to the unlikely tale. "It might do. She likes you. Only last night she said she wished you were as happily settled as we are."

Tony grimaced. "Women are so eager to have a free man shackled!"

Cyprian laughed. "She thinks you are missing life's great joys."

"Is she right?"

Cyprian looked to Tony. "My friend, your jaded soul would be refreshed even as mine if you could win a lady, innocent and pure, as my Angelea. I tell you, such women are the salvation of mankind." With a sheepish chuckle he concluded, "Why, with her at my side, I could face one of those finger-pointing preachers, and even God himself!"

Twelve

ngelea stretched her limbs under the warm, soft covers, and sighed contentedly. A marvelous sense of well-being spread from her inmost center to her fingertips. Loved by her husband, obeyed in her household, the envy of her friends, and honored by those she met, what more could she require of life?

Tangible examples of Cyprian's generosity and admiration filled her wardrobe and jewel chest. But the truest evidences of his affection were in his tone, the light she saw in his eyes, and his tender touch. Those mysterious glances between her parents no longer puzzled her. Fears over Cyprian's sincerity had receded long ago. She succeeded in fixing his affection where others failed. Someday she hoped to display his regard before the horrid women she overheard at the Simpsons'.

Even the responsibilities of the complex household proved a joy with the housekeeper at her side. During her first weeks at Omsbridge, Angelea felt intimidated by the sober, efficient Croft. But as they dealt together, she found Croft expressing helpful suggestions and hints in an inoffensive manner. Her quiet, firm control brought credit to her mistress. The lack of a frill or decoration to soften the linen cap and dark gowns Croft wore testified to her sensible character, free of frivolity. However, Angelea discovered she quickly responded to any members of the household needing care or consideration in the performance of their duties. More than once she was discovered working in the upstairs chambers or even the scullery when a maid was ill or needed in a family emergency. And Croft's rigid moral stand led Angelea to trust her absolutely in everything.

Throwing back the covers, Angelea rose and went to the fireplace, holding out her hands to the cheerful morning blaze. With a pleased smile, she reflected on her cozy chat with Helen Mason the past week at Hillview.

That was her third visit there with Cyprian. As these delightful trips entailed but a few days, she and Cyprian had ridden across the Downs and the weald into Surrey with only Feldman in attendance. On the way they dined at the Royal Oak where the host treated her with great deference.

At Hillview she paid morning calls on her mother while Cyprian discussed business with Whitley. Afternoons she entertained friends with tea and biscuits, displaying her elegant house.

This time, Helen arrived in a great flutter over her coming marriage to Mr. Josiah Rankin. Seven years Helen's senior, her parents considered him very suitable. Helen was entranced with becoming mistress of his new Elizabethan manor in Hampshire. He had assured her she would be given a free hand in decorating it.

Angelea enthusiastically entered into Helen's plans, offering sage marital advice. As she passed Helen another biscuit, she said, "Dearest Helen, I want you to be the first to know, for I am confident you shall not betray me to his lordship by the least innuendo. I have not yet confided in Mama, for she could not contain her excitement and all the world would know within an hour."

Helen leaned forward to say, "You know I have never revealed anything you told me in deep confidence. I shall not do so now."

Angelea flushed and, to prolong Helen's suspense, asked, "Can you guess my secret?"

"Have you taken a lover?" Helen asked in an awed whisper.

"No!" Feeling dampened that her friend should think that, Angelea protested, "I have not yet been married a year."

"True, but Lady Heatherfield, she was Miss Mameson, remember? She married a month after you and she took a lover at Christmas."

"She did? She cannot have loved her husband very much."

"Oh, not at all, as he well knows. It was her fortune and his rank, you know, being an earl."

"That is as may be. *My* secret is far different. Helen, I am breeding!"

"You are?" Helen nearly overset her cup in reaching to embrace Angelea. "How exciting! The heir he wants! You shall be pampered beyond anything! When will this be?"

"In the autumn. About two years after his lordship asked me to marry him. Is this not the most delightful of secrets?"

"Oh yes! How can you contain yourself?"

"It is most difficult. I only became certain this past week. Of course, I did not want to raise his lordship's hopes falsely, so I waited. And, you know, if I told him sooner, he would not have permitted me to come here, and I wanted to tell you personally. I would like to tell Mama, but she is so anxious for a grandchild that I cannot trust her in the least. If his lordship learns of it before we reach Omsbridge, I shall be coddled unmercifully and forced to ride in a horrid old coach, which I cannot abide."

Angelea moved to the window and drew back the curtains. The cloudless sky, rosy with dawn's soft hues, seemed a beautiful omen of the future. The cool morning air and even the cuckoo's monotonous song called to her. This was the day to tell Cyprian, a day bursting with the lift of spring.

Tentatively she touched her abdomen. She had concealed her slight increase, wanting to become comfortable with the idea of motherhood. Truly his interest in her transcended the bearing of children. Should this be the son he anticipated so eagerly, he would never desert her. She would tell him this morning after she went for a romp with Starlight. Once he knew, her husband would very likely hem her in with endless restrictions.

As her maid Carolyn helped her don her sapphire riding dress, Angelea imagined his surprise and delight. He would find some special way to show that pleasure. Perhaps it would be with an emerald necklace, which she mentioned needing to wear with her new gold satin gown.

The sound of voices through the connecting door to his room indicated he had risen earlier than she expected after his late night over cards with Squire Ford. Their foolish neighbor never seemed to learn that he always lost. Well, it was a harmless recreation. Cyprian could not be ruined by the modest stakes they played for, although the squire might be.

Eagerly she hurried to the stables, pausing at a bowl of fruit to select an apple for her lovely Starlight.

With her heavy riding skirt caught up over one arm, her eyes flashing in anger, Angelea hurried to Cyprian's room.

Feldman was smoothing Cyprian's coat across his shoulders as she burst in. Both men jumped at her unceremonious entrance. Feldman withdrew immediately.

Cyprian greeted her warmly, holding out his arms to embrace her. "Good morning, my dear. Did you sleep well?"

Dropping her skirt, Angelea remained a few feet from him, her eyes narrowed. "Henry said that Squire Ford took Starlight to the manor last night. That—that she is now his! Tell me that is not true!" Her voice cracked on the last words.

Cyprian sighed; his arms fell to his sides. "I am sorry, my dear. It is true. I intended telling you before you left your room, but you rose earlier than I."

"I wanted to ride with the dawn. The air is so fresh and . . ." Tears of grief and anger flooded her eyes as she demanded, "Why did you do it?"

"I am sorry, my dear. I do not always win, even from Squire Ford. He wagered a fine black mare I desired for breeding with Blue Star. He wanted Starlight." Cyprian shrugged. "He held better cards than I."

"But you had no right! She is *mine*!"

Cyprian drew himself up haughtily. "You are in error, my dear. I have every right."

His arrogance spurred her anger. "You gave her to me. She was mine!"

"All the horses on the estate are mine," he announced stiffly. "I may do with them as I choose. Starlight was for your use and enjoyment. But she was mine. Now she is Ford's. You may use another mount. There are several you would like as well. The matter is closed."

Frustrated over his attitude, she clenched her fingers tightly, declaring, "No! There is only one Starlight. I dreamed of her all my life! I loved her! How could you risk something I loved in a—a stupid game of cards?"

"That is enough, Angelea. I will not discuss it further." He made a sketchy bow and went into the hall.

Angered at her dismissal of her righteous grievance and frightened at this new side of her husband, Angelea whirled to follow him. Never had she been so treated. "It was wrong of you to do so! Starlight is mine! You *must* get her back for me!" In her headlong rush after Cyprian, her legs became entangled in her riding skirt. She fell heavily on her right hip, her head striking the corner of a chair. A flash of bright light was smothered by darkness.

Troubled by Dr. Winther's words, Cyprian entered Angelea's room. He dismissed Mrs. Croft with a nod, and went to stand beside the bed. Anxiety floated about his mind. He felt that something beautiful in their marriage was smashed in the morning's clash. Without a doubt, he bore the blame for the loss of this child, his child. He had the right to wager Starlight, but he knew Angelea's attachment to the animal, and that losing it would upset her. In truth, he had not thought of losing to Ford. He never did.

Angelea looked up, her eyes overflowing with tears. "I was going to tell you after my ride. I wanted to be sure. I could not chance raising your hopes and learn I was wrong."

He sat on her bed, kissed her hand and held it tenderly to his cheek. "I understand."

Suddenly she pulled him to her, clinging to him as a frightened child. Deep sobs racked her body. "Oh, Cyprian," she cried, "he was our son. I know—I know he was a boy!"

"Hush, hush, my dear," he said, holding her gently and stroking her hair. "We shall have a handful of sons. Dr. Winther assured me we would, once you are recovered."

"But we lost him, our son, my baby!" she wailed.

He rocked her, trying to give the comfort he sorely needed, choked by a tightness in his throat.

Thirteen

*T*ony accepted a glass of wine from Fothering and leaned back in Cyprian's new rococo gilt chair. He stretched out his legs comfortably, gave a nod of approval at the Dutch landscape hanging above the library fireplace.

Cyprian smiled as he sat down behind his inlaid desk, lavishly trimmed with gold. This was to be a pleasant evening's gossip, possible only with Tony. Six weeks earlier Tony had brightened Omsbridge with a prolonged stay after he learned of Angelea's fall. Cyprian had missed these talks after Tony left on his secret mission.

"Pitt thinks our future lies in the Colonies, not the Continent, and I agree," stated Tony, sipping his wine.

Cyprian looked at him skeptically, surprised. He well knew Tony's admiration for Pitt. "So you have claimed. But why the Colonies? They are peopled by savages and felons living in the most primitive state. Everyone knows that."

Tony shook his head. "Europe displays the grandeur of the past and the present, but the Colonies are the raw material of the future. They are not so primitive as you imagine, and their energy impressed me more than anything I saw on the tired Continent—except Turin."

"Turin?" Cyprian asked, intrigued. "What is there in Turin to rival Florence or Rome, or the fascination of Rosina?"

"You enjoy poking in dark places and gazing at ancient marbles. I prefer more refined things," Tony countered with a grin.

"Refined! Ha! What did you see in Turin to impress you more than the glories of Rome!"

Tony sat still, staring at the changing shapes of flame in the library fireplace, twirling the stem of his glass thoughtfully. He spoke slowly. "My father encountered the Duke of Savoy in a tavern when he toured Italy. They were two young men caught up in a fight not of their making. Actually, the Duke was ten years older. They were forced to draw their swords and defend themselves from a group of half-drunken brigands. As my father described it, they fought fiercely, at times actually back to back. They worsted their assailants and pledged lifelong friendship. Therefore, on my Tour, I was expected to visit there at length.

"They treated me like royalty, and they have a magnificent setting for that. Their palace is ancient, filled with paintings and sculptures collected by men of exquisite taste for generations. But the Duke's greatest treasure was his seven-year-old grandson, the darling of his life. One day while we were riding in a party, something frightened the boy's pony and he bolted. Since I was closest I chased him and snatched him off his saddle." Tony shrugged. "Anyone could have done it, but I was the hero of the day."

Cyprian chuckled at Tony's characteristic discounting of his actions. He could well imagine the dangers involved.

"Consequently, they held a special thanksgiving mass in the chapel. They're Catholic, you know." Tony leaned back and gazed at the carved beams above them. "Afterwards he ordered the shroud brought out and displayed as the greatest way he could honor me."

"A shroud? You mean a cloth used to wrap a dead body?" Cyprian exclaimed.

"Yes. This one is presumed to have been Christ's grave cloth."

"Surely you cannot be serious! What a piece of popery nonsense!"

"So I thought. But, since the old boy was showing me his most special treasure, I was determined to be the polite guest. You see, they only bring it out on very special occasions. I went to see it, prepared to put on as good a face as I could."

"And what was it?" Cyprian leaned forward.

"Actually disappointing. A long piece of old cloth, linen, I think, with some very faint brownish marks on it. It had been wrapped length-wise around a corpse, so he said. As the Duke explained the marks, I made out the shapes of arms, hands, legs, of a naked man with a wound in his side. And the crisscrosses of his scourging . . . Cyprian, they went the length of his body, clear to the calves. A clever hoax, I thought.

"Then I looked at the face. Faint as the impression was, as I gazed at it, I made out a man's features. I . . . ." Tony's voice thickened with emotion. "Old phrases I heard read countless times in church went through my mind. 'Wounded for our transgressions, he was bruised for our iniquities . . . with his stripes we are healed,' and 'God so loved the world that he gave his only begotten son.' And what the vicar says on serving the sacrament, 'This is my body, which is given for you.' I cannot describe the impact of that experience. I would stake my life it is no hoax.''

"You were so moved by faint marks on an old strip of cloth?''

"None of the many masterpieces I have admired have so affected me as those ugly brownish markings. Their only attraction lay in stark, naked reality. No artistic arrangement had glossed over the horror of what happened to Him.''

Cyprian felt a tingle along his spine at Tony's unusually intense expression.

"I felt as if He looked at me over all those centuries. I . . . I fell on my knees as if King George were to knight me.'' Tony hesitated before adding, "I have not confided this experience with anyone else.''

"You honor me, my friend,'' Cyprian said gravely, recalling a vivid memory. "There was a rainy afternoon in Lucerne in the days of my desperation. I had escaped my tutor and climbed up on the archer's walk behind the wall. As I looked back on the old town, a shaft of sunlight broke through clouds black as my mood. Like a beacon, it picked out the strange twin towers of the new Jesuit church. It appeared an invitation from God. Like one possessed I ran through the streets, across that macabre bridge of death and up the steps of the church.

"When I entered the sanctuary, I was surrounded with brilliance. White, gold, color dazzled me, washed over me—cleansing, healing, purifying even the hidden corners of my being. I was alone in that huge church, yet not alone, for it pulsed with life. And a deep sense of peace. When I finally left, I thought I should never be the same. But as I continued my Tour into Italy, it faded. And, on my return to the drawing rooms of London, I lost it altogether. But it remained a beautiful memory I longed to relive.

"When I first saw Angelea, she possessed that sense of purity and splendor I found in Lucerne. I knew I must have her.'' Noting his friend's doubtful smile, Cyprian added, "No, I know she is not perfection. Rather like a sweet child needing yet more training. But my soul rests safe with her. The purity of her innocence cleanses me and renews me. Just now she is not well. But when she is recovered . . .'' He grinned and closed his eyes. "You will see, my friend. Someday you will see— if you are lucky.''

"Perhaps you are right—if I am lucky.''

The two sat silently for some time, sipping their wine, not wanting to interrupt the intimate silence.

At length Tony cleared his throat and commented, "Angelea appears to be recovering well. She rode with spirit this morning."

"Yes," Cyprian answered, resting his elbows on the desk. "However, she grieves for our loss. She insists it was a son. As to that, we will never know, of course. Winther assures me we may have many other children in due time." Despite his forced optimism, pain and guilt made an uncomfortable knot under his heart.

He watched Tony take out his watch for the third time, flip open the cover, stare at the face, snap the lid shut and return it to his pocket. The ritual signified Tony was struggling to express an idea and he doubted its reception. Mildly curious over his friend's agitation, Cyprian waited quietly.

"I propose a change of scene for you," Tony declared abruptly.

Cyprian looked over sharply at his friend. "Oh? Winther hinted at this on his last visit."

"Yes. I heard that an ancient house was uncovered near those tombs you were poking around a few months ago, near that little town . . . what was it?"

"Resina? Where they think they found the ruins of Pompeii?"

"That sounds like it. I should think the engineer, Karl whatever you said—"

"Weber," Cyprian supplied.

"Weber? Yes, Karl Weber. I should think he would welcome your assistance in uncovering more of these antiquities. As I recall, when you met him on your Tour, he pressed you to stay and help him." Tony's voice deepened slightly as he continued dramatically, "Imagine, viewing a house and its treasures unseen since before Christ's birth, and helping unearth a statue untouched for centuries!"

Cyprian felt his pulse quicken at the vision Tony's words evoked. He reached for the marble fragment on his desk and stroked the hard fingers as he cleared his throat. "Actually Vesuvius erupted in A.D. 79."

"Well, seventeen hundred, or rather sixteen hundred, er, seventy-six years is a long time."

"You are so right, old friend, a very long time," Cyprian agreed with a chuckle. "But antiquities never interested you, other than those on your land."

"True. My stones were long in place when Vesuvius buried that town. Stukeley thinks the Druids set them up, you know, around 1858 B.C., when Abraham's wife Sarah died. I think he's rather fanciful. How could he know? It's the politics of the present, affecting my life and yours, that absorb energy." He rose and sauntered to the fireplace and examined the French china clock.

"I suspect there is more to your proposition than my distraction."

"You know me too well, dear boy." Tony sighed. "In truth, what I propose meets two needs, as I see it."

"Which are?"

"Yours . . ." Tony turned around, "and your king's."

"Ah. Tell me more. How might my exploring an ancient Italian house serve my king?"

"Our old ally, Austria, has decided not to align herself with us when the present situation develops into a war between us and France."

"You consider war is inevitable?"

"Definitely. Furthermore, she formed a defensive alliance with France should either of them be attacked. We expect they will soon sign a treaty in reaction to our agreement with Prussia last January."

"So I heard." Cyprian thoughtfully massaged the marble fingers, puzzled by Tony's recounting widely known gossip.

"That is what the world knows. What the world does not know is that Austria secretly pledged France aid if even an ally of ours attacked, and they have invited others to join their secret alliance. Specifically, they approached the kings of Spain and Naples, and Philip of Parma."

"We may take on much of the Continent if we fight with France," Cyprian observed.

"Precisely. And we shall fight, of course. Louis XV plans an invasion. I have read the documents myself. As you know, the Tsarina of Russia hates Frederick of Prussia and is determined to destroy him. We must know what Spain, Naples, and Parma will do." With surprising passion Tony demanded, "Bring us back that information."

Cyprian threw up his hands in protest. "I am no spy."

"No. You have not the talent for it."

"And Angelea could not travel so far at this time."

"I understand."

"You were not including her in your plans?"

"Not as your traveling companion."

"Of course, dear boy, of course. All the world knows of your interest in ancient Pompeii. It is not remarkable if you journey there for a few weeks. Our people will bring the news to you. Naturally, you will suddenly be overcome with longing for your bride and return home post haste."

"Angelea may consider it remarkable if I leave now."

"She might also find it easier to regain her health without your gloomy face depressing her."

"Am I so gloomy?"

"You wear a gallows look. Dear boy, I am not exaggerating in saying Louis plans our invasion along the Sussex coast. Omsbridge could well be involved. True, it was built as a fort, but consider the French firing a cannon through the chapel victory window. More than colored glass would be lost. And, your aphrodite would not survive if they attacked up the path from the river."

Cyprian joined Tony before the fire, the marble fingers clutched in his hand. "Therefore, foiling Louis' plans would spare Omsbridge from sustaining damage?"

"Possibly so."

"How long would this take?"

"A month, six weeks, depending on travel, when the treaty is signed, and how soon the kings decide whether to join the pact."

Cyprian could easily envision the French landing, guided by smugglers bought with gold. In the dark of the moon they could come around to the eastern side, where Cromwell destroyed the wall. Perhaps their guides would know the passage through the mermaid cave into the cellars, and therefore into the Hall itself. He shuddered at the ensuing destruction. Tony's proposed trip was small sacrifice if it forestalled a landing at Omsbridge.

"If Angelea will not view this as desertion, I will go," he decided.

Fourteen

C yprian stood behind the garden shrubbery of his London house, revulsion convulsing his stomach. Long buried pain triggered tears. Vivid memories of his mother in the arms of a strange man confused the past and present. He felt lost in a cold portion of reality lacking substance.

In a panic he wiped his eyes and shook his head to clear away this nightmare. Cautiously he peered around the prickly yew hiding him. Angelea, his Angelea, stood laughing with the man whose arms had held her but moments ago. Angelea, his Angelea, possessed a soul kin to all the faithless married women he had known. Her purity was merely an illusion born of his need. How absurd were his refusals of Francesca's overtures at Tivoli! Plainly his yearning for Angelea during the long weeks in Italy was not reciprocated.

Again he looked through the branches to see them coming in his direction. His heart gave a hard wrench on seeing Angelea laughing, her unpowdered hair a golden halo of curls, wearing the pink mantua he thought most became her. Then he recognized the man. Uxton! Of all the men in London, why must she make his implacable enemy her lover? Pride and anger stiffened his weak knees and stifled his emotions. Cyprian stepped coolly into the path before them and made a courtly bow. "Good evening, madam."

Both jumped. Angelea paled and swayed as if she would swoon, exclaiming, "Milord! I did not know . . ."

Uxton quickly supported her in his arms, declaring almost eagerly, "I shall be happy to give you satisfaction, Omsbridge."

Assuming a bored drawl, Cyprian said, "Uxton, your left arm already bears my mark. It will certainly give me no satisfaction whatever to run you through for *this*. I assure you, the resulting inconveniences would not be worth it. You may have her, and welcome." He turned on his heel and strode up the path.

"Cyprian, wait! You don't understand!" Angelea called. He heard her quick steps following him.

With a cold, controlled fury, he spun about to face her. "I understand perfectly."

"But it is not as—as you think. I have not—"

"Pray spare us these theatrics, madam. I am not so foolish as to deny the obvious. Did I not charge you to remain at Omsbridge until I returned?"

"Yes, but—"

"Instead, I find you in London privately entertaining a man of questionable repute and an avowed enemy of mine. Believe me, I have no interest in used baggage."

"Cyprian!" The despair in her voice and tears coursing down her lovely cheeks almost moved him to relent.

"Angelea," interposed Uxton, hurrying to her side, "speak to him later when his anger has cooled. Omsbridge, I will not permit you to insult her."

Cyprian stared steadily at his enemy, pleased to see Uxton's color rise under his scrutiny. Slowly Cyprian lowered his gaze to Uxton's shiny boots, then deliberately raised it to his face. He twisted his lips into a bitter sneer, turned and left with long, measured strides.

"I must go to him and explain," he heard Angelea say.

"Later, dear one, when he is calmer." Uxton's tone was intimately tender.

Guided by years of habit, Cyprian entered Omsbridge House through the side door, his churning emotions blinding him to his surroundings. Over and over he heard Uxton address Angelea as "dear one." The sight of his wife in Uxton's arms seemed deeply engraved on his mind. Suddenly he became aware of a man coming down the stairs. With difficulty he focused on Dagon. He heard the butler's voice, but could not make any sense out of his words.

"Feldman will arrive shortly," Cyprian said curtly. "Have him pack up *all* my things and proceed to Omsbridge promptly."

"Yes, milord," Dagon replied, masking whatever astonishment he may have felt over the sudden comings and goings of his master.

Lord Omsbridge went directly to the stables and ordered the best horse saddled. While he waited, he looked over the other cattle, giving instructions as to which were to be sent to Omsbridge with Feldman. His tour concluded at the end stall. "This bay is a fine animal, but I do not recall buying him, Dickie," he commented to the head groom accompanying him.

"No, milord," Dickie responded with an anxious side glance. "You'll not remember him. He belongs to Lord Uxton."

"Indeed. Where's that boy Charley?"

"Here, milord." An undersized lad ran to his side eagerly.

"Are you still able to ride any of my mounts?"

"Yes, milord. I works 'em all ter keep 'em fit."

"Fine." Cyprian flipped him a gold coin. "I find this one offensive. I should like him removed some distance; I care not where. Will you oblige me?"

"Yes, milord. I know just the place."

"Excellent. Please, do not tell me of your intent. And Dickie"— Cyprian turned back to the head groom—"that man is not to use any of my cattle, at any time, for any purpose whatever. Is that understood?"

"Yes, milord."

"And furthermore, he is not to make use of my stables ever again. If he chooses to call at this house, he must leave his horse in front and no one in my employ is to touch him."

"I understand. It shall be as you wish."

"Give Feldman whatever assistance he needs," he said as he mounted. "And tell him I shall expect his arrival in Omsbridge directly."

Angelea and Uxton entered the house but a quarter of an hour behind Cyprian. She hurried to his room and was dismayed to find it untouched. Frantically she ran down to the library, but it was empty. Confused, she stood in the main hall glancing about, her heartbeat pounding in her ears.

Uxton joined her, his countenance flushed. "Where is Omsbridge?"

"I don't know. I can't find him anywhere. Whatever shall I do?"

"I have not the least idea," Uxton answered unsympathetically. "He was so inhospitable as to order my horse taken elsewhere and forbid me the use of his stables! Your servant, madam. I must seek out my mount immediately."

As the footman closed the door behind Uxton, Dagon appeared in the doorway opening onto the kitchen hallway. Angelea turned to him, clasping her moist hands together. "Do you know where Lord Omsbridge is to be found?"

"He has ridden to Omsbridge, milady."

Angelea stared at him in shock. This could not be, none of it. These people must vanish and she would wake in her own bed. With a soft moan she crumpled to the floor.

Angelea became aware of sitting in a chair supported by soft pillows on either side. Moving her fingers, she felt the tapestry fabric covering the arms. A horrid smell assailed her nostrils and she opened her eyes. The oval portrait of Sir William Westover hung opposite her above the salon fireplace. She could not recall coming here. Carolyn, her maid, crouched before her, slowly passing a smoldering feather before her face, while Dagon hovered anxiously at her side, quite unlike his normal, unruffled manner.

How came she here? she wondered as she waved the offensive feather away. A burning feather was used to revive someone who fainted. She never fainted. Or had she?

The confrontation in the garden came vividly into her mind. Her eyes widened in horror, tears overflowed into rivulets down her cheeks, and choking sobs tore at her. Wildly she looked around. She needed someone to cling to, someone to give her comfort.

Through her blurred vision, she made out a figure in livery at the salon door. It must be a footman. One of Simmons' oft-repeated admonitions ran through her mind. "The mistress of a household must never appear undone before her servants. It breeds contempt and poor service."

Angelea took several deep breaths, as Simmons always made her do when upset. Using every ounce of her will power, she marshalled her shredded dignity and spoke in a voice only slightly quavering. "Dagon, please inform Mrs. Banks I will take a supper tray in my room at seven. Carolyn, come with me." She rose slowly, but steadily, and walked with a firm tread up the broad staircase to her room, her head held high.

With a strange detached numbness, she had Carolyn remove her hoops and dress her in a light gown appropriate to the summer warmth; then she dismissed her maid. When alone, she released her emotions in a storm of weeping and pacing, careful not to make a noise audible to anyone passing her door.

Hearing a drawer close in Cyprian's room, she stepped quickly to her dressing table to minimize the effects of her distress. He must not see her like this. Eagerly she opened the connecting door, her explanation ready.

Feldman was packing the personal items and clothing Cyprian normally left in his London residence. Startled, Angelea asked, "What are you doing?"

Feldman bowed with proper deference and responded, "His lordship left instruction for me to bring all his things to Omsbridge immediately, milady."

"But what—what does this mean?"

"I do not know, milady. Dagon gave me the message along with word from Dickie that his lordship selected several horses for me to take also. If I may say so, he did not expect to find you in residence. He spoke several times of his eagerness to be with you again in Omsbridge. Is he aware that you are here?"

"Yes, he knows. Oh yes, he knows."

"Then I am at a loss for his hasty removal. However, I am to follow him as quickly as I may."

"You will not leave in the morning?"

"No, milady. I will set out within the hour and travel until dark."

"Please, see me before you leave. I shall have a letter for his lordship."

Returning to her room, Angelea went to her writing desk and wrote with passionate speed, avowing her love and loyalty and explaining that friendship with Uxton never exceeded the bounds of propriety. She added she only was prevailed upon to disobey him and go to London because of his long delay, because without him the country was unbearably dull, and because, as the Season was already half gone, she could not think he intended her to miss the whole.

After completing her letter, she took a turn around the room and bathed her eyes in the basin. She was about to fold and seal the sheets when she decided to reread her letter. Its pleading, undignified tone appalled her. She had poured out her deepest feelings, skipping words here and there in her haste. Cyprian would be disgusted by this childish missal. She could see him crumple the pages with disdain. What should she do?

Never in her life had Angelea been alone, without someone available for counsel or comfort. Her parents were now at the Willows. Indeed, part of London's allure was knowing she could do as she pleased, free of supervision. She could not think of any friends or confidants she could trust for guidance in this area. *If I go to the Willows,* she reasoned, *Mama will help me and Cyprian will have but a small distance to come.*

With the decision made, she drew forth another sheet of paper. In her best penmanship, she wrote her intention, concluding with, "I shall await your soon response there." When he came, she would tell him the truth of the matter and all would be well.

Hardly had she finished sealing the note when Feldman rapped on her door. She gave him the letter, feeling it was a sound step toward repairing the breach between her and Cyprian. After he departed, she wrote notes to the hostesses of the several events she was to attend, explaining her parents needed her, and therefore she was departing for Surrey promptly. Having completed this task, she faced her supper tray with at least a small appetite.

Angelea's control nearly failed when Dagon announced Lord Uxton awaited her below. "I have no wish to see him. Send him away. Tell him I am not here." She visualized him seeking out her room. After his unexpected, rash embrace this afternoon, she knew not what he might do. "On no account is he to be permitted to remain," she added, "or— or to come up the stairs. Force him to leave if necessary."

"Yes, milady."

Anxiously she stood at the top of the stairs, listening, poised for flight should Uxton threaten to come up. Although he argued briefly with Dagon, he left with a disappointing lack of effort.

With her plans made, Angelea thrust aside her fears and focused her attention on the tasks required for accomplishing her goal. She always managed to have her way. It was simply a matter of setting about it in the right manner. Soon she would again be in residence at Omsbridge.

Fifteen

From the south window in her room at Hillview, Angelea gazed toward Sussex beyond the weald and the North Downs. If her carpet were magic, it would whisk her into the Omsbridge library where Cyprian was probably conferring with Eldridge on estate business. However, if the gossips were right, he would not welcome her. She turned away confused and dejected.

How could things go so badly? Surely Feldman gave her note to Cyprian. But he had not answered. After a brief visit at the Willows, she removed to Hillview on her mother's advice. Doubtless, Whitney informed Cyprian of her movements. Why did he not write? Why did he not come?

Despite his assurances to the contrary, when he went to Pompeii, she felt deserted because she lost his child. Lord Uxton's surprising appearance during those lonely days was a welcome diversion from her melancholy. He took a room in the Dancing Skillet at the near crossroads, and behaved with propriety while awaiting Cyprian's return. Much as she liked the excitement his daily visits injected into her routine, she took care to conduct herself in a most circumspect manner. Even in Mrs. Croft's eyes, she gave not the least cause for disapproval or servants' gossip.

She accepted Uxton's offer to escort her to London only when Cyprian's return was long delayed. As Uxton said, it was unthinkable that she should be denied the whole Season simply because Cyprian was poking his nose into buried Italian antiquities. Secretly she feared Cyprian was residing from time to time at Tivoli in the villa where the

91

beautiful, seductive Francesca lived.

London's gaiety proved illusory, emphasizing her longing for her husband. True, she enjoyed flirting with her many admirers. But she preferred the company of Tony and Uxton, her friends, to those attending her morning toilet or sending bouquets and amorous notes, a socially acceptable gesture. Uxton became more attentive in the few days preceding Cyprian's unexpected appearance. As she now realized, his manner assumed more intimacy than their friendship warranted, but, then, the change was so slight she barely noticed it.

His passionate embrace in the garden caught her unawares. Quickly, he apologized for his embarrassing behavior. As they returned to the house, he made such a comedy of his feelings overriding his sense of propriety that she was prompted to laughter, and she forgave him. She could not remain angry with so charming a man for more than the least instant.

Then she saw Cyprian.

His words shattered her life. She knew not how to extricate herself from the rubble.

Not long after Angelea's removal to Hillview, Lord Uxton arrived, grieved for the trouble his impetuous behavior had caused. But, before she sent him away, a careless remark of his hinted that Cyprian was entertaining some of the wilder members of society along with some beautiful members of the ballet at Omsbridge. Whenever Angelea thought to go to the Hall, she envisioned her humiliation in meeting those people. She would await Cyprian's coming here on business, which must be soon.

But it was Eldridge who came and begged to speak with her.

Having repaired the damage to her appearance caused by her deep disappointment, she sent for him to attend her in the blue salon, her favorite room.

Upon entering, Eldridge made his familiar, awkward bow.

Angelea always regarded his plain, freckled countenance as bordering on homely. Now he was graced with the beauty of a messenger from home. She felt herself flush with pleasure and a passing urge to embrace him as a dear friend.

Politely he inquired after her health, pulling on his long nose, patting his fingertips together, then clasping his hands behind him. These characteristic gestures provided a comforting sense of home for her.

"His lordship charged me to collect and pay such bills as you may have," the serious young man said.

"Oh, of course. I'll give them to you before you leave." She hesitated, then asked, "Is his lordship well?"

Eldridge cleared his throat and answered, "Yes, milady. He is in good health."

"I understand there are several houseguests at Omsbridge."

Eldridge shifted uneasily. "Yes, milady."

With an effort she said lightly, "I have every confidence Mrs. Croft will manage them quite well."

"Yes, milady."

"And how is she? She had a slight pain in her right shoulder when I left."

"That seems to be greatly improved."

Angelea rang for refreshment and insisted Eldridge be seated as they talked.

"And what of Henry's wife?" she asked. "She was breeding when last we spoke. This is her first child, as I recall."

"A fortnight ago she produced a fine son. Betsy Miller midwifed for her, as you requested. The mother survived and is back to her work in the creamery."

"I am glad to know that. She is a kind young woman, and I am sure she will make a good mother." One inquiry led to another as Angelea visualized the members of the Omsbridge household. Until now, she had not realized how deeply she cared for them. Mentioning their names revived vivid memories and evoked a deep longing to be among them. When the door closed behind Eldridge, she felt an oppressing isolation.

Agitated, she changed into her riding dress and hastened to the stables. For an hour or more, she rode over the countryside, maintaining such a pace that the wind dried the tears streaking her cheeks.

"Are you truly leaving me, Tony?" Cyprian asked as they strolled arm in arm along the south terrace. "I cannot understand why."

"I've been away from Stonehead too many weeks—"

"Nine days," Cyprian amended.

"Really? Only nine?" Tony scratched his head, trying to improve his excuse. As he feared, the interview was not going well. "You see, things were in a shocking state when I left. I shouldn't have come at all."

"You told me your Chambers and Perkins had all beautifully in hand."

"I did? Well, it was all a hum . . . to set your mind at ease."

Cyprian guided him along a path into the fragrant rose garden, a mass of red, gold, and white blossoms. "I'd feel easier still if you told me the truth, old friend."

Tony felt his ingenuity sorely taxed. How might he speak the truth without depriving himself of a boon companion? Then it occurred to him he would be deprived in any event since he intended to leave regardless what was said. "Cyprian, you know I'm always one for order and sense. Irregularity is something I cannot abide."

"And my household is irregular?"

"In the extreme. Dear boy, I must say you run the most ramshackle establishment. It is beyond me how you tolerate it." He peered anxiously at Cyprian. "You notice I did not say you enjoy it. It is inconceivable that you enjoy this . . . this . . . In fact, no offense meant, but that is one factor lacking, which, as you know, is indispensable to me."

Cyprian's lips tightened. "In short, you no longer enjoy my company."

"It is the circumstances—no, the people surrounding you I take exception to. These wild bucks, er, parasites drink your cellar dry and run your stable to the ground. It distresses me seeing you so used."

"Would you feel better if you knew I was using them?"

Tony fidgeted with the head of his walking stick. "No. I'd wonder if you were using me, too. I shouldn't like that at all."

They walked a few yards in silence. "What do you see around you?" Cyprian asked.

Puzzled, Tony repeated, "What do I see around me? I fail to understand you."

"Tell me exactly what you see."

Deciding to humor this strange mood, Tony turned about slowly and enumerated what he saw. "The rose garden, end of the front terrace, the fountain with your aphrodite, the edge of your lake, the hedge, the, er, uh, west wing of the house."

"And in the distance, what do you see?"

"Oh, well, to the south I suppose the Channel is out there somewhere. And to the north, there's that clump of trees several miles away."

"Those trees stand on my land. Everything you see and beyond is mine, to the sea, as you know. And there are several other properties as well."

Tony nodded, counting on his fingers. "The one in Surrey, Hillview, the house in London, the lodge in Lincolnshire, and—"

"And others. You know I love the land, especially here in Sussex."

Tony agreed, remembering the many times Cyprian spoke of the future he envisioned. At times his vision became dynastic, extending to several generations yet unborn.

"Tony, do you realize I have not one living male heir?"

Deuxbury stared at his friend in shock, then took exception to his statement. "No, no, dear boy. It ain't that bad. You've forgotten old

Freddy, you know, your cousin. He ain't much, but he's blood."

"Yesterday my solicitor sent me word Frederick failed to clear a hedge with his horse and broke his neck."

"No! Never had a good seat. Don't know why people like that insist on riding cross-country. Hunting, I suppose?"

"So Johnson said. And Emily seems not to have any children beyond her four daughters."

Tony bit his tongue to keep from speaking of Angelea. If all was well in that quarter, Cyprian would not be carrying on in this absurd fashion.

"Remember how distressed you were a few years ago before your nephews were born and you thought of strangers taking over Stone-head?"

"That I do. I lost whole nights of sleep fretting about the awful things they might do. No need to worry on that head now. Meg and Fran have six sons between them. I've been having the two eldest stay with me from time to time so they'll understand what's expected of them, and come to love Stonehead too."

"I married to have sons, to pass Omsbridge on to them. Since the days of Sir Edmund Westover, it has gone to a son. Not one master of Omsbridge was careless of the land. Each added to or improved it. Several died defending it. It's always been loved." His eyes narrowed. "I am failing those before me." With bitter intensity he exclaimed, "Would I was not tied to her!"

Tony leapt at his first opportunity to heal this domestic breach. "She was anxious for you those many weeks you were in Italy. Don't know what rumors you heard, but many's the time I dried her tears, assuring her you were well and would soon return."

"Anxious indeed!" Cyprian scoffed. "I told her expressly *not* to go to town until I returned, and she disobeyed the moment I was out of sight."

"No, you're out there. She didn't come to town 'til you'd been gone two weeks beyond your expected return. No need to glare at me. I was there. Furthermore, while I'm not one to meddle in others' affairs, you should go up and see her. She was getting pale and drugout for worry."

"I've not told any other, Tony, but I did see her. I know, the gossip is that I came straight here—that I tired of her. Let them believe that. I went to Omsbridge House and found her entertaining her lover."

"Her lover! 'Pon my word, Cyprian, no one was given the least encouragement. She was always very proper. And you know *I* would have been the first to notice anything amiss. Nothing was."

"This time you were fooled. As was I. I *saw* them. A rumor could be wrong, but the testimony of my eyes is different you will agree. I saw her in his arms." Cyprian added in a savage, low tone, "And if I *never* see her again, it will be to my liking."

"You're certain?" Tony asked incredulously.

He was answered with a withering look.

"Well, she just didn't behave like there was anyone you'd need worry about. I must be slipping, for I'd of sworn, well, no matter, you saw what you saw. Don't blame you for feeling as you do. It does put you in quite a spot without an heir."

"And I'll have none."

"You might adopt someone," Tony suggested. "I was thinking of that before my first nephew was born."

"Whom might you suggest?"

"Don't know. Haven't given it any thought for several years. It is done, you know."

"Yes, probably so." Cyprian sighed. "You are quite right, old friend. All this does not answer. I trust you are the only one to see beyond my face to my heart." He stared up at the gray clouds overhead. "Come, we must go in. I think I shall have Dr. Winther come tomorrow and inform us one of the maids has contracted the smallpox. Those not leaving immediately will catch it."

"The smallpox!" Tony exclaimed, horrified.

"No need for alarm. She has but an inflammation of the lungs. However, one cannot be certain what might develop. In fact, I shall not wait until the morrow. I will announce it this evening. Then my household may settle into its normal ways. Will you stay to see me through this plague?"

Tony bent over a yellow rose, thinking. Concern for his old friend took precedence over any other demands on him at the moment. He turned to Cyprian. "I may remain one week more; then I must consult with Pitt."

"You are expecting a message?"

"In the dark of the moon, when the tide rushes up the Oms."

Sixteen

*E*dmund Feldman sipped his hot tea, feeling its warmth spread outward from his stomach, relaxing his muscles. The new mistress had ordered Croft to provide tea on the first Monday of the month for those preferring it to their customary ale. Some of the staff clung to their ale, not holding with foreign ways. But Edmund appreciated her ladyship's generosity and enjoyed the luxury.

He leaned back in his chair, enjoying the midmorning sunlight entering the open kitchen window. Life was much easier with the London people gone. They kept the household in a constant uproar of uncertainty. However, Feldman regretted Sir Deuxbury's departure a fortnight past. He was the master's good friend.

With a nod of approval to Maggie Worth across the table, he took a second satisfying sip. Although her cooking skill did not equal Mrs. Banks', she was a pleasant woman and Feldman found her friendship of considerable value. Despite the flaming red hair escaping her mob cap, she was an even-tempered, comfortable woman.

Maggie had just cut some fresh bread for them to enjoy when they heard a pounding on the door. Feldman frowned, annoyed at the interruption just as they were settled.

With a shrug, Maggie wiped her hands on her apron and answered the summons. She returned and waved her plump hand over her shoulder, saying, " 'iggins 'e do be ill-convenient, howsumdever 'e mus' 'ave a word wid ye. I'll bring 'im some ale an' 'oney bread."

Reluctantly Feldman finished his tea quickly. As he went outside, he shed his air of spry efficiency. His posture became slouching and his step a slight shuffle.

98

Higgins stood beside the door, anxiously shifting from foot to foot. Gray hair hung like a mane about his wrinkled, tanned face. His leather breeches revealed their true color in only a few patches among the dirt stains, and his brown shirt and jacket showed evidence of long outdoor wear. Under shaggy gray brows gathered in a frown, his clear blue eyes regarded Feldman somberly. "Mornin'. 'Taint agoin' to rain terdee, I bluv."

"Mornin', Higgins." Feldman lounged against the doorframe and scanned the sky above the yard. "Looks fine enew."

"Aye." Higgins slowly looked around as if ascertaining they were alone and spit to one side. "I dunno as I should speak, howsumdever . . . I be of two minds what ter do."

Maggie joined them, with Higgins' ale and a thick slice of her bread smeared generously with honey. He thanked her, set aside his gun, and carefully took the plate and mug.

"Thank you, Maggie," Feldman said. "I'll bring in the crockery."

She nodded and withdrew.

Feldman watched Higgins eat and drink, waiting for him to explain what troubled him.

"'Ye'd best be a mort choice o'er de master," the old man said abruptly.

"Oh?"

"Aye. I 'appen' along in de ol' copse," he gestured eastward. "Mus Eldridge 'e be consarned about it along of de navy buyin' de 'ood. I seed de master and I heerd 'im shouting as loud as ever 'e could. Dere be naun else dere. 'e shoke 'is fistes, 'e did. Up-a-top-o'-de-'ouse 'e was. But dere weren't naun dere."

"I see."

"E'en-a'most any day I see 'im bein' crazy. It queers me, it do. I do'ant know as it argifies much. 'is lordship ain't 'isself."

"Aye. I be that glad ye came to me," Feldman said. "We be choice over him that he come to naun harm. He be grizzling these days, I bluv."

He'll come to no harm taking his rage and grief out on the trees and rocks, Feldman thought, bringing the mug and plate in to Maggie. *But will it end there?*

"He saw something out on the estate, and since his lordship was not here, he wanted to tell me," he explained to Maggie.

" 'iggins do be a wise gaffer. A dunnamany times I seen deer and squirrels eat outn 'isn 'and."

Feldman sipped a fresh cup of tea, staring absently at the bread before him. Higgins' warning troubled him. There were too many similarities between his lordship's behavior now and years ago on the Continent when Feldman despaired of his life.

Maggie sat down heavily and leaned both elbows on the table. "Ye be dat fretful aboutn de master? I do'ant go nabbling about, but de master, 'e bin grizzling over long. 'e be tedious and tempersome. Mus Croft do be aprayin' fer 'im, yer know. I do'ant know as it does 'im no good, but it do'ant harm 'im naun, I bluv. What's to do, Mr. Feldman?"

"I don't know. He hasn't confided in me and he's not seen any of his friends from town these past weeks. He might talk with Sir Deuxbury, but I've no idea how to bring that about."

"Mayhap Mus Croft had oughtn ter pray 'im down."

"There seems little else we can do."

Seventeen

Cyprian pulled back the curtain covering a library window. A scattering of stars twinkled between wisps of incoming fog. Smugglers liked these nights in the dark of the moon. Hopefully, Tony would return with them tonight. Cyprian remembered his youthful exhilaration in riding the tide up the Oms, then darting into the mermaid's cave and up the passageway into the lower wine cellars before the rising water cut off his escape. Tony would find it to his adventurous taste, eluding the coast guard cutter on a moonless night. Perhaps tomorrow, along with his eggs and ham, he would be treated to a colorful description of Tony's wild escapades in France.

Wearily Cyprian climbed the broad staircase and entered his room. He hardly knew how to manage himself these days. Tony was right in disapproving his reckless entertaining. That hectic activity and facade of gaiety neither healed his wounded heart nor deadened his pain. But neither was there more peace or happiness in long days occupied solely with the estate's business than in those of dissipation. Although the household was not in continuous upheaval, he had too much time for brooding on shattered dreams.

Only fools cherished their fancies. Especially his of finding a woman so pure as to be his salvation. No, miserable devil he remained. Twice miserable, for the haven he thought he had found was illusory. Devil he was, cursed of God.

Yet, Tony raised doubts of Angelea's guilt. Despite the evidence of his own eyes, he vaguely hoped for another explanation for Uxton's presence. Wherein lay the truth? How might he discover it? Go to her at Hillview? His pride would not allow it.

Pondering the situation, he prepared for another restless night.

Silently the smugglers waited as their ladened boat rose and fell with the heavy swells. Tony scanned the black sky strewn with stars as if a giant hand had tossed diamonds across it. Blank darkness over the Channel indicated the friendly fog bank lurked behind them. "Send it with us," Tony prayed.

Tense with anxious excitement, he hugged the lumpy sealskin pouch hidden under his striped shirt. Whether the landing went undetected as before, or was intercepted, these French invasion plans must get to Pitt. A red light! The landing signal from a special lantern hung in the steeple of St. Ebbs by the Sea.

His spine prickled as he became aware the boat no longer wallowed aimlessly, but moved forward. The tide had changed. The only sounds beside the wind in his ears were the soft, labored breathing of the men as they rowed, eager to make the most of the incoming force of the sea. Suddenly a wave picked them up, bearing them rapidly toward the shore.

Tony's heart thumped hard. Would they land on the rocks or be propelled up the Oms? As the rush continued, he relaxed. The experienced smugglers had positioned the boat so they were rushing past the treacherous rocks guarding the river's mouth. With the skill gained from a lifetime of practice, they occasionally pulled on the oars to avoid the lower sand bar and guided the boat around the burned out, rotted hulk of the old *Tina Marie*. Soon they would be safe in the cove and Tony would be racing into the mermaid's haven.

An unexpected light flared on shore. A musket's roar and a splash near shore shocked him. *Anxious fool,* he thought; *he should have waited until we were closer in or had started to land. Maybe they're afraid we'll pass them and they will lose us.*

The smugglers swore and began rowing rapidly to augment the tide. No need for silence now.

"Give a hand wid de casks," one said, clutching Tony's sleeve. Together they heaved them overboard as quickly as possible, lightening their load and destroying hanging evidence.

The boat veered closer to shore. The leader exclaimed "Now!" and all jumped from the boat. The two best swimmers crossed the river. Tony and the third man separated on the near shore to fend for themselves as best they might.

As he struggled out of the water, hampered by his soaked clothes, Tony heard men running on the chalk cliff above and scrambling over the rocks along the shore. He rested near what felt to be a large boulder, listening, trying to determine exactly where he was.

Some yards away a loud yell was followed by several voices, then the light of an unshuttered lantern. Evidently his recent companion was captured. Similar sounds on the far shore indicated the others were also caught.

As the lantern's rays flashed about, Tony recognized the silhouette of a flat-topped rock close to the mermaid's cave. Cautiously he began moving toward it.

A stone rattled, dislodged by his shoe. A musket fired. The harsh knock to his left shoulder forced an exclamation from him as he fell. Quickly he picked up a rock and tossed it away from the cave. Searing pain exploded in his arm and chest. Clenching his jaws together, he hurled two more stones and heard the pursuit move away.

Marshalling all his will power, he staggered across the shore and into the cave, praying, "Help me! Help me! God, help me!"

Water swirled about his knees as he felt for the high safety ledge. When he located it, he waited until the water rose, lifting his body. Using all his remaining strength, he threw the upper part of his body and one leg onto the shelf before sliding into oblivion.

Sleep had barely stilled Cyprian's fretful tossing when an irregular popping sound roused him. Puzzled, he lay wondering what wakened him. He heard distant, spasmodic popping. Musket fire! He rushed to the open window overlooking the river. Out of the darkness came muffled shouts and more shots. They must be along the banks of the Oms. Pitt's men were to arrange for the cutter out of Little Hampton to patrol another section of the coast on dark nights. Something must have gone awry, causing the landing to be intercepted.

Hastily he pulled on buckskin breeches and boots. If the soldiers came to the Hall, the nearest residence, he must be present to receive them. Tony might need his help.

As he left his room, jabbing his hands into the sleeves of his banyon, the doorbell was pulled twice, followed by noisy pounding on the oaken door. Cyprian saw Fothering come running from the servants' wing, buttoning his jacket on the way. His call brought the man to an immediate halt. "Where is Lawrence's room?"

"Up two flights, then the third, no, fourth door on the left, milord."

"Take your time answering the door. Make our guests at ease in the blue salon, then go to my room. I will be down directly."

Cyprian ran up the stairs and felt his way along the dark hall to Lawrence's door, dimly remembering exploring here as a child. He shook the young man out of a sound sleep.

"What? Is that really you, milord?"

"Yes, Lawrence. I believe I heard musket fire from the river. There is no moon tonight. I am expecting Sir Deuxbury. Do you understand?"

"Aye, milord. Do ye think de patrol's cotched 'im?"

"I pray not. Someone was pounding on the front door. I must prepare to receive them. You know these cliffs as well as I. Could you reach the mermaid's cave through the passage without being seen?"

"Aye." The young man was out of bed. He struck a light for his candle.

"See what you find. If you do not return, I will send help as quickly as possible."

"Percy, de groom, he be quick, milord. Him knows de caves too."

"On your way. And take care. If there are soldiers about, they are likely to shoot any moving shadow."

As he slipped into his room, Cyprian heard Fothering mounting the front stairs and complaining loudly to someone about his painful rheumatism. Cyprian rang for Feldman and removed his banyon.

"Yes, yes," he responded to Fothering's knock, buttoning his shirt. Cyprian noted that an army officer accompanied Fothering. With great irritation, he demanded, "What is the cause for this disturbance, Fothering? I am hardly in condition to be receiving callers at this hour."

"No, milord. I tried explaining to the lieutenant here, but he insisted on seeing you on the instant. Lieutenant Danridge says they caught some smugglers making a landing on the beach, milord."

"Ah. Very commendable, Lieutenant. I heard the noise. What has that to do with us?"

"With your permission, milord, we would like to check the Hall for any who may have escaped us. And we would like to know if all your people are here. Some may be accomplices."

"Accomplices?" Cyprian raised his chin haughtily. "Lieutenant, men engage in the trade to augment incomes inadequate to their families' needs. I pay my staff enough to discourage that activity. Furthermore, they know, should they become involved in those illegal transactions, they would bring my displeasure upon their heads. Believe me, Lieutenant, none of my staff would risk my displeasure for any amount of money."

"I am sure you are correct, milord. This is a mere formality. I may then report the search was made and nothing found."

"Precisely what do you propose doing?"

"Check any space large enough to conceal a man."

"Your men may *look*. I will not permit my belongings or those of my household to be disrupted in any way. And you are to charge your men not to touch or frighten the maids. As for accounting for the members of my staff, I should think that impossible. Your arrival was sufficiently noisy and dramatic to send them scurrying in several directions. And many are already about their morning duties. You might better search the village or the tenants. I cannot speak for their actions as I can for my household."

"Yes, milord. We will accomplish this as quickly as may be, and with the least inconvenience to you and your staff."

"Fothering, assign a special guide to each search party. Inform them of my orders, and direct them to report to me in the library at the conclusion. Lieutenant, would you please check my rooms now? I do not wish anyone going through them in my absence."

"Certainly, milord."

While the lieutenant made his search of Cyprian's and Angelea's rooms, Feldman arrived.

"Make me presentable, Feldman. It appears I must entertain the army this morning."

"Very good, milord," Feldman replied. In a few minutes he tied a simple cravat and assisted Cyprian into a dark blue coat.

"We may lock these rooms and I will instruct my men not to disturb them," the lieutenant said, emerging from Angelea's room. He paused a moment, then asked, "When I arrived, you were preparing to go out, milord?"

"The gunfire awoke me. I was preparing to determine if it signified danger for the Hall."

Danridge appeared satisfied with his answer.

Gradually the shapes of the dew-laden garden emerged in the gray dawn beyond the library windows while Cyprian and the lieutenant awaited reports. Cyprian felt strangely detached, as if observing another man in his chair conversing casually with the officer across from him. Even concern for Tony seemed imaginary, part of a grotesque illusion.

Only one group remained unaccounted for when Fothering entered with a bottle of wine. "I thought your lordship would like a glass of wine," he said.

"Quite right, Fothering. Danridge, would you join me?"

"Thank you, milord."

Fothering poured out two glasses and offered them to the lieutenant, then to Cyprian. He murmured softly, "Wounded with the mermaid."

"Thank you. Is Mrs. Croft about?"

"Yes, milord."

"Send her to me."

"Right away, milord."

Mrs. Croft entered softly, ignored the officer and made her stiff bob before Cyprian.

"I suppose all this disruption is necessary. Fortunately, it is nearly concluded. Eldridge mentioned you undertook an inventory and repair of household items some days past. What progress have you made?"

"The principal rooms are completed. Some of the guest rooms require attention. I will send to Shoreham for what is needed."

"Excellent. We are then ready to receive guests. Have you completed your arrangements for Sir Deuxbury? He should arrive most any day." Cyprian noticed the officer stiffen.

"Yes, milord. Mrs. Worth is to prepare pheasant a la orange and his favorite chocolate tarts on his arrival. His room is in readiness. Will he be remaining several days?"

"One never knows. I will try to prevail upon him to stay a week or so. He will brighten us up."

The last team interrupted their conversation to report no unauthorized person was found. The lieutenant thanked his lordship for his cooperation and apologized for the inconvenience.

Cyprian accepted the apology with condescending grace. Immediately, upon hearing the outside door close behind the officer, he said, "Ask Feldman to meet me in the dungeon. We must bring Sir Deuxbury through the passage. If the lieutenant is as sharp as he appeared, he will have our comings and goings watched. I am not sure he is entirely satisfied."

Within half an hour of the soldiers' departure, Feldman and Lawrence carried the unconscious Tony to the room kept ready for his use.

Feldman checked the wound and turned to Cyprian at his side. "Milord, the bullet is embedded beyond my reach. We need Dr. Winther."

Cyprian sighed. "I'll send right away. Stay with him, Feldman."

What excuse might he use to evade the soldiers' vigilance? On leaving Tony's room, he saw Stevenson replacing burned candles with fresh ones in the hall. Cyprian beckoned him. "Leave that. Get word to Henry in the stables to contrive a noisy ruckus, as if an accident were occurring. Have a victim carried into the house, and bring me word in the dining room. I must have an excuse to send you for Dr. Winther without arousing the suspicions of any soldiers observing the Hall."

"Milord!" Feldman called to him from Tony's room.

"Yes?" Cyprian followed him back inside.

"As we were undressing him, we found this package." He gave Cyprian a small sealskin pouch.

Cyprian turned it over thoughtfully. It must be a message for Pitt. He called Stevenson back from the end of the hall. "After you send the doctor here, stop at the Dancing Skillet for a tankard of ale. If you see Sir Deuxbury's man, give him this packet. Take great care no one sees you pass it. It is of the greatest urgency. Trust no one else in this matter.''

"Yes, milord." The young footman tucked it inside his coat and ran to the back stairs.

Cyprian returned to Tony's room where Fothering joined him, announcing Squire Ford's arrival. "He awaits your lordship in the blue salon."

"Go ahead, milord," Feldman urged. "You cannot do anything here."

Gently Cyprian touched Tony's forehead. He took a deep breath. "As you say. Fothering, prepare a partially eaten breakfast for me in the dining room. I will meet the Squire and take him there to talk."

"Good morning, Ford. How may I be of service to you?" Cyprian inquired upon entering the salon.

"Good morning, milord," his gangling neighbor responded. "I came to see if you knew of the goings-on this morning."

"Rather more than I care to. Would you join me in breakfast?"

"Oh no, milord. I ate at the manor."

"At least take a cup of coffee with me while I finish mine." Cyprian led the way to the dining room, saying, "Soldiers came with the dawn and searched the Hall."

"They didn't!" exclaimed the shocked Squire.

"They did. The lieutenant claimed it was a precaution. They caught smugglers on the beach, and they thought some may have escaped and come here. So he claimed."

Cyprian was gratified to find part of a slice of ham cut up on his plate, half a cup of coffee, his napkin thrown down beside them, and his chair pushed back at an angle. He waved the squire to the place at his right, ordered coffee for him, then resumed his apparently interrupted meal.

"I see." The squire said sitting down, adding with an air of satisfaction, "I have long maintained these desperate men would bring the King's wrath on our heads."

"I quite agree."

"I hope they hold the men for the assizes. As magistrate, I will see justice done. They will hang, and the district will be the better for it."

Stevenson entered, his blue livery smudged with blood. "Beg pardon, milord, but thee's been an accident in the stables."

"As if smugglers and soldiers were not enough for one morning! What happened?"

"Blue Star attacked Jason, the new groom."

"Is Blue Star injured?" asked Cyprian, half-rising in alarm.

"Oh no, milord. Only Jason."

He settled back in his seat. "Did Henry not warn him that Blue Star must be handled carefully?"

"He says he did. Jason is bleeding badly, milord. They brought him into the scullery. Might we send for Dr. Winther?"

"What about Betsy Miller? She is very good with herbs and things."

"She is with him now, milord, and says he's beyond her."

"Oh, very well, you may go for Winther. It won't do to have one of my men down with all that's happening."

Stevenson bowed and withdrew.

Cyprian frowned at his plate. "Smugglers, soldiers, an injured groom—all before I've finished my breakfast. I trust things are quieter at the manor."

"Oh yes. There were rumors from the servants' wing this morning about an interrupted landing. I thought I'd best learn the truth before the tale grew out of proportion. If they caught all of them, the lanes will be safe come the next dark night."

"True, true. Would you care to join me for cards tonight?"

"I should like to, but my wife's sister is still with us. She departs in a few days time."

"Fine. Then we shall have a game at the end of the week. Extend my greetings to your lady, Ford."

Immediately upon Ford's departure, Cyprian went to the scullery to view the victim. Jason, a tall lad, thoroughly enjoyed his role. He moaned, and winked at Betsy Miller and complained about that devil gray horse.

"Watch how you blacken my steed's reputation," Cyprian cautioned. "I regret you must act the invalid a few days to lend credence to our play and outwit the army."

"Der be naun to it, milord. De sojers be larmentaable bothersome I bluv."

"I've no doubt you will make the most of it, young man."

Dr. Winther arrived within the hour and calmly cared for his two patients. With Feldman's assistance, he probed for and removed the bullet, then bandaged Tony tightly. He left laudanum to keep him quiet and instructions for his care with Feldman. Then he went down to the groom, bandaged him, and told him how to play his part.

Both Winther and Feldman assured Cyprian there was nothing he might do for his friend. Therefore, he departed for the Dancing Skillet to discharge the normal business of the district, trying to pretend nothing at the Hall merited his concern.

Eighteen

*E*arly the following afternoon, Tony's green coach, accompanied by two outriders, rolled to a stop before the Hall. Having been alerted by his staff of the arrival, Cyprian met it on the outer steps. He gave a warm greeting to the dandy in puce disembarking as a second coach loaded with baggage arrived.

"We may be watched," Cyprian murmured to the astonished footman dressed in his master's garb, "so act your part well."

After they entered the hall, Cyprian explained what occurred the day before, adding that Sir Deuxbury remained in a state of delirium. The anxious footman was shown to his master's bedside, then went with Cyprian and Feldman to Cyprian's room for consultation.

"You may stay until your master is well, of course," Cyprian began, pacing thoughtfully before his fireplace. "According to Dr. Winther, it will be some weeks before Sir Anthony may return home. He may give us a better understanding of what we might expect when he comes this afternoon. Be assured the alert Lieutenant Danridge will be watching and asking in the village concerning the happenings at the Hall."

"Milord," Feldman said, "Sir Deuxbury usually appears to visit but a day or two at a time these past weeks. It might be remarked upon if he lengthened his stay now."

"I agree. It might not be best for you to remain so long. Unless Dr. Winther gives us cause to change our plans, I suggest that you, er, Wilkins isn't it?"

"Yes, milord," the footman answered.

"Sir Anthony has remarked that you carry off his part very well. I

108

suggest that this afternoon we stroll in the garden, arm in arm. Tomorrow morning we will ride side by side about the estate, and the day after tomorrow you depart for Stonehead. Surely any watchers will be satisfied that he has arrived for a brief visit, as expected, and continued on.''

"Very good, milord," Wilkins assented.

"We must also be careful not to be too obvious in showing his presence," Feldman cautioned. "As the oft-quoted bard—"

"Protesting over much, you mean?" Cyprian interrupted.

"Exactly, milord."

"Once we are returned to Stonehead, will you send word for us to come for Sir Deuxbury?" asked Wilkins.

"No. We shall contrive something. I come and go on occasion with several servants. I may well choose to go to one of my other properties for a prolonged visit, taking my staff with me. We will bring him to you as soon as he is able. Should anyone appear looking for him, I am confident your Chambers is able to turn them away on some pretext."

"Oh yes, milord," Wilkins grinned. "He is well practiced at staring down any callers asking impertinent questions." He dropped his voice, mimicking the haughty Chambers. " 'Sir Deuxbury does not take me into his confidence.' Or, 'Sir Deuxbury is not accountable to his staff for his comings and goings.' Yes, milord, he does it very well."

The conference was interrupted by Fothering. "Lieutenant Danridge is asking to see you, milord. I showed him into the blue salon."

"Very good. It would appear we are, indeed, being observed," Cyprian commented. At the door, he turned back to Wilkins. "I shall attempt to fob him off, saying you are resting from a strenuous journey. However, be prepared for an interview in the library. Where have you been?"

"Chichester."

"No farther? Well, I shall assure him you are easily fatigued. Very likely he will meet us tomorrow while we are out riding."

Cyprian looked up with a frown as the lieutenant entered the library. He leaned back from his desk littered with papers and waved Eldridge aside. His greeting was polite and cold.

"Good afternoon, milord," the lieutenant replied. "I thought you would wish to know the results of our search in the district."

"Yes, of course."

"We have accounted for all but one of the smugglers."

"How do you know one is missing?"

"We wounded one, and none of those we captured is wounded."

"Ah, I see. Was the wound serious? Mayhap he crawled behind some rocks or bushes and died."

"That is possible," the lieutenant answered skeptically. He then asked, "I understand you have a visitor?"

"Yes. My friend Sir Deuxbury has arrived."

"May I speak with him? I should like to know if he observed anything out of the ordinary in the district."

"That will not be possible at this time. He is resting. On no account may he be disturbed. I will inquire of him for you."

"That would be kind of you, milord, if it would not be an inconvenience."

"None at all. Where might I reach you with his answer?"

"I am staying at The Rose. Has Sir Deuxbury traveled far?"

"For him, yes. He came from Chichester. And yes, he always requires a large amount of baggage to maintain his appearance as a recognized man of fashion. Is there anything else, Lieutenant?"

"No, milord. Thank you for your time."

"I trust you apprehend the missing man shortly, or locate his body."

Cyprian hurried up to Tony's room as soon as the officer left. He was troubled by his friend's constant restlessness and distracted muttering. He would like to halt the charade and summon Dr. Winther to remain until Tony passed his crisis. But such exposure of Tony's mission would be tantamount to betraying his friend's trust.

For an hour, Cyprian stayed at Tony's side, hoping for an indication of improvement. He walked with Wilkins in the garden while they planned what he would do and say if the lieutenant met them the next day. And after some discussion, they agreed the message to send to The Rose was that only a tinker was seen some miles distant.

The officer did not meet them while they were riding the next morning, nor did he call before Sir Anthony's entourage departed the following day. Wilkins left assured that information of his master's progress would be sent as soon as possible.

That evening Squire Ford arrived for supper and whist. He was especially testy for the inconvenience the soldiers caused in the district. "The lieutenant insists he is looking for the leader of a large smuggling ring. I think he is searching for a shadow one of his men fired at. They are notoriously poor marksmen. If they have not found any trace of him by now, they should move on and do something useful. And so I told him this afternoon."

"Did you indeed?" Cyprian responded.

"I did for a fact. And he agreed with me. A very smooth young man. Too smooth by half. I've no doubt he intends using this unimportant incident to advance his position. And he bedevils all of us in the process. I've a notion to write his commanding officer, or even Pitt. Let them send him to the colonies, maybe India, and let him make his way out there where he can do less harm."

Cyprian took a sip of wine and nodded agreement. He would let the peppery squire fight the army for him.

Waking early, Cyprian donned his banyon and slipped quietly into Tony's room.

As he closed the door, he was startled to hear Tony complain, "Dear boy, I thought you had deserted me!"

A burst of relief clouded Cyprian's eyes and strangled his speech as he crossed to Tony's bed and clasped his hand. When he recovered, he declared, "Such a show of gratitude to begin my day! You have no idea of the hours I spent in this room worrying over you."

"I am delighted you consider my well-being of such import."

"Oh, not at all. It would be of the greatest inconvenience if you died here. Very likely you would haunt the Hall, frightening all my servants."

"Oh, I should make a dramatic ghost. Would you have me appear without a head?"

"You may appear any way you wish so long as you do not moan and rattle chains. I may sleep through appearances, but not noises."

"Very well. I should become the silent shade of Omsbridge."

"But not just yet, if you don't mind. I prefer your company in the flesh rather than as a phantom. You worried me and my staff these last days, old friend."

"Being on the mend, I shall worry you even more," Tony promised him.

"Very well, I must warn the staff. Oh, the pouch you were carrying was sent on through your man at the Dancing Skillet." He then informed Tony of the events surrounding his injury.

"Such fun as you had, and I missed it! But then, I was having some experiences of my own."

"What do you mean?"

Tony paused, and looked seriously into Cyprian's eyes. "I must sort it out first. Then I may tell you a marvelous tale, which you may not believe."

Carefully Tony eased himself onto the narrow seat in the chapel choir. He braced his good shoulder against the wood back and gazed up at the Victory window. The morning sunlight made it appear as if the majestic Christ was ascending into a sky of broken sapphires.

Closing his eyes, he inhaled, expanding his lungs to their fullest.

After holding his breath a moment, he exhaled slowly, feeling all his tension flow out his fingertips. At last, in this dim corner, he felt an echo of the intense peace he knew before recovering consciousness a week ago. When he tried explaining that powerful emotion to Cyprian, his friend looked baffled. Perhaps no one who had not experienced it could understand.

He recalled the soft darkness enfolding him and a radiant curtain of spun silver. And he saw Grandmere, smiling as when he shared his boyish adventures with her. Fantastic joy thrilled him.

Her voiceless words had greeted him lovingly, "Tony, my child!"

He moved across a spaceless distance, reaching for her.

As he was about to touch her hand, she said, "No, my pet, not yet. You must go back. In time you will join me, but first you must serve our loving Savior, as I taught you. Do you remember?"

Grandmere had come to England in her youth, a young Huguenot fleeing persecution in Lyons. She treasured her relationship to God, a relationship she sought to share with her little grandson. He believed everything she said until that unforgettable day in the garden. Suddenly clutching her head, she grimaced in pain, cried out, and died.

Crouching beside her, Tony had held her hand and screamed until a gardener came running. Everyone declared her death a stroke of God's. Angry, he shut his heart against the horrible deity who stripped him of his dearest friend, leaving him in a cold, comfortless world.

With shaking fingers Tony brushed away the tears of longing streaking his cheeks. Again he felt the devastating loss of her death two decades past.

When he saw her again, the wall about his heart shattered. Grandmere died in pain, but she was happy and in an astoundingly peaceful place. Her expectation of his joining her there comforted him.

Nineteen

*C*yprian cantered down the muddy winter road on horseback, tatters of his black mood clinging about him. Only a few days past he had returned Tony, disguised as a groom, to Stonehead. Cyprian made that trip reluctantly, fearing the loss of his friend's companionship would leave him prey to recurring despair. And indeed it had. Pitt had asked Tony to take a dangerous winter crossing to the colonies. It would be many months before Cyprian could enjoy his friend's presence again.

The noise of a crowd gathered at Ox Hill Cross ahead claimed his attention. Another of those crazy preachers he kept encountering of late. Had the world lost its senses to go after such unsanctified persons?

As before, a lean person stood at the foot of the ancient stone cross, an open book in one hand, the other gesturing alternately at the sky and his audience. Brown hair hung about his face beneath the broad brim of his hat. His open brown coat flapped in the light breeze.

Cyprian slowed, then stopped at the edge of the crowd, musing on the folly of his fellows. Unlettered, without proper instruction, they could be led easily by any speaker with a strong personality. He was about to continue his journey when he heard a few of the speaker's words: ". . . your sins!"

Speaking in clear, ringing tones, he declared, "Because of them, you are condemned in the sight of Almighty God! Therefore, you must be born again!"

Stunned, Cyprian felt cold and immobile, as a statue. The words blazed in his mind—great, flaming letters.

The crowd began to murmur, not liking what they heard, either. They moved restlessly, shaking their heads and talking softly with each other.

"Him no-ought ter make such a noration!"

"Him be a foreigner, naunbut a sheere-mouse, I bluv!" exclaimed another.

"Be off wid ye!" a man yelled.

As in a dream Cyprian dismounted and picked up a stone from the road, even as others were doing. He threw it with all his strength, feeling a sense of satisfaction when it hit the preacher's right shoulder, his pointing arm.

The preacher dropped his book to clutch at his injured shoulder and turned to look at Cyprian. Late afternoon sunlight illumined his features: a long nose, deep set eyes, a jutting forehead, and lean cheeks. Another stone struck him in the abdomen and he bent over, falling to his knees.

Men and women closed in around the man. "Take him to the gaol so's he can meditate awhile."

"Aye, dese here Methodists do like meditating."

As Cyprian mounted, he heard a shriek of pain. The shoulder was probably broken and the people were being none too gentle.

Continuing on to the Dancing Skillet, Cyprian felt troubled by the absence of anger or bitterness in the preacher's expression. A normal man should be fighting mad at being stoned by the crowd. But then, anyone preaching at a crossroads must be demented. Regret at stooping to behave in the common spirit of the crowd superseded his brief satisfaction at hitting his mark.

Cyprian determined to shake off his black thoughts as he rode under the newly repainted sign of the Dancing Skillet and into its spacious yard. He must concentrate on the monthly business at hand. An oustler sprang to hold Blue Star as his lordship dismounted.

"Rub him down and feed him," Cyprian directed, tossing him a coin. "I will be inside for some time."

"Aye, milord," the man replied with a tug of his forelock.

The host of the Dancing Skillet, a man nearly as broad as he was tall, met him at the door to the coffee room. A wide grin creased his fat face into a collection of fleshly bumps. "Milord Omsbridge, an honor that you come to my poor house. The Venus and the Mars are ready an' you wish."

"Thank you, Holmes. The Venus will do very well. I always prefer the goddess of love to the god of war."

Holmes laughed. "Aye, milord. She do be a deal more comfortable."

"If anyone mentions wishing to see me, tell him where I am. And send up a pitcher of your fine brown ale."

"Aye, milord. Dracly minute."

Cyprian was turning toward the stairs when an angular woman of spare, tall proportions appeared in the doorway leading to the kitchen. She dropped a curtsy when she saw him and pulled the corners of her thin lips back into a sour smile. "My lord, you honor our humble inn. Did I hear you say the Venus?" She selected a taper from the oak mantle as she spoke and lit it at the fire. "Permit me to attend you and open the windows. Betsy is drawing a pitcher of ale and will bring it up shortly."

"Betsy?"

"A new girl. I'm sure you'll find her satisfactory. She's a good girl and a hard worker, not like some of the chits as has been here." As she clambered up the stairs, she added over her shoulder, "And I'll send up a plate of biscuits I've taken from the oven within this hour. I'm sure your lordship will find them light and tasty."

"I am confident you are right, Mistress Holmes," Cyprian answered. "And I would like your tasty game pie for dinner." He gave a friendly nod to her bowing husband and followed her upstairs.

Despite its name, the Venus had no claim to beauty. A table, adequate to serve eight or ten people, was placed to one side. Several scarred chairs stood about in no particular order. Using her taper, the landlady quickly lit the neatly laid fire in the blackened stone fireplace. She flung open the two windows overlooking the cobbled yard, then crossed the room to open those facing the main road. After checking the tall cupboard to make sure the chamber pots were in place and ready, she picked up the violet-sprinkled pitcher on the table near the door, saying, "I'll bring up some hot water right away, milord. If you wish anything at all, ring, and Betsy or I shall attend to it promptly." She dropped another curtsy and left.

With a frown, Cyprian stared at the door a moment. Why was it that, regardless of her efforts to make him comfortable, he felt an immediate hostility when she came into his sight? He pitied her husband, who seemed happy enough. It was well known that the Dancing Skillet's wide reputation for cleanliness and fine food and drink was due to her energy and skill. While the local people granted her a grudging respect, they held her in no affection. There was something bristly about her that reminded him of a porcupine. Perhaps it was her grating northern accent constantly identifying her as a foreigner, what the locals called a "sheere-mouse."

Cyprian faced the long day with a heavy sense of duty, lacking his usual buoyant anticipation of social interchange and zestful battles of wits. Like everything else in his life these days, his duties were not as they should be.

Within the half hour people were climbing to the Venus to lay various projects or problems before him, seeking his support or ruling. During the afternoon three separate men came to discuss their desire to stand for this seat in the House of Commons. All knew whomever Omsbridge chose would win. He promised each he would give careful consideration to his candidacy.

A wizened old man and another farmer came with a young neighbor to lay a boundary dispute before him. Cyprian was tempted to find for the young man, whom he felt would be a good ally in the future, but he decided to follow his sense of justice in this case and find for the old one. As they left, Cyprian clapped the loser on his shoulder, saying he would gladly find for him the next time if his case was better prepared, without such evident wrong-doing as moving a landmarker in the plain view of several farmers.

By midafternoon, his duties oppressed him as lead weights on each shoulder. Neither countless mugs of ale nor Mistress Holmes' excellent dinner served by the shy, but comely, Betsy lightened his burden. A pressure in his forehead indicated a headache was in the making when two men entered.

Cyprian invited them to be seated. Mr. Harold Fairfield, known in the district as a sharp, enterprising businessman, introduced the younger man as his nephew, James Fairfield. They bore a strong resemblance in their narrow faces and sandy hair. The senior Fairfield's was well seasoned with gray.

After a few polite generalities and a mug of ale, the subject of the deplorable state of the roads was raised and the new turnpike trusts being established to improve them. "The road passing the Dancing Skillet joins two market towns and is usually left in a poor state. It would be a blessing to the district for it to be maintained in a more responsible manner."

Cyprian nodded agreement. Carefully he listened to the plan they described to form a trust for this roadway headed by himself. A tollgate would be placed at each end in narrow locations where it would be impossible to bypass them. The revenue would be used for a minimal periodic upkeep of the surface of the road. To aid in preventing its deterioration, passage would be banned to any heavily laden wagons which would tend to dig ruts in their road. Of course, the people would complain about the added costs, but they had no legal recourse. A tidy profit was projected for all three members of the trust by the end of the first year. Income would increase dramatically after the initial cost of the gates and upgrading of the road.

"And who would propose the bill in Parliament?" Cyprian asked.

"James here would," the older gentleman responded promptly. "If he wins the election for this seat, he will propose it."

"I see. Was this scheme of your making, James?" Cyprian asked.

"Yes, milord."

"I think an energetic person, as enterprising as yourself, would be an asset for our country should he serve in Parliament. You have my hearty support."

"Thank you, milord," James said enthusiastically.

"May I propose a toast to our new business venture?" Mr. Fairfield suggested. Cyprian assented, and a bottle of good vintage wine was ordered. They drank toasts to the trust's success and their enrichment, then to James's term in Parliament and his service to the district. The half-empty bottle was overset, spilling its contents on the floor, and Betsy was summoned to bring another.

As she placed it on the table and bent to mop up the wine, Cyprian's attention was directed to her lissome, feminine young figure and neckline. He rose unsteadily, braced himself against the table, saying, "I can think of no more pleasant seal to our venture than a kiss from Betsy here, a beauteous wench if ever I saw one." He attempted a smile. "A kiss all around," he paused, and raised his eyebrows, "and a special one for me, heh, Betsy, my girl?"

"Hear, hear," James agreed, pounding the table with his mug, and Mr. Fairfield roared his assent.

Cyprian leaned forward, reaching for Betsy's waist.

Her eyes widened in fright. "Oh no, please, milord!" In her attempt to avoid Cyprian's grasping hands, her foot slid on the spilled wine, catapulting her through the open casement. Her piercing shriek ended with a dull thud on the cobbled yard below.

At first immobile in their shock, the three men stared at each other; then, coming to their senses, they all rushed to the window. She lay as a doll tossed aside, with an ugly red stain spreading on her white blouse and mob cap.

A man in black, dismounting from a fine chestnut in the yard, hurried to kneel at Betsy's side as Mistress Holmes ran out and bent over her. She straightened and looked silently up at the men leaning out of the window. Her angry, accusing glare seemed focused on Cyprian. The stranger also looked up at him. Although shaded by the broad brim of his hat, his expression seemed in some way softer.

"I didn't touch her!" Cyprian exclaimed. "I didn't touch her. None of us were near her. It was the—the wine. There was wine on the floor. She slipped."

"Of course, milord," Mistress Holmes said in a level tone that Cyprian felt denied his explanation. "Is she dead, Dr. Knight?" she asked of the man beside her.

He nodded. Gently he closed Betsy's staring eyes and crossed her hands on her breast.

A subdued, mournful atmosphere shrouded the taproom as the Fairfields and Cyprian gathered with a few villagers. The stranger in black quietly took charge of the situation. He directed the ostlers to lay Betsy out in an empty room and sent messages to Squire Ford, the local magistrate, and to Betsy's parents.

Cyprian inquired after the stranger's identity.

"Him be a proper gentleman, de vicar of Tyne-at-de-Crossroads. Anywhen he come anigh he stop here. He justabout got de fore-horse by de head, surelye. Dis be larmentaable ernful."

Dr. Knight left a group of people and turned toward Omsbridge's table. His blonde hair was drawn into a queue tied with a plain black ribbon. The white squared ends of his cravat, emphasized by his neat, dark suit, showed his position as a clergyman. Again Cyprian was struck with the lack of condemnation in his expression when their eyes met.

Abruptly Cyprian rose, saying he wanted to check on Blue Star. On good days, Rev. Pettigrew's platitudes were hard to bear. He was not in the mood to stomach them from a stranger. Let the Fairfields hear them. Harold was trying to calm his shaking with Mr. Holmes' brandy, and young James seemed immobilized with fear. If his nerve was so easily shaken, he might not prove a strong ally in the House of Commons.

The pungent odors of the stables and rustling of horses eased his tension. Blue Star nickered softly and shoved his nose against his master's vest, expecting a treat. Cyprian smiled, giving him the apple taken from a bowl in the taproom. Two stalls away he saw the spirited chestnut stallion Dr. Knight rode and paused to note his fine points.

"A remarkable mount for a country parson," he commented to the stableboy.

"Aye. He be from Lord Rockivale's stable, I bluv. Dey be neighbors together an' come here now an' agin."

Knight and Rockivale, in combination—those names reminded Cyprian of a tale making the rounds in his undergraduate days. Insolent Ezekiel Walton, recognized as a peerless swordsman, suffered a humiliating defeat in an irregular duel at a ball. Could the mild parson inside be the undefeated Black Knight of Oxford? Impossible. It was also unlikely Rockivale had two close friends named Knight.

The vicar was still talking with the Fairfields when Cyprian returned to the taproom. Both seemed in an improved state. A middle-aged couple entered, sparing Cyprian the necessity of exchanging civilities with the clergyman.

The woman rushed to Mr. Holmes, crying, "Where be our Betsy?" The man followed, dragging his right foot as he limped across the room.

Dr. Knight took the woman's hand, spoke softly to both, and accompanied them to the room where Betsy lay.

"What did you tell him?" Cyprian asked of Harold Fairfield.

"Everything, milord."

"Everything?" Cyprian exclaimed, shocked. "Surely not our business dealings!"

"Oh no, milord. Everything about poor Betsy. He were right comforting, weren't he, James?"

The young man nodded.

"Have no fear, milord. We'll not be seeing much of him again, more's the pity. Kind he is. Not one to say fancy things without much meaning."

"What do you mean 'we'll not be seeing much of him again'?"

"Him's been appointed vicar to St. Jude's in London. He moves his family there directly."

Squire Ford arrived and went to Cyprian promptly. "My apologies for this unfortunate interruption, milord. Pray do not trouble yourself further."

"I should like to contribute to her burial."

"Very generous of you, milord. It will be a poor affair. Betsy was the sole support of her parents, their only child. As you know, her father was injured some time ago while hewing wood, and has been unable to work since. Her mother does spinning when she can."

Anxious to be gone, Cyprian gave him a gold coin and departed. His memory of the pretty girl gushing blood on the stones beneath the window haunted his ride to Omsbridge. He was all too aware that she was trying to evade his grasp when she slipped.

Twenty

*C*yprian walked a few steps from Blue Star to the crest of the High Down. Betsy's accidental death burdened his spirit. Since Tony's return to Stonehead the past fortnight, no one remained to distract Cyprian from his dark thoughts and chafing loneliness. Tony had spoken of being near heaven after being shot. Whatever he thought he had experienced, Cyprian envied the deep peace he displayed during his convalescence.

Staring at the clouds shrouding the swelling green Downs, he strove to pierce their veil, and see past the North Downs and the weald to Hillview. Eldridge last reported Angelea was still in residence there. The last note he delivered said once again she would await his coming. His immediate response was to go. But, on rereading her message, the lack of any indication of contrition snuffed out his impulse. Doubtless she thought to charm him into restoring her, only to betray him again and again.

Gusts of January wind tugged incessantly at his heavy cape, making his stance uncertain and interfering with his brooding mood. Absently he wound the cape around him, clasping the edges securely against his chest. The chill air stung his eyes, generating streams of water from the outside corners, matching the tears on his cheeks.

Rage at her betrayal warred with intense longing to see her graceful form, hear her rippling laughter, touch her soft skin. A tiny, stubborn voice reminded him that he felt the agony of a cuckold, such as he imposed on others. But, the rest of his being revolted with an explosive "No!" He threw his arms upward, fists clenched. "No!" he shouted again.

The wind caught his freed cloak suddenly, throwing him onto the

120

grass, wet from a recent squall. He struggled to his feet, flung himself into his saddle, and wheeled Blue Star away from Surrey. With more passion than judgment, he left the High Down and galloped among his beloved, rolling Downs, attempting to flee his emotions.

At last, sensing Blue Star's fatigue, he permitted a slower pace and turned toward the Hall. Despair shrouded him. In all these months, nothing provided more than fleeting relief from his pain. Shattered hopes cluttered the emptiness he felt since Angelea left.

As he crossed a path leading to the village half a mile distant, he heard someone singing. Looking to his left, he saw a young woman walking briskly toward him.

Cyprian roused from sleep with an odd sense of unease. He drew back the bed curtain enough to see the fire well established in the grate. He felt an inner revulsion, as if he had eaten something bad. He winced at the distasteful memory. What possessed him to behave so despicably in a muddy field? If Angelea had been here, he would not have done it. He had never forced his attentions on a woman. This maid was not even pretty. He could still hear her screeches. How could he fall so low? Somehow he must learn who she was and make amends, or he could not bear his own company.

"Feldman!" he called as he rose and reached for his banyon.

When there was no response, he strode angrily to the bell pull and gave it a hard tug. That should bring action from below stairs.

He ran his hand over the stubble on his chin and his shaved head. Pulling back the fringed curtains over the east window, he looked on a gray world through depressing rain beating against the panes. This morning he must meet Eldridge and review the accounts, a disagreeable task he could no longer delay. He would wear the old brown wig he hated. It fit his mood.

Cyprian heard the door swing open. "Ah, there you are, dear fellow. I must admit I've risen more than a little blue deviled this morning." He turned around and gaped at the footman standing before him holding a copper pitcher and towel. "Stevenson! Where's Feldman?" Then he added anxiously, "Is he ill?"

"Nay, milord," answered the young man stiffly.

"If he's not ill, why is he not here?" Cyprian demanded irritably.

The footman poured water into the flowered basin on the stand. "Him be wid de parson, I bluv." He began stropping the razor vigorously.

"With Pettigrew! So early? In the middle of the week? Why, Stevenson? Tell me the whole."

"Aye." The young man cleared his throat, then answered slowly, "It be on account of Hetty aneedin' to be put-in, surelye."

"Little Hetty? She died? She's but a child." He reflected a moment, then added, "Well, I have not seen her in some time. But, in any event, she is very young. My poor Feldman. He loved her dearly. When was this?"

"It were in de night, I bluv. Ifn yer sit here, milord, I'll not scraze yer moren a leetle, surelye."

"Yes, of course." He eyed the sharp razor warily as he sat down. "What happened? Was she taken ill?"

"Nay, milord." As the footman began shaving him, Cyprian could feel Stevenson's fingers trembling. "She hunged herself, I bluv."

"She did what?" Involuntarily Cyprian jerked, endangering his neck from the razor.

"Hunged herself. Turn again, milord, ifn you please. I allow as we're most done."

"My poor Edmund. He was planning to retire with her as his house-keeper. He said she would soon marry one of the grooms, Percy I think it was. He was a good hand with my cattle. This is terrible. I shall see what may be done to assist him as soon as I am dressed. Does anyone know why she did this?"

"Aye. She writ it down. She learnt her letters in de dame school agin de village, I bluv. Up a leetle wid yer chin, ifn yer please."

"And? Why must I pry each piece of information from you?"

"Ahold yerself still, milord. Happen I cut yer throat."

As soon as the footman finished his work, Cyprian demanded, "Out with it, Stevenson. She is one of my people. I must know."

"Aye." He wiped the razor on a towel, placed it in its leather case with care and fastened the clasp before explaining. "Yest'day she were a-comin' from de village and a man atop a horse cotched her. She shruck and she shruck. It be larmentaable purty bad. He raped her."

Cyprian turned to stare at Stevenson. "Little Hetty? No! Not Feld-man's Hetty!" He felt a stiffening chill, his fingers clenched about the arm of his chair, his dry throat constricted. "I must see Feldman," he whispered.

"Mr. Feldman he sent me. He . . . I allow as he'll not be a-comin' agin, milord."

"I see . . ." Cyprian rose and strode about the room, trying to order his thoughts. Finally he told Stevenson he would wear his dark blue riding clothes. "And inform the staff I will not be taking breakfast," he added as he was dressed.

He hurried to the stables and ordered Blue Star saddled. While the grooms sprang to do his bidding, he paced the flagged courtyard, slap-ping his gloves impatiently against his thigh. If he knew the truth, Feld-man would not wish to see him, but he would go to Pettigrew and make the arrangements as easy as possible.

A shout interrupted his thoughts. Spinning around, he found himself attacked by a knife-wielding madman. The struggle broke off, permitting Cyprian to recognize his assailant. Percy. Other grooms tried to grab him to stop the fight, but Percy forced them back with jabbing motions. Again he jumped on Omsbridge, yelling, "I'll kill you! I'll kill you!"

There was a tearing sound, and Cyprian felt a stinging streak on his left upper arm. He grasped Percy's wrist, attempting to turn the knife away from either of them. Suddenly they were falling and rolling on the uneven stone pavement. Jabs of pain exploded in his chest. Abruptly the young man made a groaning cry and ceased struggling.

Eager hands pulled them apart with exclaims of dismay. "De blood, der be a tedious lot of blood!"

"Be dey gone?"

Dimly Cyprian heard someone call for Dr. Winther, followed by the sound of hooves. *I hope they used Blue Star*, he thought, sinking into thick blackness.

Out of the blackness came an awareness of sharp pain, deep pain, jabbing at him in several places. Nothingness alternated with agony and intense heat. Cyprian felt like a loaf of bread in Maggie's oven. He wanted to yell, "I'm done, let me out!" But, like a glob of dough, he lacked the power of speech.

Abruptly a clammy draft came over him, as if a door was thrown open on a winter day. A robed figure drifted toward him. Its dark garment seemed like an absence of color, yet radiated a greenish luminescence.

He peered at the face obscured by the cowl, expecting a smoky spectre or a skull. His chill deepened on seeing nothing. One handless, full sleeve beckoned to him. Drawn against his will, he followed the figure. The eerie robes retreated, lighting the thick blackness of a starless night.

Unintelligible sounds swirled around him, wordless voices—harsh, threatening, foreign. Although he strained to resist, the figure pulled him along. A bloody flickering appeared like reflections from a fire pit, fueling his terror. Then he saw the flames.

A commanding voice reverberated, as in a long, vacant hall. Again the call came, this time clearly. "Omsbridge! Omsbridge, come back!"

The figure halted. Cyprian felt he hovered on the pinpoint of decision. "No!" he shouted, striking against his guide with leaden limbs. Again he heard his name called. Exerting all his will power, he turned, leaving the awful figure behind. It was hard going, like swimming against the incoming tide with iron fetters.

Suddenly he heard Dr. Winther's comfortable, deep voice, "I think he's coming back. It was a near thing."

Cyprian regained aching consciousness, his left arm and ribs bound by bandages. As his eyes adjusted, he made out a white cap beside his bed. It was highlighted by a near candle. Croft's cap. What was she doing? Kneeling? She was too still to be searching for something. Sleeping? He made out her forehead leaning against her clasped hands. Praying?

In response to a moan, she looked up, rose, and brought the candle close to his face, peering at him anxiously. Her serene compassion seemed to flow around him. She smiled and murmured, "Thank God!" After a moment, she gently slipped a hand beneath his head and pressed a glass of liquid to his lips.

"You're past the crisis, milord," she said in soothing tones. "Dr. Winther said although your wounds were deep, your body would soon heal, if allowed. You've had a touch of fever, but that is to be expected. He ordered rest."

"Thank . . . you." Oblivion swathed his mind, parting at brief intervals. Always Croft was there providing support and ministering quietly to his needs.

At last he opened his eyes to bright daylight. He wrestled with his thoughts, trying to marshall his reason. Why was he in bed trussed like this, hurting so badly? Gradually he recalled the fight. The lad had a knife. "Percy?" he murmured.

Mrs. Croft touched his forehead with her cool hand, and straightened his covers. "He is with his Hetty. God rest his troubled soul."

Cyprian puzzled over her meaning before he understood. "No." He forced the word out over his thick tongue. "Should not . . . harm."

"He fell on his own knife during the fight. No one holds you to blame, milord. He and Hetty were buried together."

He frowned and blinked, struggling with wayward thoughts. "When?"

"The fever deranged you for a time. Doctor Winther ordered lanaudum to let you sleep. Lie quiet, milord. Young Stevenson or I will be here for anything you need." She hesitated before adding, "We all depend on you to regain your strength quickly, milord."

Obediently Cyprian closed his eyes, giving in to the astonishing weariness besetting his body.

Then the spectre was there, accompanied by Hetty and Percy. Others followed, indistinguishable people, advancing in a menacing manner. Cyprian began scrambling up a steep hill to the Hall. Just as Percy was reaching for his foot, he reached the steps, raced up them and swung the heavy front door shut. At the clang of the bolt, his eyes opened. For some time he lay rigid; his heart pounding, his body shaking.

Twenty-one

"How is Feldman?" Cyprian asked Stevenson as he bent over the bed to remove the beard grown during Cyprian's illness.

"Well enow, milord, considerin'."

"What manner of answer is that?" Cyprian exclaimed petulantly. "What do you mean 'considering'? Is that because he is mourning his niece, or something else?"

"Aye."

"Well, which? Don't fence words with me. I've no heart for it. Tell me plainly, why is Feldman not, in truth, very well?"

Stevenson gently turned Cyprian's face away to work on the near cheek as he replied slowly, "Him be grizzled for hisn Hetty, surelye. But . . . Ifn ye please, do'ant be amovin' so, milord. I be afeard o' de blade slippin'."

"You must be one of the few. Most wish you'd happen to slit my throat," Cyprian said drily. "If you continue to keep me waiting, I swear I will slit your throat with my razor!"

"Aye, milord. He be low on account of her wasn't put-in proper like, in de churchyard."

Cyprian lay still while Stevenson finished one side of his face. When the apprentice valet turned his head to complete the shave, Cyprian grasped his razor hand with his good right hand and held it away from his face. He saw the young man blanche and felt his fury almost escape control. "Why?" he exploded.

"On—on account o' de vicar allowed as how she couldn't."

"What! Why?"

125

"On account o' she—she hunged herself, I bluv."

"It is unthinkable that one of my people should be buried outside. My poor Feldman. I'll not have it. Send for Pettigrew. I will speak with that pompous cleric immediately, within the hour. Has he forgotten he owes his preferment to me?"

When Stevenson returned from sending a message to the vicarage, Cyprian permitted him to finish his shave. Next he ordered him to help him remove to a nearby armchair.

"Nay, milord," the young man answered with a tremor in his voice.

Cyprian glared at him haughtily. "I cannot believe I heard you correctly. Do you think I will receive the vicar in my bed?"

Stevenson turned crimson but did not move to his master's side.

"Well, come give me your arm."

"Nay, milord."

Cyprian glared at him, shocked at his stubborn refusal, angered by his own weakness. Never had he faced this blatant refusal of an order. "Then you are dismissed from my service!" he declared hastily. "And my face will be the better for not suffering your inept scraping. Send in Croft as you leave."

"Aye, milord." Stevenson bowed and left the room quickly.

Cyprian plucked peavishly at his sheet, irritation at his lack of control growing. He smiled at Mrs. Croft as she entered. "Ah, there you are. Give me your arm so I can move to that chair. I am to receive the vicar."

Mrs. Croft stopped several feet from the bed and said, "Milord, no person in your employ will assist you. Dr. Winther ordered us on no account to allow you up for the next few days."

"Must I dismiss all of you?" Cyprian exclaimed angrily. Even to his own ears his voice sounded less thundering than his intent, more querulous.

"There still would be no one to obey you," she replied.

"Have you forgotten you are in *my* employ and not that fool Winther's?"

"No, milord. We do not wish any harm to come to you. If you must receive Rev. Pettigrew, you will do so in bed. In a few days' time you could receive him sitting in the chair."

"I cannot wait. I must see him now."

"Very good. Word has been sent to him."

While still angry at being disobeyed, an unaccustomed weariness flooded over Cyprian. Grudgingly he admitted in his heart that a move to the chair would not have left enough strength to deal with the vicar.

With a start Cyprian opened his eyes, unaware they were closed.

No one was within sight. With an effort he recalled the morning's events. Frustrated by his condition, he sighed heavily.

Mrs. Croft appeared at his side. "Would you like some barley broth, milord?" she inquired, laying her cool hand on his forehead.

"In a bit, thank you. Has Pettigrew arrived?"

"Yes. He is in the garden salon, having a dish of bohea."

"Have him come up. I must see him."

"Yes, milord." She promptly went to tug on the bell pull.

Pettigrew entered with a stately step, his expression as sober as if about to read a service. He inclined his head and asked, "How are you feeling, milord?"

"Curst uncomfortable." Cyprian waved the vicar to the chair. "I have need to speak with you."

"Yes, milord. A brush with the wings of the angel of death often brings us to a serious appraisal of our lives and we begin to see things more sharply. What do you wish to tell me?"

Cyrian stared at the clergyman leaning forward in the chair. What did the man think? Then it became clear to him. "You are laboring under a misapprehension, Pettigrew. I am not about to confide my many sins to you. I have something to ask of you."

The vicar moved uneasily. "In what way may I be of service, milord? I shall be happy to do anything within my power."

"Hetty must be buried in the churchyard. If it's her tithe that's owing, I'll pay it. I will not have this grief added to Feldman."

Pettigrew frowned anxiously. "But that is impossible, milord. I cannot do it."

"What do you mean, you cannot do it? I warrant digging up a coffin is not a pleasant task. I'll pay Simmons, or whoever you have to dig graves. I'll pay him well. It must be done."

"But it cannot. There is no place for her."

"Nonsense. I am confident you will be able to find a plot for her, and the poor box will be heavier for it."

Pettigrew shifted in the chair, pulled thoughtfully on his lower lip. "I fear I have not made myself clear, milord. It cannot be done. Not for you or anyone else. Not for any amount of money. Her willful act of suicide makes it impossible. It is not allowed to bury her in hallowed ground. It was not allowed to bury Percy in hallowed ground since he died while attempting to commit murder. If it is a comfort to you, they lie side by side, together in death."

"It is not my comfort I am seeking. Have you no feeling for Feldman? Do you know how you have increased his pain and sorrow? She must be buried in the churchyard."

"I am sorry, milord. It cannot be done."

"You are aware I control your living? If need be, I will have you moved and find a cleric who will do this."

"You may remove me, but you will not find an ordained man to do this thing. Your concern for Feldman is most commendable. If it were possible, I would do this gladly. But it is not."

Suddenly Cyprian felt pressed down with a great weariness. "Leave me." He closed his eyes, disgusted at his inability to bend even this pompous man to his will. When the Blue Devil was ill, the world conspired its revenge.

Again, the spectre led a crowd pursuing him across the roofs of Omsbridge and along the parapet. He tried to fight them off, but suddenly he was falling . . . falling . . . falling . . . like Betsy fell. He woke with a convulsive jerk, dry-mouthed and trembling. Something must be done to appease the shades of those he wronged so he could rest. How? His accusers were beyond his counting.

Twenty-two

yprian shifted uncomfortably on his narrow seat in the front pew, deliberately blocking out Rev. Pettigrew's homily. He attended Sunday morning service on this, his first venture from the Hall, because his people expected him to be there. True, he was profoundly grateful to be alive and should give thanks to God. But must it be such a bore?

Solemnly he stared at the old altar painting of Christ, seated on a hill overlooking the Channel and the Isle of Wight, blessing Saxon children. The faded colors were speckled with white where the paint was chipped. It was said that in Cromwell's time the lord of Omsbridge hired an artist to whitewash a gory crucifixion scene and produce this picture. As Cyprian recalled the tradition, it was done as a penance for striking a servant, a young boy, and killing him. The child's spectre haunted the master of the Hall. When the painting was completed, it vanished.

Suddenly Cyprian focused more intently on the painting. It was penance. *He* must do a penance for poor Hetty. He would order the painting restored. Then the demons plaguing him would be satisfied. And, hopefully, he would not encounter that ghastly spectre on his death.

Following the benediction, leaning heavily on his beribboned staff, he walked slowly up the stone aisle between rows of respectfully standing parishioners. Thoughtfully, he noted the generally dilapidated condition of the church. Restoring the painting might atone for Hetty, but other faces plagued him.

As he stepped off the south porch into the sunshine, he concluded that renovating the entire church would be penance enough for all his sins. The decision made, he was eager for action, but rapidly ebbing strength denied him.

Lawrence assisted him into his coach, where he leaned against the cushions and closed his eyes. A rap on the door caused him to look out.

Rev. Pettigrew stood below. "Milord, we rejoice with you on your recovery and are grateful for your presence among us this Sabbath morning."

"Yes, I, too, rejoice in being here." On impulse Cyprian asked, "Would you and your good wife join me for dinner today?"

Obviously startled by the unusual invitation, Rev. Pettigrew replied, "Dinner? Yes. Oh my, yes. We should be delighted, milord."

"Very good. On Sundays we dine at five."

"Thank you for your kindness, milord. We shall be there."

Cyprian slept deeply on returning to his room. When Stevenson roused him to dress for dinner, he felt more refreshed than he had in days. Surely this confirmed that his penance was appropriate.

The Pettigrews arrived in their cart at a quarter before five. Cyprian found Mrs. Pettigrew aggressively overbearing. Her rose gown in the style of several years past emphasized her large, boney form. A demure lace cap rested on chestnut hair, its waves straining against a tight knot in back. No curls softened her strong jawline or slightly protruding brown eyes. Forthright honesty radiated intimidatingly from her.

Subsequent to her withdrawing to the salon after dinner, Cyprian noticed a definite easing in Rev. Pettigrew's manner. As he poured a glass of port for each of them, Lord Omsbridge began explaining his intent to repair and improve the church.

The vicar beamed enthusiastically. "Thank heaven!" he exclaimed. "The leaks worsen each year, and the parish is too poor to effect the repairs."

Vaguely Cyprian recalled some previous mention of leaks.

As the men discussed the project, it assumed proportions beyond Cyprian's original vision. However, when embarking on a penance, one could hardly be cheese paring.

On the morrow, Cyprian laid the idea before Eldridge. Always quick with figures, the man of business came up with an estimate of the expenses likely to be incurred, a shocking total.

Cyprian took a turn around the small office, then sank into a chair. "I know what you are thinking, Eldridge, and of course you are right. My sister's settlement, my father's debts, refurbishing the Hall," he paused, reflecting cynically about the effort wasted on his adored bride. "All that and more, but *this must* be done. Find the funds some place.

You are resourceful. Only consider, I am no longer entertaining lavishly."

"Yes, milord."

"With the improvements we made in the estate, and the renting of Lane's End Farm, income should be higher this quarter. And the new copse is ready for cutting. We will realize quite a sum for that."

"Yes, milord. In fact—"

Cyprian interrupted with an impatient wave of his hand. "Take care of the details as you see fit." He sighed, adding earnestly, "This is my penance for the evil I have done. It is essential this be done over all else, and that it be done without stint. Do you understand, Eldridge?"

"Yes, milord. I understand."

"Good. Then I place the matter in your capable hands. Locate a painter of the first order to do the work. Bring him over from France if necessary.

On leaving Eldridge's office, Cyprian felt the distance to either the library or his room beyond his strength without a rest. Leaning heavily on his stick, he entered the nearby chapel and settled in an old, dark choir stall. Although the seat was narrow and hard, he twisted into a fairly comfortable position and leaned back, his eyes closed. Time and time he hid here as a boy to avoid censure for some escapade.

The creak of the door and footsteps on the stone floor caused him to look around.

Mrs. Croft was placing a bowl of early snowdrops on the altar. She went to the old Bible resting on the carved lectern, turned several pages, then read silently, her lips forming the words. She knelt before the altar and bowed her head. Morning light filtered by the Victory window scattered brilliant colors about her. After several minutes, she left.

Cyprian stared at the stained glass portrayal of a majestic Christ ascending from the High Down. The grandeur of the subject and the beauty of the clear colors seemed to exude healing rays. Tony mentioned this effect during his recovery.

From his shadowed seat, he observed Betsy Miller, Sally, a new footman, and one of the grooms enter one by one for a few minutes of prayer. Gradually, as the morning sun moved higher, the colors disappeared.

Energized by a new inspiration, Cyprian returned to Eldridge's office. "Is the church altar on the east wall?" he asked without preamble.

Eldridge looked up from the huge estate ledger with a puzzled frown. "I am not sure, milord." He rose and faced several different ways, as if imagining entering the church. "I believe it is on the east, milord, but I am not certain."

"Find out immediately, then tell me. If so, we will turn the painting into stained glass."

Within a week of learning the altar was on the east wall, letters were sent to a Venetian artist whose work Cyprian had admired in Florence, offering a generous amount for him to design and oversee the project. Cyprian then journeyed the quarter mile to the church to inspect the wall personally and inform the vicar. At first its magnitude overwhelmed the vicar. However, when assured the other work would not be curtailed, he developed a guarded enthusiasm for it.

As they left the sanctuary, Cyprian noticed a man weeding beyond the graveyard fence. Leaving the vicar, Cyprian walked to the man's side, knelt awkwardly on the soft, damp ground, and tugged at a weed. "How are you these days?" he asked Feldman.

"Very well, thank you, milord."

Two unhewn stones marked the site. "A fence is needed to protect this place from trespassers, don't you think?" Cyprian observed.

Feldman peered at Cyprian. He resumed weeding and answered, "Aye."

More. There must be something more. "And a rose bush by the headstones?"

"She might like that, milord. She was partial to the pink roses at our cottage."

Cyprian tried to rise, but the effort made him dizzy and brought on a momentary blackness. He fell heavily on one knee, then he felt Feldman's firm grasp on his left arm.

"Allow me to assist you, milord."

"Thank you, Feldman." He stood leaning on Feldman's arm and his walking stick until the world ceased moving. "I had best return to the Hall. My intentions exceed my capacity."

" 'Twas ever so, milord. Have Mrs. Croft prepare her herbal tea. 'Twill renew your strength."

"I will, thank you."

Supported by Feldman, Cyprian rejoined the vicar and took his leave. As he drove off, he watched Feldman return to his lonely labor, his back and shoulders more stooped than he remembered. Guilt for causing his long time friend such grief pained him, and he had to look away.

Following Feldman's suggestion, Cyprian requested Fothering to send Mrs. Croft to his room with a cup of herbal tea. After Stevenson had settled him comfortably in bed, Cyprian sent him for Eldridge.

"Yet another task for you," Cyprian said, setting aside his tea as the man of business entered. "Do not cringe so, Eldridge. I merely wish to have a damask rose bush planted and a strong, beautiful iron fence made. Who would do the best work?''

"Judson, the blacksmith," Eldridge answered unhesitatingly. "He enjoys doing fancy things with iron, although there's little call for that. He'd welcome the money. Business is slow since the smugglers were caught and he has four children and a wife to feed."

"Ask him to come today. I want to tell him directly what is to be done. I leave payment in your capable hands. Make it generous."

Feeling his personal attention was required for his penance to be effective, Cyprian drove frequently to the church to follow its renovation. When he became stronger, he rode the short distance. In a fortnight, he was gratified to find a sturdy iron fence surrounding Hetty and Percy's graves with a gate of beautiful scrolling design.

Exhausted after inspecting the new fence, Cyprian retired early, satisfied at completing an important step. He closed his eyes, fully expecting the reward of the dreamless rest reserved for owners of clear consciences.

Against a black backdrop he saw a girl running away. She looked over her shoulder at him, and he recognized Betsy. Then she was falling. A girl with Hetty's tear-streaked face hit at him, then dropped her hands limply to her sides and her head lolled to one side. The preacher beside her clutched his shoulder. Slowly he raised his injured arm and pointed at him, shrieking, "The sins of Omsbridge!" Familiar women of various ages and positions advanced upon him chanting the preacher's words. Tradesmen and others in the shadows joined the chorus. Lurking behind them the luminous spectre incited the mob. Suddenly Percy leapt out, slashing with a gigantic sword.

Awaking, Cyprian sat up shaking, his nightshirt clinging to his wet body. As he made out his furniture in the predawn light, and realized his accusers were gone, rage welled up inside.

Raising both fists above his head he shouted, "I am doing my penance! Is it not enough?"

He heard only his pounding heart.

Unwilling to risk facing the phantoms again, he rose, donned his banyon, and lit the fire. Restlessly, he warmed himself before the flames, stalked around the room, gazed out the windows at the reddening sky, then sank into his chair beside the hearth.

If his demons were not appeased by his intentions, his only hope of relief lay in completing the project. He would impress the Italian artist with its urgency immediately upon his arrival.

—— Twenty-three ——

"Milord, may I confer with you?" Eldridge inquired on entering to the library.

Cyprian turned from the window. "Yes, certainly." He went to sit at his desk.

Eldridge stood before him uneasily, fingering a sheaf of papers.

"Yes?" Cyprian prompted.

"Milord, I fear . . . I think you must sell Hillview."

"Sell Hillview? How so?"

"Outside of the Hall, it is the only property you own not mortgaged to the limit."

"Am I truly in need of so much money?" Cyprian inquired, confident Eldridge was overly alarmed.

"Your debts, including the work on the church, have reached that sum."

"Are you not impressed with the sketches of the window? It will be most beautiful, will it not?"

"Yes, milord," Eldridge responded, adding emphatically, "it is also expensive."

Then why, Cyprian wondered, *does it not give me more pleasure and why does it not buy the demons' silence?*

"Hillview must be sold to meet the costs of the window and past bills," Eldridge persisted.

"And if I refuse to sell?"

Eldridge frowned. "Richards will foreclose on the Lincoln property. When the other creditors hear, they also will take action."

"And I should be wiped out to the boundaries of the Hall?"

"Exactly so, milord."

"What of the new copse? The shipbuilders will pay well for the oaks."

"They did, milord. While you were ill, I sold them to meet the most critical bills."

"I see." Cyprian clenched his teeth and reached for the marble fingers. He resented being forced into this position. A series of mortgages had financed debts from his father and mother's extravagance, and his sister's dowry. A significant turn-around was nearly completed when he began preparing the Hall for Angelea and upgrading the Hillview property. Those costs far exceeded expectations. And, of late, his entertaining reckless young bucks and remodeling the church worsened the situation.

With a deep sigh and shake of his head, he said, "Very well. Sell Hillview. Offer it first to Sir Matthew Byngstone, in the event he wishes to expand his holdings. I will send word to Lady Omsbridge to remove whatever she desires to keep. I believe she is in London. Make certain all my furnishings are removed." Cyprian paused. "There is no need to sell more than the land and the house, is there?"

"Not at the moment, milord. If we practice strict economy, I think we shall come through until the rents are due."

"I shall indeed practice such economy," Cyprian assured him.

On returning from a fruitless shopping expedition, Angelea was surprised to have Dagon present her with a note bearing the Omsbridge crest. Her heart thumped hard on recognizing Cyprian's hand. "How did this arrive?"

"A footman from the Hall—Lawrence, I believe."

"Yes, I know him. Make sure he is well fed. Very likely I shall wish to send a reply."

"Very good, milady."

Angelea hurried to the drawing room. With shaking fingers she tore open the envelope. Was he coming? It was yet some weeks before the Season. Business in the City might bring him. Better, was he asking her to return home?

"Oh, let it be that!" she murmured, unfolding the stiff sheet. For a moment her tumultuous emotions stripped the words of meaning. "Hillview" sharpened her attention.

Dear Angelea,

I regret to inform you that it has become mandatory for me to sell Hillview. Please make certain all your possessions are removed from the premises. We do not wish the buyer to gain more than he bargains for.

I trust you are in good health.

I have the honor to remain

Your ladyship's obedient servant,
Cyprian Westover

Tears of disappointment mingled with anger over the loss of her refuge. Where could she go when not in town? Her recent tour with her mother demonstrated it no longer pleased her to live with her parents. After visiting Helen in Hampshire, they removed to Bath for a few weeks. Angelea found that quiet town not at all to her taste. Hillview was home. In his autocractic manner, Cyprian chose to dispose of it, ignoring her wishes. How cruel of him. No fear about his selling the London house. It meant more to him than property won on the turn of a card. It was just like gambling with Starlight.

She crushed the heavy paper in her fist, wadded it up, and hurled it across the room. Then she ran to retrieve it, not wanting an inquisitive servant to read it. Carefully she smoothed the crumpled sheet, folded it, and tucked it inside her bodice. She was mistress of this house and Hillview only at Cyprian's pleasure.

When she felt in command of her feelings, she wrote a cold, formal note, thanking Cyprian for informing her of the impending sale and assuring him she would take steps to secure her personal belongings. Then she sent for Lawrence.

The young footman's face reminded her of the time he showed her Freckles' newborn puppies and his eager response to any request. She almost thought of him as a dear friend.

"It is good to see you again, Lawrence. I hope your journey was not difficult."

He smiled. "Nay, milady, howsumdever it were quick. De master allowed as how I must be back nexdy, surelye. De master said yer justabout be anxious ter have it."

"Yes. I am glad to receive this so promptly. It is important. Tell me, how is Fothering going along?"

After absorbing the news of the staff, Angelea gave Lawrence her note, saying, "I trust his lordship is well."

"He do be done-over soon, but generally-always 'im be naun de better fer bein' set upon."

Angelea felt a knot form in her stomach. Quickly she gasped in as much air as her stays would permit, trying to calm her rapid heart. "I do not know what you mean by being set upon. I have been some weeks in Hampshire and Bath with Lady Byngstone. Was he injured? Please, tell me the whole."

She sat very still, clutching the arm of her chair, horrified at his account of Percy's attack and his master's slow recovery. When she thought she could speak with a steady voice, she said, "Be sure you deliver my note to his lordship's hand, personally."

"Aye, milady."

"And tell him—tell him I *deeply* regret his—his accident, and am relieved, no, *pleased* to learn of his progress. Tell him that I—I hope he is soon fully recovered."

As he held his master and mistress in respect and great affection, Lawrence was deeply troubled over their separation. Frequently one of the household discovered the master during the day, sleeping deeply in a salon, the music room, even the chapel. Unaccountable for an active man. Lawrence attributed this and his lordship's continued lack of appetite and shadowed eyes more to pining for his lady than convalescence. Her ladyship had behaved in a way similar to his sisters and other village women when they claimed they suffered the pangs of love.

Thinking the note he bore might be a means of healing their breach, Lawrence pressed his mount hard and shortened his rest stops on the ride to Omsbridge. Immediately on his arrival, he sought out his lordship in the library and delivered Lady Omsbridge's note.

After reading it, his lordship looked up, saying, "You said this was urgent?"

"Milord, de mistress askt me ter give ter yer dracly-minute I come."

"I see. Well, you have done so."

"Her wanted ter know how ye go on," he continued, anxious over the cool response.

"That was kind of her."

"I said ye was easy done-over, but generally-always be naun de better fer bein' set upon."

"True."

"She were quite non-plushed, she were. She allowed as how she were here an' there a dunnamany weeks an' wasn't knowin' yer was particular."

Lord Omsbridge leaned back in his chair. "And?"

Encouraged by this show of interest, Lawrence said, "I told her Percy cut yer wid 'is blade an' we be afeard ye be put-in the church nexdy, surelye."

"I am gratified you did not contemplate placing me in the churchyard."

"Hem-a-bit!" Lawrence exclaimed, shocked at the suggestion. "Ye be hither de altar!"

"It is a relief to know my final resting place would be there."

"She tol' me ter say, 'I *deeply* regret yer accident an' am relieved ter larnt ye be . . .' An' her wants yer ter be stocky soon."

"Thank you, Lawrence. It is commendable for you to deliver her message so promptly."

"An', milord, her went white like a sheet when I tol' her ye be hurt bad, and her eyes was wet."

"Oh." His lordship quickly looked down at the note he held, although it was shaking so badly he could not possibly read it. "Thank you, Lawrence."

Twenty-four

*B*lue Star loped in an easy, rhythmic pace along a lane near the western boundary of Omsbridge. The breeze stung Cyprian's cheeks pleasantly, its cold edge softened by impending summer. Bright greens and a joyful lark above added zest to his ride. A red squirrel dashed up a pine before him and scolded as he rode past. Countless times during his nearly forgotten age of innocence, he had sought this secluded area to escape anger or pain.

Angelea's betrayal. That hysterical girl's fall at the Dancing Skillet. Now Feldman's departure. It was inconceivable Feldman was gone for any reason other than death. His death. Much as Cyprian needed a man of his skill, he delayed replacing Stevenson, hoping Feldman would return. Perhaps the graveyard fence and rose bush would make amends.

Why did that stupid girl hang herself over . . . and why had he lowered himself to behave thus? She wasn't even pretty. Before, when staggered by life's blows, he at least kept his sense of honor. Now, his inner core was stained.

If his costly penance failed to silence the demons of darkness, what more could he do? The Italian artisan estimated many more months for completing the window. Would he be denied respite from the spectre's hoard until then?

Suddenly the powerful gray stallion shied. The world spun upside down, vanishing in a shower of bright stars. Cyprian found himself lying on the path momentarily disoriented. He shook his head and slowly struggled to his feet, cursing his foolish preoccupation with his troubles. Taking a few stiff steps, he was relieved no bones were broken.

As he picked off chunks of mud and brushed the leaves from his breeches and coat, Blue Star returned, stopping a few feet away. He tossed his head and snorted as if disgusted that his master left his seat so easily. Puzzled at the cause of Blue Star's unmannerly behavior, Cyprian scanned the trees and brush about the area.

A movement behind a beech caught his eye. He detected a crouched figure. With a surge of anger, he cautiously moved past the tree, then lunged. His fingers closed on the skinny arm of a young boy. Cyprian raised his left arm ready to deal the urchin a ringing blow as he spun him around exclaiming, "What are you doing here, frightening my horse? You nearly killed me!"

The lad's tangled black hair fell across his face as Cyprian first jerked him about, then stood back to look at him. Amazed, Cyprian stared at a face very like his own boyish reflection in a sunlit pool.

Cyprian's arm remained raised as if transformed into marble, then fell to his side. "Who are you?" Cyprian demanded with thunderous frown.

"W-William, s-sir," the boy replied, cowering.

"William? What is your surname?"

"I dunno . . . sir."

"You—do not *know*? How is it your mother permits you to run loose scaring horses?"

"I dunno."

"Where is she? Where do you live?"

The boy stared up at him, wide-eyed.

"Answer me. Where do you live?"

William pointed vaguely in an easterly direction.

Maintaining a firm grasp on the child's arm, Cyprian strode to the restless gray and gathered up the reins. "Take me there," he commanded. Then, reflecting that the way may be longer than his patience, he added, "Stand still." He swung into the saddle then leaned down, extending his hand to the boy. "Here, step on my boot and come up behind me."

William remained motionless, staring at the man and the horse.

"Come, take my hand." Cyprian moderated his tone as he added, "I've no wish to hurt you, much as you may deserve it. Show me the way to your home."

Obediently William took his hand and leapt up behind Cyprian. The child weighed little more than a feather. Following William's directions, Cyprian nudged Blue Star into a trot down the lane.

The lad pointed to a small cottage hardly visible through the trees. Often as Cyprian had ridden this way, he could not recall seeing it before.

As he dismounted, he noted the thatch roof needed repair and the dingy wattle and daub walls could use a coat of whitewash.

William stood at his side, his gaze fixed on the door, one bare foot restlessly scraping the ground. Cyprian observed a tear in William's worn, faded shirt, and several in his breeches.

"Bring me your mother," Cyprian commanded. "I wish to meet her."

Scowling, the boy went to the door and shoved it open. He paused, looking back, as if asking Cyprian to change his mind, then disappeared inside. Following a loud discussion, William appeared in the doorway with a glum woman who squinted at her visitor. She brushed back her stringy gray hair, saying, "Well, what's 'e done naow?"

Taking in her slovenly appearance and the nearly empty gin bottle in her hand, Cyprian erased any thought of censure against the child. "I asked the boy to take me to his mother."

"Did ye naow?" The woman steadied herself on the doorframe. "Well, dat be a good 'un. I'd lik ter see 'er too, ungrateful wench. Ran off years ago, leavin' her byblow. Poor way ter treat de 'un what giv her life, I say. Poor way."

"Yes, that is, er, ungrateful. Did she have employment before— before William was born?"

"Aye, she did. Her be de upstairs maid at the Hall, 'til they turn 'er out fer her im, immoral character. An' it be de young master, she say. A handsome devil what had 'is way wid 'er, an' turn 'er out fer bearin' 'is child."

"I see," Cyprian said uncomfortably. "May I know your name, good woman?"

"Good 'ooman!" She threw back her head in loud laughter, revealing the few teeth remaining in her mouth. "Good 'ooman! Well, naow, ain't yer de one! Dey calls me Granny Simpson, dat's what dey calls me."

Cyprian doffed his hat and made a slight bow. "I must take my leave. Good day, Granny Simpson, William."

He mounted and started down the path. Her laughter followed him, punctuated by a sharp cry from William. When he reached the familiar lane, he pulled Blue Star to a stand and stared back at the tip of the chimney barely visible through the undergrowth. He might not locate it again without a marker. He searched his pockets for something to use as a sign. The best he could find was a red cord. Standing in his stirrups he tied it to a branch pointing toward William's home. And William was his son!

Satisfied that it was secure, he rode home deep in thought. He seemed to hear that wild preacher again jabbing a finger at him. "The sins of Omsbridge'' sounded in his mind. "Your sins will find you out" formed a counterpoint to the first phrase.

Preoccupied with thoughts of the boy, he entered the library and went to the fire. Holding out his cold hands for warmth, he gazed at the flames, then at his hands. They looked bloodred. Like Lady MacBeth's. He turned around, clasping them behind him. The load of his past misdeeds assumed crushing proportions.

His wealth and power aroused envy among those who knew him. They named him the Blue Devil, a reputation he used cynically for his own ends. Now, he felt surrounded by accusers—Hetty, Percy, Betsy, the preacher, Becket, and countless other shadowy figures, dominated by the spectre—accusers he longed to escape.

At least William's mother was not among them. He could not recall her face. An upstairs maid, how long ago? She meant little to him, yet he marked her life and caused William's birth, a child despised for the lack of a father. Yet, his son.

Throughout the night Cyprian tossed in his bed and paced his room, wrestling with his predicament. Gradually a plan evolved, becoming complete as dawn tinted the sky. Exhausted, he fell across his bed and surrendered to dreamless slumber.

It was nearly noon when Cyprian roused, finding a cover thrown over him and a fire blazing. As Stevenson shaved and dressed him, the plans shaped with the new day came to his mind. Fresh energy coursed through his body. Most of his wrongs were past righting. But one was not. Perhaps in this matter he could end his suffering.

Learning that Higgins, the gamekeeper, had been seen nearby, he sent for him to come to the dovecote. As a child he had often followed him about, learning of the animals populating the estate. The man could be trusted to execute this task discreetly and honestly.

Higgins seemed more gray and bent than Cyprian remembered. He pulled his forelock and stared at the ground while Cyprian detailed his errand. Placing two fat coin purses in Higgins' earth-stained hands, Cyprian told him to keep one and give the other to Granny Simpson in exchange for William. He was not to reveal the identity of her benefactor at any time. William would no longer be a charge against her. At the next full moon, Higgins would bring her a like sum.

William could bring any treasure or pets he desired. Higgins was not to tell the boy anything other than that he was being taken to a new place where he would receive proper care. As soon as possible, the child should be brought to the kitchen door.

After Higgins departed, Cyprian sought Mrs. Croft. He startled that prim woman by declaring he was bringing a child into the household. The nursery must be prepared and a seamstress charged with making shirts and breeches. Soon the boy would arrive at the kitchen, where he was to be scrubbed and dressed properly. Cyprian told her he would buy the necessary garments from anyone with a child that size.

Impatient to be about his good deed, Cyprian went to the stable and talked with Henry about acquiring a pony. Great pains must be taken to make the boy a first-class horseman with instruction beginning within the week.

When notified Higgins was in the stable yard, Cyprian hurried to meet him. Higgins sat astride his brown cob, firmly holding a pale, trembling boy. Cyprian reached up to take William. The boy shrank from him.

"Here naow, ye hadn't oughtn ter act so ter de master, nipper!" Higgins exclaimed roughly. " 'im be a hard un ter cotch up, I bluv."

"He didn't want to come?" Cyprian asked in disbelief.

"Aye. 'im be afeared yer aboutn ter eat 'im dis night, surelye."

"William, I give you my word you will be well fed and cared for."

The boy's dark eyes stared sullenly down at him from a dirty, tear-streaked face. He looked at the grooms and kitchen servants standing about the yard, and his body sagged against Higgins as he fainted.

"I'll take him, Higgins. Please wait for my return." Gently, Cyprian carried him into the kitchen. He gave the boy to Mrs. Worth with instructions to treat the child tenderly and make every effort to calm his fears. The boy was to be brought to him in the library when washed and fed.

Cyprian rejoined Higgins to ask about Granny Simpson.

"Dat one, de gold be bettermost fer her," was the gamekeeper's comment. "I said I be back wid more at de full moon, an' she be dat glad fer him ter come wid me. Why 'e be afeared, I do'ant know. Boys do take up odd idees."

"Thank you, Higgins. Tell me, have you seen Feldman? How does he fare?"

"Well enow."

"Has he need for anything?"

"I be seein' him tdee, I bluv," Higgins assured him.

As Cyprian entered the Hall through the side door, he met Fothering, who requested his supply of Spanish snuff for young William.

With raised eyebrows, Cyprian replied, "So much for such a small lad! Has he acquired a strong habit?"

"No, milord. It's for lice. You do not seem to fancy the Spanish, so I thought you would not mind."

"No, no. Of course not. Take all you need." He looked down at his coat and started to brush it off. "Save a cup or so for me. I took him from Higgins. Lice. I should have realized."

Over an hour passed before Maggie escorted William into the library. Warily, William eyed the strange man, maintaining a position near the door. "He's naun so clean as he ought," she said, "but Higgins said he be afeard we'd eat 'im. We tried washin' 'im up widout he hip tub, thinin' he'd think it a kettle to boil 'im. He oughtn ter have more soap an' water an' snuff. De nipper's naun been washed since birthin', I bluv."

"Thank you, Maggie. Forgive me for upsetting your kitchen."

"Think naun o' it, milord. De nipper be lean as a rake."

"Did you feed him anything?"

"Aye, a mug o' ale and a bit of tasty pie afore we touched him wid soap or rag. Ye must have a care, milord. He be set ter eat de bettermost o' all in de kitchen and der be naun fer de rest o' us." At the door, she paused to add, "Milord, ye'd best take a look at hisn backside."

After Maggie left, Cyprian rang for Mrs. Croft. She surprised Cyprian by kneeling before the lad and holding out her hands toward him, palm upwards. "William," she said kindly, "I should like to be your friend. We will deal well together, I think."

William stood still, head lowered, looking at her under his brows. Stiffly, tentatively, he placed his left hand, then his right hand in hers.

"If you will come with me, Master William, I will show you your room."

"I will bear the candle for you both," Cyprian said, taking one from the mantel.

The three of them climbed the stairs and walked through the halls slowly, giving William an opportunity to take in his magnificent surroundings. His awe was painfully reminiscent of Angelea's introduction to Omsbridge Hall.

The nursery had been aired and dusted and a bright quilt tucked on the cot. Cyprian showed William his old rocking horse standing nearly to the boy's shoulder. "I used to call him Charger," he explained. "But, I expect you are too old to ride such a steed. This will be your room. However, tonight you will stay with me. Mrs. Croft, please assign a maid tomorrow to care for William and to sleep on a cot here. This is a strange place in a very large house."

"Sally is just the girl. She's the oldest of several children, and knows how to deal with the little ones."

"She'll not be harsh with him?"

"Have no fears on that score, milord. Sally's kind to a fault."

Later, in his own room, Cyprian watched Stevenson help William change to a hastily fashioned nightshirt. An astonishing crisscross of scars marked the child's back from his shoulders to his buttocks. One pink stripe looked to have lost its scab but recently. Silently Cyprian vowed only the tenderest care for this boy, his child.

Cyprian awoke as the curtains were thrown back. Anxiously he leaned to one side to look at William sleeping on his cot.

"Milord, will you wear the camlet frock this morning?" Feldman inquired.

"Yes, that will—" In shock, Cyprian stared at the man laying a small sized shirt and breeches on a chair. This must be a dream, but a pleasant one for a change. For a moment he dared not speak, fearing Feldman would vanish.

Finally he asked softly, "Are you real?"

"Yes, milord." Feldman calmly began arranging his shaving implements as he had done for years.

"You are truly here?"

"Yes, milord."

Cyprian smiled and relaxed against the pillows. "Yes, I will wear the camlet frock." He thought he must still be weak, for his voice sounded tremulous, his vision clouded, and he felt a trace of wetness on his cheeks.

Two days later, at breakfast, Cyprian announced, "This morning we will see Henry in the stables."

William looked up from his generously filled plate and asked anxiously, "Am I to live out there?"

"In the stables? Of course not. You live here, in the Hall."

Fothering entered, with the hint of an anxious frown. "Milord, a female child was found tied to the hitching post in the yard this morning."

"A female child?" Cyprian exclaimed in surprise. "Whose is she?"

"We are not sure, but Maggie thinks she might be Nellie Swingham's child. Nellie was an upstairs maid five years ago."

Cyprian stared at the floor, trying to recall such a person. "Nellie Swinham. Five years. Oh, yes . . . Where is she?"

"In the kitchen, milord."

With a wry smile Cyprian said, "I'd best see her. Excuse me, William, I must needs visit your friend, Mrs. Worth."

In the center of the kitchen a little girl stood clutching a cloth doll, tears streaming down her cheeks. She took deep sobbing breaths as she looked wide-eyed from one to another of her growing audience of maids and footmen. Her patched dress was clean, and the black ringlets falling to her shoulders appeared newly washed.

Remembering Mrs. Croft's gentle approach to William, Cyprian squatted in front of the child and asked softly, "By what name are you called?"

She shrank back from him, regarding him soberly with dark eyes under black brows very like his own.

He held out his hand, asking, "May I be your friend?"

The little girl turned to run, but found herself surrounded with skirts and legs. A loud wail burst from her mouth. "Mama!"

Sally crouched at her side and drew her into her arms. "Dere, dere, wee one." She patted the child's back and stroked her hair while rocking her slowly from side to side. "Yer mama had ter goo away. Ye be safe wid me. Dere, dere." Humming a soothing melody, Sally continued holding the crying child.

Cyprian rose. "Does anyone know where her mother is?"

Maggie answered, "She be Nellie from upstairs five year ago, I bluv. She an' John Swingham was wed last year. Nellie died in birthing a month since. I do'ant know as who cared fer de child. John misliked her, surelye."

"Could be someone in de village," a maid suggested.

"Aye, Mrs. Beacon or Mrs. Gilly, dey be good 'oomen."

Cyprian shook his head and smiled. "In any event it appears you have another charge, Sally. Feed her when she is calm and prepare another bed in the nursery. William and I will be in the stables discovering a new pony."

Twenty-five

A s the footman took her velvet cloak, Angelea spread her painted chicken-skin fan and scanned the magnificent entry hall of Burlington House. With head held high, she entered the assembly room. Glancing about anxiously, she paused inside the door and fluttered her fan as the warm stuffiness of the room enclosed her. Familiar people were gathering for the Season's first major social event, people she wanted to impress favorably. Angry, hurt from losing Hillview, she strove for an appearance of unruffled indifference.

Suddenly she realized she was seeking Cyprian. In fact, she selected pale blue silk for her gown knowing he preferred it. Intense longing spread its ache to the tips of her shaking fingers. She blinked back the tears threatening to mar her carefully painted face. She regretted coming alone this night.

"Good evening, Lady Omsbridge." Lord Uxton's rich, smooth voice interrupted her unhappy thoughts.

Relieved at the distraction, she gave him her hand and looked up, smiling in her habitually gracious manner.

He bowed formally. "You are in exceptionally good looks this evening, Angelea."

Soothed by his attention, she altered her decision to banish this charming man from her presence. Long ago, he had apologized for being overcome by his emotions in the garden. He did not make Cyprian leave. That was her husband's foolish pride. Just now Uxton's offer of renewed friendship rescued her from making a public display of her feelings. It was time she forgave his small part in her painful past.

"How very gallant, milord," she responded and placed her fingertips on his arm. His warm smile strengthened her self-confidence. A man so considerate was certainly no enemy as Cyprian claimed. It must be a misunderstanding. After all, Uxton often referred to the longtime friendship between their fathers, and always spoke of Cyprian with warm regard.

"Lord Uxton!" Cyprian exclaimed, looking up from a letter he was writing to his sister. "Uxton, here to see me?"

"Yes, milord," Fothering replied. "On a matter of business."

"A matter of business! What can he mean? How did he arrive?" Cyprian picked up the marble fingers and rubbed them thoughtfully.

"He drove his phaeton."

"Any baggage in back?"

"None, milord."

"He must be staying at the Dancing Skillet or the Royal Oak to arrive at this hour. Send Eldridge to me. Inform his lordship I am occupied at the moment and will see him shortly, when I ring."

When Eldridge entered the library, Cyprian was standing at the window, staring at the gardeners. "Lord Uxton is here on a matter of business. What might he mean?"

Eldridge paused before answering, "I can think of nothing connected with him. Someone may have been his agent without our knowledge in the sale of Hillview. Might he have bought paper from your creditors?"

"I think not. Before leaving for the Colonies, Sir Deuxbury mentioned he had come into funds of late, but only sufficient to permit him an easier style of living." Cyprian returned to his desk and placed his sister's letter in an open upper section surrounded by gold scrollwork. "Ring for Fothering," he directed. "I wish you to remain. I do not trust the man."

Lord Uxton entered with a degree of confidence verging on a swagger.

He is convinced he has beaten me at something, Cyprian thought.

The two peers exchanged civilities as duelists testing each other. Cyprian directed him to a gilt armchair, upholstered in blue and cream brocade. Despite its comfortable appearance, the springs were poorly tied, encouraging its occupant to speed the business at hand.

After being acknowledged, Eldridge withdrew to the side. Cyprian sat, his back to a window, keeping his face shadowed while he freely observed Uxton's.

"The other day a box of my father's papers was discovered. In going through them, I came across this." Uxton gave Cyprian a folded sheet and shifted his position.

You'll find no ease there, Cyprian thought. Upon opening the paper, he stared, stunned, at his father's familiar scrawl. On the second reading, he understood Uxton's confidence.

> As surety for the loan of £100,000, by my good friend Elias Uxton, should the said loan not be repaid within five years of this date, I grant the land between the River Oms and the post road, containing the house known as Omsbridge Hall, its gardens, and park.

Cyprian glanced at the date, eight years old, before handing it to Eldridge. With rigid self-control, he commented calmly, "Very interesting," as a chill began working through his body.

Uxton shifted again. "No doubt you are aware I am in reduced circumstances and find it necessary to press for payment. It is, as you see, more than due."

"So I noticed."

"I assume you are as surprised by its existence as I."

"Yes. Our fathers considered their dealings the honorable matters of two close friends that need not involve anyone else."

"True." With a bitter twist of his lips, Uxton added, "My father always thought himself in your father's debt for being rescued from drowning in the Thames. No doubt that explains the reason for a loan of that size."

"Very likely. My father valued yours as his dearest companion. Odd, is it not, that we have ever been rivals?"

"Perhaps. Your virtues were compared to my failings. Without the least effort, you pleased my father as I never could. I hated you before we went to Eton. After I joined you at Oxford, everything confirmed my feelings."

Cyprian nodded in understanding. He felt his limbs fastened to the arms of his chair. "And you desire payment."

"Yes. A suitable house in town has come up for sale. I need it for a residence and these funds for its purchase. The present owner wishes to conclude the sale at the end of the Season."

"Of course." *I have but two months,* Cyprian thought.

Uxton shifted his position again. "Although mention was not made of interest on the loan, I am certain you will agree it is appropriate. Since they were good friends, I think the rate at that time of 5% would have been considered too high. However, 3% would not be excessive, do you think?"

"Which would increase the debt by £24,000."

"Er, yes."

"And should I fail to pay you the whole £124,000 within the next two months, you will foreclose and take possession of the Hall."

Uxton shrugged. "That is my sole recourse, is it not?"

"Very well. I shall confer with Eldridge regarding this matter and inform you when you may expect payment." Cyprian rose stiffly and nodded to Eldridge, who rang for Fothering and returned the document to Lord Uxton.

Fothering entered on the instant and held the door open.

"I trust you have a pleasant drive back to town," Cyprian said drily.

"Thank you. I shall."

Cyprian continued standing beside his desk, staring at the closed door. "He swore his son would live in the Hall," he murmured. "Now he thinks he can make that happen." Turning to Eldridge, he asked, "Were you aware of this agreement?"

"No, milord. I found no reference in your father's papers. Might it be a forgery?"

Cyprian shook his head. "That was my father's hand. Of course, we must consider the possibility, but I doubt it will save us."

"There is no payment to Lord Elias Uxton recorded in the last ten years other than the settling of small wagers."

"I see. How might we raise the funds in two months' time?"

"We have exhausted all your ready resources. A private loan from Sir Deuxbury and other friends might be adequate."

"Deuxbury is in the Colonies on business. Tell me truthfully, Eldridge, in all likelihood I shall have to sell the Hall to clear this amount?"

"I fear so, milord."

"Then Uxton would purchase it. He would far rather possess the Hall than any London house, no matter how grand. Search diligently for an escape, Eldridge. Inform me the moment you discover it, night or day."

A fortnight after Lord Uxton's startling disclosure, Lord Omsbridge entered Eldridge's office. With sick dread in his heart, the little man watched his master stalk about the tiny room. The tall, elegant figure lacked his normal vitality and force. Shadows around his eyes emphasized the gauntness in his face.

Eldridge's arms trembled with weariness as he leaned on his desk. The succession of late nights and early mornings had taken their toll. Lord Omsbridge ran his fingers over the worn leather ledgers recording the estate's business since his grandfather's time. Most of their pages were newly etched into Eldridge's memory.

Picking up a candlestick holding the stub of a guttered candle, Cyprian asked, "From last night?"

Eldridge nodded.

Cyprian sighed and sat down. "You found nothing?"

"No, milord."

"I am certain there is no scrap of paper in your keeping which you have scrutinized."

"True, milord."

"I, too, have searched through everything at hand where he kept papers or things of value. Nothing."

"Perhaps it is fraudulent, milord."

"I think not, much as I wish it. I was on my Tour at that time, requiring fairly large sums of money. My mother's extravagance knew no bounds, and my sister was being presented at Court. They redecorated Omsbridge House for that purpose. And, on occasion, my father indulged in speculation. It is fortunate for us he was not given to gambling for large stakes. Yes, he could have needed such a sum. And he would have turned to his closest friend. No doubt he had a means in mind for repaying it, but he died before executing it or telling me."

"He made no mention of it?"

"Only that he did not want to renew the entail on my inheritance, claiming I would have a freer hand with buying and selling the land. He said, 'I know you love Omsbridge and will do all in your power to protect it.' And he hinted at some important estate matters he must review with me that even his man of business was not privy to. Unfortunately he was thrown from his horse first. I thought we unearthed all such matters and resolved them years ago."

"And your friends, milord?"

Cyprian shook his head. "I asked two, but they were fully extended also. Between them, they could raise but £25,000. I dare not talk with others, fearing if the word gets around, other loans would be called in."

After an uncomfortable pause, Lord Omsbridge continued. "I rode out with William this morning. The lad is learning rapidly. I believe he has a natural feel for the land. And little Jenny is a bright and pleasing child. Would you please pull together funds to ensure their education and care should we be unable to save the Hall?"

"Certainly, milord." Eldridge replied, relieved at a task he could handle with dispatch. "Such sums are not difficult for me to manage."

"Have whatever papers I must sign ready after dinner. Is that too soon?"

"No, milord."

"Good." Cyprian rose, a determined set to his shoulders. "I will return immediately after dining. Then I must . . . I must ride to the village this afternoon."

Cyprian ate his dinner slowly, savoring the flavor of each mouthful. He sent word to Maggie Worth that her meal was excellent. Having conferred with Eldridge on the papers funding William's and Jenny's education, he signed them and went up to his room.

He stood for several minutes before the mirror, staring at his reflection, seeing himself as a small, eager, innocent boy, an energetic youth, and a disillusioned undergraduate. All his life there was Omsbridge. With a sigh, he opened a drawer and removed the pistol he purchased in France. Thoughtfully, he examined the grip carved with the fierce face of a hawk. The weapon attracted him because of its fine workmanship and the shopkeeper's assurance it possessed an extremely sensitive trigger and was deadly at close range. Carefully he primed it, then dropped it into his coat pocket. With deliberation, he went to each window, absorbing the views of Omsbridge. From his earliest memory he had loved this place. It was more important to him than anything or anyone else. Its traditions were part of his being. During his times of doubts and stress, it was a solid foundation, a sure haven. This was his, a sacred trust to be cared for, improved, and passed on to his heir.

Leaving the Hall on Blue Star, he rode slowly down the drive noting the glories of early summer, letting memories of his old adventures flow through his mind uninterrupted. Hardly a tree or rock existed on the estate that did not have some particular association in his memory.

Stopping at his favorite lookout, he tied Blue Star firmly to the far side of a large beech. He went to the spot affording an unobstructed view of his home. Tears distorted the familiar sight of Omsbridge Hall.

He could not prevent its going to Uxton. He failed all those who labored and died for it. This humiliation, added to his other woes, made life intolerable. As that crazy preacher said, he was condemned by God, cursed as a blue devil. His sins were beyond anything he could do to atone. Grasping the pistol firmly, he removed it from his pocket and slipped off the catch.

Twenty-six

The old white pony blew gustily as he reached to nibble the grasses sprouting beside the road. His rider stared apprehensively at the ancient stone gargoyles flanking the entrance to an estate. Their fierce mien had eroded into an evil cast. Should he venture between them, they seemed ready to pounce upon him, rip his dusty coat to shreds, stomp and tear his floppy black hat, and chew his worn boots to pieces.

The lumpy little ball at the end of his long nose quivered. Beads of perspiration moistened his jutting brow line, joined together, ran around his deep-set eyes, down his concave cheeks, and dripped from his sharply pointed chin. Goose flesh raised on his thin arms and back. The mousy brown hair hanging to his shoulders jumped as he jerked his head from side to side.

The inner urge halting his journey abruptly could not be from the Lord. It must be a temptation aroused by his base desire to see the great and wealthy and so deter him from his preaching assignment in Sussex.

Again the inner voice urged, this time sharply. "Go down that road."

"It looks to be a grand place," the man argued. "I was called to preach to the poor, the outcasts, and the prisoners. This would be casting the Lord's pearls before heedless swine." Determined not to be led astray, he kicked the pony into a trot down the highway.

"Go!" the Voice commanded.

Anxiously he scanned a distant gathering of clouds. It was coming on to rain. A side trip would almost certainly mean arriving at the inn very late, in a May downpour. Or worse, he would have to spend the night under a wet hedge. His flesh quailed at the prospect.

The white pony halted, pitching the rider forward on his neck. The account of the prophet Balaam and his uncooperative ass came to his mind. "Lord, I have not the learning or the appearance. They won't listen to the likes of me."

"My servant, you are to go where I command and speak only My words. I did not say they will like you or heed you. Jeremiah was a faithful servant, great in My sight."

The shabby little man looked upward, half-expecting to see a great thunderhead crisscrossed with darting lightning. He studied the pleasant road ahead, then glanced over his shoulder at the fearsome statues. Jeremiah's path held no attractions for him. He, too, might be cast into a deep well for trespassing.

"I have chosen the foolish things of the world to confound the wise; I have chosen the weak to confound the mighty," the inner Voice reminded him.

"Lord, I am indeed foolish. I am weak. But are You *sure*?" He clutched the reins tightly in his trembling, boney fingers, and with a deep sigh, tentatively laid them on the pony's neck hoping he would not respond. Promptly the perverse animal turned and trotted back to the drive. The rider leaned slightly and his mount headed between the carved figures as if he was going home.

Majestic, ancient beeches arched above, forming a gothic corridor. Golden light streaked between their branches. Blind to this grandeur, he looked right and left, fearing the charge of some wild beast, or the challenge of a gameskeeper.

"*I* have not given you this spirit of fear. Mine is the Spirit of power and love and a sound mind," the Voice reprimanded.

As the pony's trot became a confident gallop along the curving drive, the tremor left the man's hands and knees. Ceasing his anxious peering to the sides, he gazed expectantly ahead. He was committed to this road. The Lord was with him, as He had been with Jeremiah, Daniel, and all the others. He raised his pointed chin and breathed deeply. His palms prickled with anticipation.

Upon rounding a bend, he came upon a man standing alone, gazing across a valley toward a sprawling castle. His hands hung limply at his sides. One held a pistol. His head was slightly bowed, his shoulders slumped.

"Tell him he is My child," the Voice directed.

The elegant cut and cloth of the blue riding coat came into focus. "I—I don't know him."

"*I* know him."

The rider reined in the pony and cleared his throat. In an abnormally high and squeaky voice he said, "Sir, uh, I beg your pardon."

The man started and whirled around with an intimidating frown. "Yes? Who are you?"

The little man nearly strangled trying to swallow the painful lump in his throat. "I, sir? Er, I'm John Michaelson."

"I do not know you, but . . . you do seem familiar." He asked in a cold, repressive tone, "What do you want?"

John's cheeks flushed bright red and he felt a sharp twinge of recognition in his newly mended right shoulder. He moistened his lips and replied, "Sir, you are God's child. He loves you."

Just as he had feared, the man threw back his head and laughed a bitter, scornful sound. Silently John reminded God he had known this would happen. He laid the rein on the pony's neck and kicked his heels to make him turn about, but his mount stood still. He jerked on the rein and the pony took one step, half-turning from the man before them.

"Do you know who I am?" the stranger demanded.

"No, sir."

"Do you know what I've done?"

"No, sir."

"Then, how in God's name can you come here and speak as you did?"

John cleared his throat again. "I do not know, sir." Hearing his voice a little lower, he relaxed slightly. "I was on my way to Chichester, and it seemed as clear as clear that God told me to come down this drive. Believe me, sir, I did not want to. When I saw you, that's what He said I should say."

"You must be mad!"

"I'm sure I appear so, sir."

"Are you some special saint that God himself speaks to you?"

"No, sir. I'm a preacher. Once in a while He speaks plainly, like He did today. But it's not often."

"You must be a *great* preacher." The man's cynical eyes traveled over John's unimpressive clothes.

"No, sir," John replied, thinking of three separate stonings, the last causing his broken shoulder, and two miserable sentences served in jails shared with rats and cursing felons.

"Yet God favors you by speaking directly to you. How do you account for it?"

"I cannot, sir."

"What happens when you act on these special messages?"

"Well, sir, uh, many things." He cleared his throat. This time his voice was almost its normal baritone as he spoke. "It usually develops that someone needed that message."

"Really!" The man laughed again. "You're quite out here. If your voice said I was his child, it was not God speaking, but the devil."

"Oh no, sir. I'm not on speaking terms with him."

"But I belong to the devil. I am his child."

"Oh. How do you know?"

"Because no matter what I do, God does not forgive me. I am cursed of God as a child of Satan."

"What have you done?"

"Everything! I rebuilt the parish church at my own expense. I attend service every Lord's Day and Holy Day, although they are so deadly dull I can hardly stomach them. I pay the vicar out of my pocket and have him often to dinner. I care for my people when they are sick, injured, or aged. I have taken in my illegitimate children, two of them, and am giving them a decent home. I have not been drunk or gambled these six months. Yet the burden in my heart is not eased."

"No, sir. It won't be."

"But this is what Rev. Pettigrew preaches!"

"Sir, St. Paul wrote, 'By the deeds of the law there shall no flesh be justified in his sight: for by the law is the knowledge of sin. But now the righteousness of God without the law is manifested, which is by faith of Jesus Christ, unto all and upon all them that believe.' And Jesus himself said, 'This is the work of God, that ye believe on him whom he sent.' "

"I believe there is a God."

"James wrote, 'Thou believest that there is one God; thou doest well: the devils also believe and tremble.' But, did you know, sir, that the great God, the Creator of the universe, loved you so much He sent His Son to die for you? As Paul wrote, 'God commendeth his love toward us, in that, while we were yet sinners, Christ died for us.' For you. He was delivered for our offenses, which are many and heavy, and was raised again for our justification. The only work for you to do is repent and believe the one whom God sent. He did all that needs be done."

The man stared at him as if trying to grasp what was being said, then laughed again, bitterly. "And rebuilding the church, sitting through those dull sermons, caring for my—my *by-blows* . . ."

"Isaiah said, 'All our righteousnesses are as filthy rags.' And Paul wrote, 'For by grace are ye saved through faith; and that not of your-selves; it is the gift of God: Not of works, lest any man should boast.' This faith is God's own gift. He is holding it out to you. All you must do is accept it. Then Paul continues, 'For we are his workmanship, created in Christ Jesus unto good works, which God hath before ordained that we should walk in them.' While good works do not earn God's forgiveness, we must do them to express our thankfulness to Him for what He has done for us, and to show others that God truly loves them too.''

The laughter was gone. The man's black eyes regarded Michaelson soberly, probing for the truth in what he said. After a while he turned to face the distant castle. "It is too simple for the burden I carry."

"Oh, it's not easy, sir. It involves repentance, turning your back on what you were. You will live for God, not yourself. That is not at all simple or easy."

"Change my ways? I know no other way than to live for myself. That is all I have ever done."

"I, too, once lived only to satisfy my desires."

The man made no response, but gazed again at the castle.

Respecting the stranger's air of thoughtfulness, the little preacher remained silent. He took heart that, perhaps, this was not a senseless mission and that the voice had indeed been God's. For a moment, he allowed himself to enjoy the surrounding natural beauties skillfully embellished by the planting and tending of men sensitive to the potentials in creation. Briefly, he reflected on the marvelous possibilities when man cooperated with God in His work.

Rousing from his meditation, the man asked, "John Michaelson, where are you bound?"

"I go to Chichester, sir."

"Would you break bread with me, even spend the night? There are yet many miles for you to travel. The day is far spent and I feel a gathering storm."

"You are kind, sir, but—"

"The message you brought me is one I must hear in more detail," the man interrupted, his voice firm and authoritative. "I should indeed like to believe it, but find it impossible." He continued with some hesitation. "The recent deaths of several people lie heavy upon me. Do you see the magnitude of my burden?" His tone softened to entreaty as he added, "Stay with me awhile. Let me consider your words carefully."

Hastily Michaelson sent a petition upward for guidance. Now the Voice was silent. Without doubt it was too late to go much farther. The last word he had was to speak to this man. Nothing was said regarding his leaving. In fact, he was sent to preach in Sussex, without any specific location. He assumed he should meet with the society in Chichester. His interpretation of the command may have been in error. Obviously, here was a soul in deep need. Certainly his own body would rest far better this night in a bed under a roof than on the ground under a hedge.

"Thank you for your kindness, sir. I will be happy to stay if I may be of assistance."

The man fired his pistol in the air.

John jumped at the noise. His pony sidestepped and backed nervously.

"Please forgive me . . . it was already cocked. Come, my horse is picketted on the far side of that beech."

As they rode slowly down the curving avenue, the strange man told of his past debaucheries. Michaelson felt repelled by the sordid revelations, yet compassionate for the soul sorrow of his host. Although this man wore fine clothes and rode a highly bred, beautiful stallion, his heart needed comfort as surely as the dirty felons in jail.

"This afternoon I concluded that anyone sinning so long and heartily as I was beyond the pale of God's notice," his guide explained. "For me there was no forgiveness. I brought my gun to put a period to my bitter existence. You claim your message is from God, that I am His child, that He loves me. I laughed because it is impossible. But I want to believe it. This evening, tell me more how this can be. Show me where these things are that I may read them for myself."

As they rode into the stable yard, Michaelson felt almost flattened by the height of the ancient stone walls looming above. His host gave instructions for the care and feeding of the pony and directed that his guest's dusty baggage be carried to the green room immediately.

These orders were promptly acknowledged with "Aye, milord," and "Dracly minute, milord."

Leaving his mount in expert hands, Michaelson followed his host through a small door swinging easily on well-oiled hinges into a long hall with massive hewn beams spanning its high, arched ceiling. A man of lordly dignity appeared and was directed to show the honored guest up to the green room. There being no one else in sight, John concluded he was the honored guest. "Thank you, milord, sir," he responded and trailed after his impressive guide.

Refreshed, but troubled, John Michaelson descended for supper. His shabby clothes were thoroughly brushed and even mended while he soaked in a warm bath. His shoes never shone so brightly. The attention of several servants in the midst of luxury such as he never imagined worried him lest he be spoiled for the rough days ahead. He would feel easier in a room in the servants' wing with a tressle bed.

His host stood in the middle of a richly furnished drawing room, gloriously arrayed in blue satin, a cascade of snowy white lace ruffles falling from beneath his chin. A plump little woman gowned in black with a stiffly starched white cap on her head listened intently as he spoke.

As John stepped across the threshold, he was greeted with, "Ah, there you are, my friend. Mrs. Croft, this is the Rev. John Michaelson. You are a Reverend, aren't you? You must be."

"No, sir, er, milord. I am a lay preacher. A Methodist lay preacher. One of Mr. Wesley's assistants."

His host raised his eyebrows, gave a nod of acceptance, and said, "His every wish is to be regarded as my command."

The woman ducked her head as she curtsied. John was acutely aware of her sharp, quick scrutiny.

"Mrs. Croft is my housekeeper, a good, devout woman." John made his clumsy bow, sensing her disapproval. After she left them, he turned anxiously to his host and said, "Sir, milord, I do appreciate y-your kindness, your generosity, but I am not accustomed to such—such . . ." He flung out his hands to encompass everything. "I am in a quake that I shall embarrass you before your many servants. Really, sir, milord, a simpler room would be adequate to my needs. No offense meant, but most nights I sleep on the ground."

The tall man chuckled. "Do you find your room too confining?"

"No, sir. It is too grand for me."

"I hope you will not find it an intolerable burden. That room is but a few steps from mine. I should like to know you are near at hand. As for embarrassing me, you shall rather bring credit to me in the eyes of my household."

"I? Bring credit to *you*? How, sir?"

"With one exception, you are the most respectable guest to visit here in some time."

"Most respectable?" Bewildered, John was glancing at his old brown coat and shoes when the door opened and his dignified guide entered to announce supper.

Following an astounding assortment of tasty dishes, which John feared had lured him into the sin of gluttony, the men retired to comfortable chairs before a pleasant fire in a room of rich, dark paneling. A thick, red oriental rug covered the floor. Leather-bound volumes filled the bookcases across the far wall.

"Do you wish a brandy, my friend?" asked the gentleman host. "I noticed you did not find the port to your taste."

John licked his lips before replying. "Sir, milord, please, please do not offer me any such. I have been over fond of it—of wine, of gin. I beg of you to aid me by not offering it."

His host cocked an eyebrow, then asked, "Does my drinking bother you?"

"Oh no, milord. It is just that sometimes I find it hard to resist, and I must."

"I see. Would you do me the favor of calling me Cyprian?"

"Cyprian?"

"My name. You do not yet know my name!" He shouted with laughter. "Let me present myself; Cyprian Westover, Lord Omsbridge."

"I am honored, milord. Now I understand."

"And what is that?"

"The 'O' on the table service and the linen."

"My name is not familiar to you?"

John apologized hastily. "You see, sir, milord, er, Cyprian, I do not move in your circles. The people with whom I associate are not . . . you would not know them, nor would they know you."

"Who are these associates? Preachers? I do know some of them."

"Well, yes. But mostly, well, vendors of various kinds—tradesmen, harlots, innkeepers, shopkeepers, apprentices, er, felons of various sorts. They live in London, around Westminster, and in the towns and villages on the way here."

"How came you to Sussex? Did your God send you?"

"Well, er, in a manner of speaking. At our conference six months past, Mr. Wesley directed me to preach in Sussex."

"Six months? Were you in York or Ireland?"

"No, sir, er, Cyprian, sir. I was detained along the way for several months."

"Detained?"

John shifted uneasily in his chair. "Yes. I was, you see, well . . ."

"You were in jail?"

John nodded glumly.

"Let me guess the charge." Cyprian regarded the intricately carved beams above through narrowed eyes. "You are a preacher, but not ordained. Lacking a pulpit, you spoke outside, in a field, perhaps, and a crowd gathered. They became unruly. Naturally you were held for disturbing the peace. Possibly you were also charged with inciting to riot?"

Again John nodded, wondering if this fine gentleman would permit him to pack up his things before having him leave, or simply have them thrown out the window.

"Do not look so downcast. I have heard of several such incidents." Cyprian paused, then asked, "Have you preached at Ox Hill Cross?"

"Yes, sir."

"Oh, my friend, forgive me for throwing that stone. I fear I injured your shoulder. Was it serious?"

"I, er—it was broken."

"How might I make amends?"

"You have done, sir." John hesitated, then said, "You are forgiven, Cyprian . . . gladly. You were kicking against God's pricks. I understand, for I, too, kicked hard."

"Drinking?"

"Yes, sir. And other things. I was a wild one until the Lord caught and tamed me."

"Ah, then you do understand my distress. I nearly ended my life this afternoon. Please, tell me more that I may gain a reason to live. And show me those words you quoted, for I must read them for myself."

John Michaelson took a deep breath and made an urgent prayer for guidance as he took his battered Bible from a deep pocket in his coat and opened it to the book of Ephesians. Cyprian drew his chair beside him, and seriously gave his attention to the words pointed out by John's brown finger. "For by grace are ye saved through faith; and that not of yourselves; it is the gift of God. Not of works . . ."

Twenty-seven

As the two men talked before the library fire, Cyprian became increasingly burdened. The lift he experienced with Michaelson's startling declaration of God's love dissipated.

He exclaimed, "Oh, John Michaelson, I have sinned! Those against whom I sinned are pursuing me, crying for vengeance. What must I do to escape them? I am no child of God, for He is holy and righteous. I bear no resemblance to Him. Briefly, when you appeared this afternoon, I hoped . . . but now you remind me of God's greatness. I am far from Him! Truly there is no good thing in me! You are in error. God cannot love *me*!"

"But He does! He does indeed," countered Michaelson emphatically. "Hear these words." He turned rapidly to a well-thumbed page in the Epistle to the Romans. " 'There is none righteous, no, not one: there is none that understandeth, there is none that seeketh after God.' And here"—he moved his finger down the page—" 'For there is no difference: for all have sinned, and come short of the glory of God.'

"I am no different from you," Michaelson explained. "In God's eyes I was as guilty a sinner as you. I was a drunkard, destroying the lives of my wife and children, caring for nothing but my next bottle of gin. But, as you see here, Paul does not stop with this general indictment. He continues. . . .'And are justified freely by his grace through the redemption which is in Christ Jesus.' Not only are all guilty, but all may be redeemed, including you and me."

"But, how can this be?" Cyprian broke in. "How can a righteous God even *look* at me? You do not understand. My hands are stained with blood."

"Because He *loves you*." John turned a page and read, " 'But God commendeth his love toward us, in that, while we were yet sinners, Christ died for us. . . . For if, when we were enemies, we were reconciled to God by the death of his Son, much more, being reconciled, we shall be saved by his life.'

"Why He loved me, I know not, for I was unworthy. I—I bore the blood of my own dear daughter." Michaelson's voice cracked and faded. He coughed and wiped his eyes. "But, God washed it away. While I was far from Him, the Lord Christ himself suffered on the cross and died for me. There could hardly be greater proof of His love. I do not understand why, but he loved me and does still today."

"Then how can I . . .?" Cyprian shook his head and raised his hands in a gesture of futility. "I have tried. I have done all that came to mind as penance for my sins, but have no sense of forgiveness. What must I do?"

"Believe. You have repented. Now believe." He moved his finger up the page, then read, " 'For what saith the scripture? Abraham believed God, and it was counted unto him for righteousness.' That is, God accepted him as if he was altogether righteous. 'Now to him that worketh is the reward not reckoned of grace, but of debt. But to him that worketh not, but believeth on him that justifieth the ungodly, his faith is counted for righteousness.'

"And over here"—he turned another page—"it says, 'For the wages of sin is death; but the gift of God is eternal life, through Jesus Christ our Lord.' As the thieves who were crucified with Christ, the evil works you did merited death. But God's gift to you, if you believe, is not earned, but free. Even as the thief who believed was promised immediately life in Paradise. With his hands and feet nailed to a cross, he could do nothing to earn that or even prove the truth of his belief."

Again Michaelson turned quickly to a page much smudged from use. "When asked by followers what works they should do to do the work of God, our Lord himself is quoted in John's gospel as saying, 'This is the work of God, that ye believe on him whom he hath sent.' Milord, sir, Cyprian . . . do you now believe?"

Cyprian stared blankly at the page before him, bemused by an inner conflict. This was too simple. The preacher, a man of no real importance, was a presumptuous fool to think he could convince Lord Omsbridge of such an overly simple proposition. He recounted all he had done for the church and his offspring. Surely these considerable deeds were more impressive than an unsubstantial thing like faith—like belief.

But, if they counted so much, why was he bound with chains of guilt and pursued by ghosts? He repented of his past sins, but how could he change? As the days progressed, he would certainly return to his old ways, for he knew them well.

His eyes focused upon the words John Michaelson read. "This is the work of God, that ye believe on him whom he hath sent." Other words on the page caught his eyes, as if printed in thick black type. "I am the bread of life: he that cometh to me shall never hunger; and he that believeth on me shall never thirst." And again, "This is the will of him that sent me, that every one which seeth the Son, and believeth on him, may have everlasting life: and I will raise him up at the last day."

Slowly Cyprian raised his gaze from the page to meet Michaelson's. Firmly he replied, "Yes. I believe . . . I can do nothing else."

He felt the chains snap and the oppressive weight slip from his shoulders.

Twenty-eight

The morning sun, streaming through the open kitchen door shone on John Michaelson as he doubled over with laughter, then straightened to wipe his eyes. Maggie Worth stood beside the marble-topped table, floured hands on her hips, laughing heartily. Several maids were giggling. The scullery boy, bellows in hand, added a pipping shout.

Small Sam, the cause of the hubbub, had whisked John's hat out of his hand and clapped it on his own head. Whereupon it covered his ears and rested on the tip of his nose. The toddler then reached out, crying, "Were be de sun? It's darksome!"

John recovered himself, removed his hat from the child's head, then picked him up. Using the end of his cravat to blot Sam's tears, he carried the child to the doorway, saying soothingly, "There's the sun, in God's heaven above, as it always is. It's there even when we cannot see it. 'Tis only when something comes between us and Him that we are in darkness. My hat covered your eyes and made it dark." Taking up his black hat, he held it over his own face. " 'Tis very dark in here." Gently he held it over the boy's face and removed it quickly. "See?"

Small Sam took another reassuring look at the sun, then soberly put on the hat again, causing his audience to laugh with delight. He shoved it up above his forehead. It fell off into the flour on the table, rocking in a half circle until it came to rest on its crown.

Anticipating John, Maggie picked the hat up and gave it to him with a mock curtsy. The sight of floury fingerprints on the floppy black brim startled John into thinking, *What would Mr. Wesley say, wanting us to look neat and tidy all the time?*

165

Mrs. Croft entered from a back passageway and surveyed the riotous scene. Her presence dampened the air perceptibly. "I merely looked in at all the noise," she said primly. "I expected to see a broken platter at the very least." Then she noticed the household guest. "Rev. Michaelson! I did not think to find *you* here! Lord Omsbridge is asking for you in the dining room."

"He is? I was given to understand he would not rise for an hour yet!" John lowered Small Sam to the floor, feeling guilty at upsetting the kitchen staff and not being immediately available to his generous host. "I will join him promptly, ma'am—Mrs.—er—Croft, ma'am."

On the instant he was the center of activity. The blonde little maid snatched his floured hat from his grasp and darted away, exclaiming, "I'll fresh it wid de brush, sir."

The plump dark one took to brushing off his coat skirts with her hands while another straightened his cravat. The scullery boy dropped the bellows, caught up a rag and briskly dusted John's shoes. Maggie overlooked this wholesale desertion of duty with a tolerant chuckle. She nodded toward Mrs. Croft. "Dis be a purty start! Dere, ye be fittin' fer his lordship."

"After enticing my kitchen staff from their rightful duties!" Cyprian complained from the door to the passageway. "We may not have our dinner until half the afternoon is past! Is that any way to treat your host, John?" his lordship inquired severely.

John saw the frozen shock on everyone's face as he turned to face Cyprian. He felt his face redden as he prepared to apologize.

A charming smile replaced Cyprian's stern expression. Immediately the women were bobbing their curtsies and tried to outdo each other in explaining what had happened.

John stood still, growing hotter each second, clutching his refurbished hat, heartily wishing himself elsewhere. Why had he come here and so disturbed a well-run household?

"If you've won Mrs. Worth's favor this morning, John, you have done very well. She is an excellent cook. I look forward to a very special dinner," Cyprian said, patting John's shoulder and gesturing toward the inner door.

John paused to speak a word of appreciation to each of those repairing his appearance, addressing them by name. Jim, the scullery boy, beamed at the attention. Small Sam burst into tears when John turned to leave and tugged on the skirt of his coat. John bent to assure him he would come to see him again. He thanked Maggie for the excellent food he enjoyed the previous evening, then smiled at Mrs. Croft. "The maids have been most kind and prompt, ma'am, a credit to you."

She smiled stiffly as she bobbed a curtsy when he and Cyprian passed.

"I trust you are not displeased, milord, Cyprian, sir. I, you see, sir, they said you would not be about this hour, and I took a walk, and went to see my pony, and then"—he swallowed—"there were voices raised in argument, and I, well, sir, I seemed drawn here, and . . . you see, sir," he began afresh, "I have been in kitchens more often than above stairs."

"John, I understand. Do not feel ill at ease with me. You are free to go any place you choose in my house. Now I shall know where to find you when you are not readily visible."

The little preacher relaxed at his host's understanding and pleasant manner. "Thank you, you are most kind."

"John, my friend, last night I slept as deeply as a newborn—which I am! My leadened spirit is become as a sunbeam passing through our Victory window. Everything about me shines with newness. Truly, this is my Father's world, and as His child, I am no longer at odds with it!"

"Is there no reasoning I may advance to convince you to remain longer at the Hall?" Cyprian asked hopefully as he and Michaelson left the breakfast table two days later.

"Much as I should enjoy tarrying here, I must press on. There are many places I must preach in Sussex. With your permission, may I address your household once more?"

"Certainly. Would two hours from now be agreeable?"

"Yes, thank you, Cyprian."

"I will ask Fothering to gather the staff in the old main hall. The dias there will make it possible for them to see as well as hear you, and it will not be so crowded as the chapel yesterday. May I also tell him to set a cover for you at dinner?"

"No. I must meet with the society at Little Hampton as soon as I may, and then on to Chichester."

After making his request clear to Fothering, Cyprian led Michaelson to the library. Standing together at the tall window overlooking the garden, they watched the early morning mist rise to the warming of the sun, leaving a sparkling dewy cover glistening on grass and shrubs. Cyprian pulled the window open, permitting the chirping of several birds invisible in a nearby tree to be heard.

"You have a beautiful home," Michaelson commented. " 'Tis the closest to heaven I have been on earth."

Cyprian smiled. "It is as much a part of me as my right arm. I love the Hall, the park, the feel of this place, the Downs." He breathed in the garden scents deeply, enjoying the peace, wholeness, and joy new to him these past few days. Nature sang and bloomed before him, and he was at one with it.

"Sir, Cyprian," Michaelson began hesitantly, then paused to clear his throat. "Before I leave, would you share with me the special burden driving you to contemplate taking your life? I should like to know how I may best pray for you."

For a moment Cyprian frowned, puzzled. He felt he was trying to recall events related to another person he hardly knew. What could have brought him to such a place? Then his agony over the pending loss of Omsbridge flooded back. Tears filled his eyes. He gestured toward the garden and the room. "I am to lose all this."

"Tell me, that I may provide support during your coming trial."

Cyprian sat heavily before his desk, took the marble fingers, and turned them over thoughtfully. In recounting Uxton's visit, his father's note, and the unfruitful search, he felt his spirit increasingly oppressed. "So, in a few weeks, I must raise £124,000 or surrender the Hall to my greatest enemy," he concluded.

Cyprian felt Michaelson's hand on his shoulder and the little preacher's sympathy for his plight. He covered John's hand with his own, appreciating his kindness and understanding.

After a few minutes, Michaelson asked, "Please, tell me about your wonderful library. Have you read all these books?"

Taking a deep breath, Cyprian looked around, assuming his role of host. "No. My father read most of them. The collection was begun by my great-grandfather. My father added to it considerably. The different colored bindings indicate the sort of books they are. Histories are in brown, philosophy and theology are in red, biographies in green, poetry in blue, and his diaries in black. My father chose black over yellow because he did not want to leave his finger marks on the covers. He loved writing in his diaries, and often had ink stains on his fingers from his quill."

"A wise choice." Michaelson walked along the shelves, reading the titles. Every so often he tapped one, murmuring, "Ah yes, a good man," or, "One of my favorites."

Cyprian joined him to point out those he liked. When they came to a shelf filled with thin black volumes, Michaelson asked, "Have you read these?"

"I tried to, but they are boring. He filled pages with the minutia of life, saying little of his thoughts or feelings. They are like account books."

"*Are* they . . ."

"I found them very disappointing, for I hoped he would express his mind as some of the great diarists. But he did not."

Michaelson stared at the row of volumes stamped with decorative gold bands and the number of a year. He tugged thoughtfully on his lower lip. "One volume a year. He kept detailed records in his diary?"

"Yes. How many miles he traveled, what he ate and what it cost, the birth and death of stock, servants, a meticulous account of repairing the west wing when rot was discovered and some beams replaced. That sort of thing."

"And what was the date on the note you were shown?"

Cyprian stared at him blankly. "The date?" Then he realized what Michaelson was thinking. "But of course. I looked through his papers everywhere, but not here." Eagerly he pulled down the next to the last volume and flipped through the pages. A loose, folded sheet slipped out and would have fallen to the floor but for John bending quickly to catch it.

"What a sorry day is this," Cyprian read in the diary, "that I must place a mortgage on the Hall. But, I am grateful to a loyal friend who gave me the funds cheerfully and freely—the true mark of friendship." He opened the folded paper. Spidery curlicues of an unfamiliar hand made reading difficult.

I have this day agreed to place the sum of £100,000 for the use of my dear friend, Edmund Westover, Lord Omsbridge. No interest is to be charged for the life of this loan. Although a note pledging Omsbridge Hall was given as surety, every leniency is to be shown in permitting repayment rather than foreclosing. I owe Edmund my life since he pulled me from the Thames outside Eton. I would not, in turn, deprive my friend of his family home.

Unable to speak, Cyprian handed the note to Michaelson. Two close friends. It must have grieved them to see their sons become enemies. How ironic that in giving timely aid, his father's dearest friend also provided the means of destroying his own godson.

"Does this not change things?" John asked eagerly.

Cyprian smiled and shook his head. "Some. The debt is reduced to the original £100,000. But I have no resources to meet that amount."

"But God does! His resources are limitless!"

Cyprian raised a skeptical brow.

John looked down at his worn apparel, reddening. "I have modest needs, and my Lord supplies them. Sometimes He supplies them in peculiar ways. But I am grateful. Take heart. He will supply *your* need as well."

"My friend," Cyprian said, placing the precious volume on his desk, "I hold you in great affection and am eternally grateful to you for bringing light into my dark life. That God should deliver me from the demons plaguing me and remove my guilt is enough. I have no faith in His producing a sum like this."

"But *I* have faith, and I shall pray accordingly. When I return in two months' time, I shall expect to hear how He accomplished it."

Twenty-nine

"$\mathcal{M}$ ilord, may I have a word with you, if it would not delay you overmuch?" Rev. Pettigrew asked as Cyprian left Sunday morning worship a few days after Michaelson's departure.

Cyprian looked down at Rev. Pettigrew, his short, plump figure emphasized by his white surplice. "Certainly, Vicar. What may I do for you?" Odd, the pompous cleric now seemed imbued with an earnestness formerly unrecognized. Freed from his burdens, it was as if Cyprian saw new facets in everyone.

"I have been given to believe that there are substantial alterations at the Hall. That is to say that the tone of life has undergone a fundamental change."

Cyprian raised his eyebrows. The rapidity with which news of the Hall spread always amazed him. "That is true."

"I understand that you are not likely to entertain some of the er— that is to say, those of the er—"

"Wild, young bucks?" Cyprian supplied drily.

"Oh dear, yes, well as you say, some of the wilder element of society. Although I am confident they come from excellent families."

Cyprian frowned. "What are you trying to say, Vicar? I would think if my establishment has achieved respectability in Mrs. Croft's eyes, it is beyond the least censure."

"Yes, yes, of course. You are quite correct. Mary Croft informed me of the improved circumstances. And I must express my pleasure at this change. If it were not for this I would not speak—I do have a responsibility for the members of my family."

"Without doubt," Cyprian agreed, mystified.

"I understand that you are looking for a governess for two children now residing at the Hall."

"You have someone to suggest?"

"Dear me, yes. That is what I am trying to say. My brother, Dr. Perceval Pettigrew of Milton's Cross, was blessed with five children. His second, a daughter, is nearly eighteen and would make an admirable governess."

"I see. What has been her education?"

"You should know, my brother had rather unusual ideas. He undertook the instruction of all the children on his own shoulders. Marianne is well grounded in mathematics, geography, history, philosophy, and theology. I am certain she can read in Latin, and very likely French."

"An exceptional education for a woman."

"Yes. Well, music and art have not been encouraged. But I am confident she will be able to instruct the little girl in needlework at the proper time."

"She may do very well. Have you seen her recently?"

"No, milord. Not for two or three years. But she was a pleasing kind of girl, with nice manners. My brother wrote me regarding finding a place for her only this week."

"Be so good as to ask him to send her as soon as she may come. Eldridge will pay her a fair wage. I will instruct Mrs. Croft to ready a room and tell the children their holidays are at an end."

"Oh, thank you, milord. Thank you. I am sure you will be very satisfied with her."

Cyprian gazed out the library window to the wood on the far side of the neatly trimmed lawn. He imagined Angelea emerging, carrying a basket of berries, her pink skirts blown about, revealing her slender ankles, and her shining curls forming a tousled halo. His long-suppressed yearning for her broke loose from its deep prison. She *should* be here, but he knew not how to achieve that end. A discreet tap on the door interrupted his reverie. "Come in, Fothering."

"Beg pardon, milord. Miss Pettigrew is here."

"Miss Pettigrew?" A female version of his short, stout vicar came to mind. "Oh yes. Excellent. Has she been taken to her room?"

"Yes, milord."

"Ask her to sup with me tonight. She may begin her duties in the morning. Has she met the children?"

"I do not believe so, milord."

"Very well. I wish to introduce them myself."

Shortly before the evening meal, Fothering stepped into the drawing room and announced, "Miss Pettigrew, milord."

A demure, slender young lady entered and spread her gray skirts in a proper curtsy. Frivolous chestnut curls escaped her muslin cap. She looked up with sparkling brown eyes, and greeting him with a timid smile, creating an adorable dimple.

Astonished, Cyprian found her sole similarity to the good vicar in her stature. A physical attraction not felt for months charged through his body. Struggling to control his response, he greeted her stiffly. "Fothering, have Mrs. Worth set supper back half an hour while I take Miss Pettigrew to the nursery." He tried not to look at the attractive young woman as he explained, "The children will be asleep before we arise from the table."

Sally brought the children to Cyprian and Miss Pettigrew, dipped a curtsy, and stepped back. William bowed solemnly and Jenny made her curtsy with a shy, curious glance. To Cyprian's dismay, they seemed absorbed in the rug's design, and neither child could be brought to respond beyond "Yes, ma'am" or "No, ma'am."

Later, at supper, Cyprian concentrated on his plate while he discussed his children. "You see, they need a good deal of social training as well as instruction in history and mathematics."

"Yes. They do not seem at ease, even with you."

"I know," Cyprian said regretfully. "I have tried to make them feel at home." In a quick glance, he noted her look of surprise. He added hastily, "I must explain. The children only recently became part of my household."

"Oh? They are not yours?"

"Yes. They are mine," he admitted uncomfortably. "That is, they are, well . . . I fathered them. I only came across them in the last few months. They were living in very poor circumstances. I felt," he shrugged, "responsible." He flicked his gaze upward to determine her reaction.

"Of course." Her cheeks flushed a becoming pink.

"Not 'of course,' " he objected, frowning at the roast duck before him. "I am not usually given to concern for the consequences of my actions."

"I see."

"Do be gentle with them. I want them to be happy as they never were in their former homes."

"Certainly, milord. I will do my best with them."

Alone in his room, Cyprian paced restlessly. The fresh innocence of the young governess attracted him as Angelea had. But, beyond the physical, he was drawn by an inner beauty, a serenity of soul new to him. He longed to reach out and touch her, to possess her as he had many other women. Except, she would not be as other women, and he was no longer the man he once was.

If he was unmarried, he would woo her for his bride. Had she come to his household a few months ago, he would have begun a campaign to seduce her. No wonder the vicar was anxious to ascertain that life at the Hall had changed. His niece would not have possessed her virtue long in former days.

Now such thoughts aroused a strange conflict. To contemplate the pleasure of claiming this delightful morsel of womanhood produced an anxiety in his mind. Part of him accepted the idea. Another rejected it.

This struggle against his natural urge deprived him of sleep the greater part of the night, for the first time since Michaelson's appearance. In the morning he made an extended tour of the estate, returning tired and irritable. For the next several days, he deliberately avoided the children and Miss Pettigrew. As Feldman, Eldridge, and Fothering grew increasingly aloof and formal in their behavior, he wished he could explain his anger was not with them, but himself.

On Michaelson's last visit, he asserted that the Bible spoke to his common problems of life. In desperation, Cyprian searched out the old, thick family Bible and began reading Genesis. But God did not meet him there. He turned to the middle. The Psalms reflected his anguish, but did not give him any answers other than to trust in the Lord and to praise Him. Further on, the prophets spoke to an ancient people, providing no insight for him.

A fortnight later, Cyprian met Fothering in the entry hall after his morning ride. Miss Pettigrew was requesting a conference regarding the children's education.

Feeling cornered, Cyprian stared at the floor. At all events, he must avoid meeting with this charming young woman. He shook his head, saying, "It is a reasonable enough request." Then, with a gesture of helplessness, he added, "I do not know what to tell her. Surely she understands the instruction of children. She seems very competent. I do not wish to see her. Fothering, I *must* not see her."

Fothering replied, "Yes, milord. I will explain that you trust her judgment implicitly in matters relating to the children's instruction. I will endeavor to prevent any uncomfortable encounters."

"Thank you, Fothering." With a sigh of relief, he entered the library and went to his desk. He dropped into his chair, picked up the Herculaneum fragment and rubbed the fingers gently. Fothering's understanding and assistance helped with the outer pressure, but not the inner.

As an emphasis, he heard the sudden burst of Marianne's laughter combined with the children's voices outside his open window. They were discussing plants and flowers! Immediately, her voice conjured up her face and form and the attraction he so sternly resisted. Springing up, he shut the window, reducing the sounds to a murmur. He returned to his desk, his pulse quickened and his mind agitated.

Frustrated, he glanced at the Bible on his desk open to Zechariah where his fruitless search for enlightenment ended. He flipped through Matthew, Mark, and Luke, saying, "There must be something for me here, but where, where, where?"

Abruptly his eyes focused on some words that leapt from the page and burned themselves into his heart. "Verily, verily, I say unto you, Whatsoever ye shall ask the Father in my name, he will give it you. Hitherto have ye asked nothing in my name: ask and ye shall receive, that your joy may be full."

Faintly he heard Marianne's laughter again.

"Oh, Lord God," he whispered, leaning his forehead against his clenched fists, "save me from this torment! I am trying, but I need Your help." Then, from the depths of his being he cried, "Oh, Lord, restore my wife! Bring Angelea to me to help me resist this temptation! You are a God of miracles. Grant me this miracle."

A discreet rap on the door interrupted his prayer. He dabbed his moist eyes with his handkerchief before calling, "Yes, come in."

Fothering entered bearing a note on a small silver tray. "I beg pardon for intruding, milord, but a messenger awaits your reply. He indicated it was a matter of urgency. He is the common sort who brings Sir Deuxbury's letters."

"Thank you, Fothering. You were quite right in bringing it to me immediately." Cyprian recognized Tony's elaborate script. He tore it open to read: "I am returned from the Colonies and must spend time in town. When may I expect you for dinner?"

"A moment and I will give you my reply."

Cyprian scribbled, "Noon, the 20th," in two days' time. Then he rang for Feldman.

After instructing Feldman to continue on and meet him at Ox Hill Cross, Cyprian rode up the High Down alone. The thyme scented the air brushing across his face. He scanned the green humped downs until the swells ended in a shimmer of sunlight where sky and sea merged. The thrill and pride he normally experienced in surveying much of his land from here was augmented by an awesome sense of God's presence.

The joyous carol of a soaring lark caught his attention as he dismounted. Searching for the invisible singer, he looked into the deep blue of a heavenly window surrounded by gray clouds. Infinity stretched beyond his range of sight. Vastness pressed upon him, shrinking him to an antlike being. He turned toward all points of the compass. Everything evidenced careful, loving handiwork, untouched by man.

He always considered this his land. But he did nothing to gain it, only maintain it and use it for his personal satisfaction. Truly, this was God's land. He was but a steward.

Words from an oft-repeated psalm blazed across his mind with new meaning. "The heavens declare the glory of God: and the firmament sheweth his handywork." Kneeling, he experienced a new reverence as the Presence pressed about him, a solid reality. Who was he to raise his will against the Creator's majesty? In the psalmist's words, his spirit asked, "What am I that Thou art mindful of me? Who am I that Thou visitest me?"

This is God's land. If He chooses to give it to another, so be it. I am in His hands and loving care. The wonder of John Michaelson's shocking announcement struck him afresh. "You are God's child. He loves you." He was the beloved child of the almighty Creator! The tense string binding his soul broke. Tender warmth enfolded him, freeing an upward rush of emotion. Raising his arms skyward, he exclaimed, "O Lord, my Lord, how majestic is Thy name in all the earth!"

After some minutes savoring this strange exaltation, he rose, mounted, and proceeded toward Ox Hill Cross. His expanded view from the High Down lingered. Each shepherd and villager he saw now seemed to bear God's mark. Upon meeting Feldman, he sensed a new, deeper appreciation and affection for his loyal retainer.

As they traveled to London, he marveled at his altered perception. The high moral path he determined as suitable to his new relationship to God no longer seemed filled with rocky obstacles of things he must not do. His vision of a bleak future endlessly struggling with old habits and his baser nature was replaced with a glowing awareness of infinite love.

Even if he lost Omsbridge, he would survive and build a new life. Perhaps Tony's tales of his adventures in the Colonies would give him a direction. Many who went found a fresh start there. Suddenly he was free to explore new possibilities. Excited, he urged Blue Star forward, saying, "Feldman, tonight we'll put up at the Brown Bear near Sir Deuxbury's rooms."

Thirty

The invitation to Lord and Lady Melfords' ball provided Cyprian and Tony with an evening's occupation following their lengthy visit. Tony's tales of his adventures were a delightful diversion for Cyprian from his struggles of the past few weeks.

They arrived near ten o'clock knowing most other guests would be present and the activities already begun. After greeting their hosts, the men separated to speak with various friends.

Cyprian moved through the colorful crowd, struck by the artificiality around him. A multitude of candles cast noon-bright light over the night scene. Satins and silks shimmered in the most fashionable hues. Cascades of light feminine laughter flowed over masculine tones, ringing forced and false against his ear. Heavy perfumes combined to form the aroma of an improbable bouquet. He sensed an underlying boredom and anxiety—even desperation. In all the years he participated in these affairs, he had never *truly* seen these people.

"Cyprian, my dear!" broke into his reverie.

"Aunt Matilda," he responded with a bow.

The rotund little woman, festooned in lavender ruffles, smiled at him as her eyes pled for his attention. "How fortunate to see you. Come, you must meet your Cousin Melissa. I promised her mother I would sponsor her this Season. A dance with you would be the capstone of her evening."

"My pleasure, Aunt. Please tell me, how many cousins do I have? You always have a new one in your care."

"Unlike your poor, dear mama, the rest of us, all four, are remarkably healthy. We seem to have been breeding girls almost like rabbits. So, what with my three, Chester's five, Martha's one and Miranda's one, I've been kept busy. The others have lived in the country too long to do this properly, and so I am granted the responsibility of introducing the family to society. It is a mercy our daughters were born in different years, so I've not had to shepherd more than one at a time. And, of course, your Uncle Henry has the care of the boys. This is Melissa, your Uncle Chester's next to the youngest daughter.''

Like those his aunt introduced in other seasons, she was somewhat pretty, proper, and eager to please. He also realized she was worried. Undoubtedly, the family expected her to catch a respectable husband of some fortune. With the Season coming to a close, she was probably aware that she lacked the looks and rank to succeed.

Deliberately, he favored her with his full attention, intending to make the ball less trying. She knew her steps well, and managed to hold up their conversation in a reasonable manner. At the close of the dance, Cyprian beckoned to a young man of his acquaintance, and introduced his partner.

"Charles, you must meet my cousin, Melissa Plimpton of Nottingham. *The* Plimptons, you know."

The startled young man looked from Cyprian to Melissa, and made his bow. "Plimpton. Oh yes. It would be my pleasure if you would stand up with me for the next dance, miss."

Cyprian directed the couple toward his aunt and continued through the crowd with a chuckle. If the girl had her wits about her, with a hint here and there, she could turn that introduction into a most enjoyable evening.

With a new sensitivity, he chatted with his friends, finding the atmosphere charged with intense emotions and little real gaiety. None of the sounds carried the jubilance expressed by William and Jenny when he had taken them to the fair a month earlier.

Sipping a cup of punch, Cyprian leaned against a pillar and slowly looked over the scene, person by person, troubled by the pervading anxiety he sensed. He might join Tony in preferring the country to these pressured gatherings. Then, with a painful start, he saw Angelea across the room, flirting with a handsome young man.

Artfully she tapped her companion's arm with her fan and laughed in much the style of other young women. And once she had intrigued him with her innocence and lack of pretense. As she turned from her admirer, her glance met Cyprian's, and his heartbeat quickened. Her fan slipped from her grasp, her movement arrested. The young man gallantly retrieved the fan and presented it with a flourish. Angelea thanked him prettily, sent him on an errand, and began making her way to Cyprian. Well aware that their meeting would be noted and discussed in every drawing room on the morrow, he was uncertain whether he wanted this encounter.

"Cyprian, you came!" Angelea clutched his arm, closed her eyes and took a deep breath. "Oh, Cyprian!" She opened her eyes and gazed up at him, tears trembling on her eyelids. "I've prayed so for you to come! Please, please, take me away from here!"

Shocked by her passionate plea and his own disordered emotions, he asked, "Where do you wish to go, Angelea?" as he placed his cup on a near table.

"*Home!*" she answered, a tremor in her voice.

"It is rather early. Don't you think our hosts will be offended if we leave so soon?"

"I don't care! Take me home. Please, please take me home."

"As you wish."

Angelea pled a frightful headache as they bade farewell to Lady Melford. Cyprian scrawled a note to Tony while Angelea's carriage was summoned and a footman brought her red, fur-trimmed cardinal.

Hardly was the door closed and the steps raised before Angelea threw herself into Cyprian's arms, weeping. Puzzled by his wife's behavior, he awkwardly patted her shoulder. For a moment, kindness and tenderness melted his defensive reserve. Then the painful memory of the garden intruded. Bitterly he said, "I think Uxton will take exception to your departing with me at such an early hour."

"Uxton! Why should he have anything to say? Oh, Cyprian, dearest Cyprian, he never, *never* meant anything to me."

"Do not lie to me, Angelea. I saw you in the garden, or have you forgotten?"

"I am not likely *ever* to forget that horrible event! But, as I've tried times out of mind to tell you, it was not as it appeared. We were talking in a friendly manner when suddenly he caught me in an embrace. And then you were there. I was unprepared for either his strange behavior or your appearance. And you left, allowing no opportunity for explaining."

"No explanation seemed required, considering what I saw. You did not appear displeased. You were laughing."

"He claimed his emotions overcame him, and he begged my forgiveness in such a comical way that I laughed. I—I believed him."

"And you disobeyed my wishes. I expressly forbade your coming to town without me, or did you forget?"

"No, I know I did," she said between sobs, "but you were delayed beyond expectation. And Lord Uxton arrived, declaring his long friendship with you and offering me his escort so I might enjoy some of the Season, and I did so want to go to the parties and shop and do all those delightful things."

"Uxton claimed to be my *friend*?"

"Oh yes! He said you were very close. He pointed out several improvements in the Hall that you did at his urging."

"A lie!" he exclaimed, his anger rising.

"And, he said he had been on a long trip inspecting his Irish properties and had only just returned. His first interest was to call on you, only to find you away."

"Did he stay at Omsbridge?"

"About ten days. He rode over from the Dancing Skillet daily. We expected you would come at any time. Then your letter arrived saying you would be above a month later. His presence was required in Town, and so he offered me his protection, confident you would want me to see the sights."

Wrath at Uxton's deception and his own impulsive conclusions choked Cyprian's response. He would gladly have killed his old foe had he been present. With Angelea, the hapless victim of his animosity, in his arms he patted and stroked her trembling form attempting to comfort her. Gradually, her sobs lessened.

"And he was only a friend to you?"

"Nothing more, until you went down to Omsbridge."

Foreboding settled on his heart. "And then?"

"I refused to see him, even when he followed me to the Willows and Hillview. Oh, Cyprian, I have been so torn, and *wretched* with loneliness for you!"

The memory of her flirtatious behavior when he first saw her at the ball stifled his compassion. He commented drily, "I gather you found some young men to console you."

"Oh yes, they are kind and amusing because I am pretty. I really think some of them have the idea that being seen with me will lend them some consequence, although I cannot imagine why."

Cyprian could easily picture the conversations in the coffeehouses and at White's where they boasted of fictional conquests of his wife to an appreciative audience. No doubt Uxton insinuated a great deal beyond the facts and then, having blackened her character, left her prey to young fools aspiring to win a baseless reputation. His guilt over erroneously condemning his wife encouraged his desire to believe her innocent of any wrong.

By the time the carriage halted before the manor in the Square, Cyprian and Angelea were in a tight embrace.

Thirty-one

A ngelea poured a second cup of chocolate for Cyprian. The pleasant, familiar ritual gave her the feeling of slipping back in time. She handed him the cup with a smile and a tender kiss on his prickly cheek. Leaning back in her chair, she studied him, carefully maintaining her smiling expression. She knew her pink silk mantua enhanced her complexion and the morning sunlight she felt on her back would be shimmering on her hair.

In the coach, with Cyprian's arms about her, she experienced the most glorious feeling of safety, protection, of homecoming. She intended to secure that position. Nothing must happen to thrust her outside again into the heartless, mocking world. Nothing must deprive her of Cyprian's strength. Yet, she sensed a new tenderness in his manner, and his arrogance seemed softened. If this indicated weakness when she needed strength, it might be a problem. For the moment she set the puzzle aside.

The anguish and fears suffered the past week were resolved beyond her dreams. Instead of dreading months of deception and possibly social ostracism, she now anticipated restoration as mistress of Omsbridge. It was like waking from a hideous nightmare to a beautiful day. She would not permit anything to threaten her new sense of well-being.

Cyprian reached across the tiny table, took her hand, and placed a burning kiss in her palm. One by one he folded her fingers over, as if to protect it or keep it from being lost. "My dearest. How I've longed to have you near me!"

"And I have longed for you. Oh, please, may we go home to the

Hall today? I have so missed being there with you. We must begin again, my love."

"Your wish will be granted immediately," Cyprian answered, starting toward the bell pull. He stopped, returned to his seat, and took her right hand between his hands, caressing it gently. "We will go, but it will only be for a few weeks."

She frowned. "Only a few weeks? But why?" This sounded ominous.

"It seems my father took a large mortgage against the Hall, and I cannot find a way to lift it." He sighed heavily. "The Hall will shortly go to the holder."

"I do not understand."

"My father did not inform me. When Lord Uxton presented the note, written in my father's own hand, I could not deny it. Already, it is years past due."

"Lord Uxton!" Realizing her voice had taken on a sharp edge, she tried to temper it. "What has he to do with the Hall?"

"Our fathers were close friends. Several years ago, his father lent mine a large amount of money. The Hall was pledged for its repayment. Uxton only recently discovered the note. He says he needs the money to purchase property in town."

"Langford House."

"Perhaps so. Eldridge and I have searched every possible avenue, and have not been able to raise the sum owed. Losing the Hall to Uxton makes it an especially bitter blow."

"After what he has done to us!" Angelea exploded. She rose and began pacing the length of the Chinese rug in great agitation. "It must not be! It cannot be! Of all people in the world!"

Cyprian tried to intercept her pacing. "My dear, calm yourself. We shall contrive to work through it. We may need to retrench in Lincoln, but now that we are together, I know we shall succeed."

Engulfed with passionate hatred, she shook off Cyprian's hand, maintaining her stride. Repeatedly she struck her right fist against her left palm. "He must not! *We* must live there. Cyprian, surely you understand! That is the place for us to raise our children. Not in Lincoln or any other place. Only at Omsbridge Hall."

"My dear, I feel as you do. But it is not possible. We may raise them wherever we reside—even in the Colonies. Tony told me marvelous stories of his experiences there."

"No! No! No! It must be at the Hall. There must be a way!" Suddenly she whirled to face her husband. "My father!"

"Your father!"

"But of course. He will give me that amount. He has never denied me what I wanted."

"Could he? He might, now. I will see him immediately after we reach Omsbridge."

"No." With a solution in mind, she brought her emotions under control. She laid her hand on his arm and looked up with her most pleading expression. "No. Please, let me talk to him."

"This is a matter of business, my dear. I will attend to it."

"Please, Cyprian. I—I want to do something for you. He was very angry when you left me in London. Let me explain. Let me tell him how important it is to me. Please." She stroked his cheek gently. "It is important to me to do this . . . for you. Accept it as—as a token of my love."

"I should not," he said, placing his arms around her.

She nestled against his body, wanting to relax in the security of his care. After her agonizing uncertainty of recent days, this blissful haven must be protected. The Hall must be retained. She knew that, while her father would give Cyprian a cold reception, he must yield to her arguments.

"My dear, I must attend to my business. The Hall is my business."

With a flash of inspiration, Angelea suggested, "Then let us stop at the Willows on our way to Omsbridge. I will visit with Mother while you and Father discuss business. Once we reach the Hall, I should not like either of us to leave it for some time, as I have already been gone too long."

Thirty-two

*J*ohn Michaelson rode slowly toward a gracious paladian manor. Concern over his coming interview blinded him to the beauties of Lincolnshire. He surveyed the structure's trim, modern lines uneasily, estimating it might be a third the size of Omsbridge Hall. After mounting the steps, he hesitated, then banged the knocker. Its dull thuds sounded ominous.

His concern eased when Fothering opened the door. Surprisingly, this august man's frosty dignity melted on the instant of recognition. Fothering very nearly smiled, giving the preacher a warm sense of welcome.

After a brief wait in a green salon, Fothering conducted him to the library. In tones verging on triumph, he announced Michaelson.

The oak panelled room was cluttered with the furnishings from the spacious Omsbridge library. Lord Omsbridge's ornate desk was obscured by an assortment of chairs. Gold framed paintings stood on the floor, leaning against the far wall. Stacks of books in a near corner bore mute evidence of inadequate bookcases.

"John, you found me! I'd no way to reach you to inform you of my changed direction, or to ask you to come," Lord Omsbridge exclaimed, weaving around several chairs to meet him with an outstretched hand.

"I learned your whereabouts from Holmes of the Dancing Skillet, and came directly," John answered, gripping his host's hand and smiling.

"Had you been to the Hall?" Cyprian asked, directing him to a comfortable arm chair.

"Yes. I went there first."

"And how did you find it?"

John cleared his throat. "I did not pass beyond the front door. The outside was unchanged."

"And your journey. Have you been well? Have you been able to stay outside the gaol?"

"Yes. I fear I must have tempered my message, for not once was I stoned or arrested since last I saw you."

"Were you not!" Cyprian laughed. "You must be weakening indeed!"

At this point Mrs. Croft entered bearing a silver tray with coffee, biscuits, and a decanter of wine. She poured the wine for Lord Omsbridge and coffee for Michaelson in her crisp, efficient way. As she offered the plate of biscuits to Michaelson, she murmured softly, "I'm that glad you came, sir."

"I ordered a room prepared for you, and expect you to remain at least this night," Cyprian said.

"Thank you, sir. You are most kind."

"Nonsense. You are very important to me."

After the door closed behind Mrs. Croft, Omsbridge leaned forward and asked intently, "My friend, why am I here?" The soft, anguished words pierced John's heart as the scream of a gravely wounded man.

Omsbridge set his glass upon a table, rose, and began stalking agitatedly about the room. "Originally I could have accepted it as punishment for my evil life. But I have changed, and you said God honors that."

"True. In Ezekiel He expressly says if a wicked man turns away from his sins, he shall live and not die."

"My life *has* changed. I pray to God frequently each day. I earnestly seek to live as His child. And that is not easy for me. But I am here!" exploded Lord Omsbridge. "I implored God Almighty to save Omsbridge from Uxton's grasp, but he did not. Was I failing in something? Was I too weak in my faith that He did not hear me? How could a good God allow *Uxton* to triumph? Why would He not have thwarted Uxton's taking of Omsbridge?"

"Milord—"

"Cyprian, please."

"Cyprian, I do not perfectly understand you. When last we parted, you indicated you were resigned to this possibility and seemed set on arranging matters to make your removal a smooth one. What has happened to change this?"

"Many things. Lady Omsbridge has returned!"

"She has! God be praised!" John responded fervently, gratified that this prayer was granted, although the Hall was not saved.

"Yes, she is here. I cried to God from the bottom of my heart that He would restore her to me. And, forthwith, I was given a note from a good friend to meet him in town the next day. I did so. There I saw Lady Omsbridge at a ball. She begged me to take her home, and we were reconciled. It was truly the most amazing miracle!

"On learning the Hall would pass into Uxton's hands, she became very upset and insisted I apply to her father for a loan. I thought I saw God's hand in this to save the Hall. However, his funds were fully invested. He could do nothing until some six or more months after the time I was to redeem the note."

John nodded, firing a hasty prayer heavenward for wisdom.

"I did not realize how deeply Lady Omsbridge loved the Hall. She was inconsolable, having set great reliance on Sir Matthew providing the ready. Then she became adamant that nothing but bare walls be left for Uxton. She is breeding, you know, and is very emotional. Dr. Winther recommended I humor her. So this place is overcrowded with furnishings, and the rest is stored various places.

"Seeing those ancient rooms laid bare of things I had known all my life, was most . . . painful, as if I myself was being stripped of my past and my heritage. The last week was a horror of bare rooms and boxes I hope never to relive. I feel cast out of my home, an orphan."

Ceasing his striding on the far side of the room, Cyprian faced John and asked, "Why am I here? Why has God not answered my prayers? Is He deaf? Is He powerless?"

John reached in his pocket for his Bible and cleared his throat.

Cyprian continued, "I feel so—so alien. This place is mine, yet I am in exile."

Thumbing through his Bible, John said, "He did answer your prayer, my friend."

"How so? I begged him for the Hall and my people."

"Because He did not grant you what you asked does not mean He failed to hear and answer."

"I do not understand." Omsbridge returned to his chair.

"If I asked you for something and you said no, that would be an answer. That you deny my request does not mean you do not regard me or are indifferent to my well-being."

After a brief pause, Cyprian nodded. "That is true. It may not be possible for me to grant, or I may consider it to be not in your best interests. But how could the Hall not be in my best interest?"

"You said you felt as if you were in exile."

"Yes. True, this is my house and my land, but it cramps me. I have never spent above a few weeks in residence here at one time. It is as if I do not belong."

"God may well have sent you into exile."

"Sent me! How can this be? How can a loving God do such?"

"We can only guess what His purpose might be. But we do know that He does this from time to time. Here, the prophet Jeremiah wrote, 'Thus saith the Lord of hosts, the God of Israel, unto all that are carried away captives, whom *I have caused to be carried away from Jerusalem* unto Babylon, Build ye houses, and dwell in them and plant gardens, and eat the fruit of them . . . and seek the peace of the city whither *I have caused you to be carried away captives*, and pray unto the Lord for it: for in the peace thereof shall ye have peace.' "

Cyprian sat quietly, his narrowed eyes staring toward the window, his lips pursed.

John continued, "You see, sir, for whatever purpose He may have had in mind, He sent you here. Perhaps it is a better place for you to grow. Possibly here, away from other associations, you may better pursue your new life in Him. He may have other reasons. But, you are not here against His will. You are not here apart from His love and care. You are simply in a different place."

Cyprian frowned and sighed.

John resumed reading. "Hear these words of the Lord, 'For I know the thoughts that I think toward you, saith the Lord, thoughts of peace, and not of evil, to give you an expected end. Then shall ye call upon me, and ye shall go and pray unto me, and I will hearken unto you. And ye shall seek me, and find me, when ye shall search for me with all your heart. And I will be found of you, saith the Lord; and I will turn away your captivity, and I will gather you from all the nations and from all the places whither I have driven you, saith the Lord; and I will bring you again into the place whence I caused you to be carried away captive.' "

Cyprian shook his head slowly. "That is as may be. But what am I to do here? I do not feel at home, as if I belonged, as if I had a place."

"You belong wherever the Lord has placed you, sir."

After a pause, Cyprian asked softly, "But what am I to do here, in this small place?"

"The most that you can."

"What do you mean?"

"Time and time I have heard Mr. Wesley exhort us 'to do all the good you can to all the people you can in all the places you can as long as you can.' Sir"—John leaned forward earnestly—"God has not cast you off. He *placed* you here to do His work. Search it out and do it with all your heart. Your people here, your family, the child soon to be born— they need your ministry. God loves each person in your household, from the stableboy and the scullery maid, to yourself and your wife, and your unborn child."

Cyprian shook his head and made a gesture encompassing the room.

"Neither our happiness nor our spiritual growth is measured in the abundance of our possessions," John continued. "We think of ourselves in terms of what we own or do. Frequently we seem to find ourselves tangled in the trappings of life. However, from time to time God strips those away. He shows us our reality lies solely in Him. From the depths of a Roman prison, the Apostle Paul commanded the Philippians to 'rejoice evermore.' Martyrs discovered the glory of God's presence in dank dungeons. In the midst of death by torture, they felt God's loving touch and the support of His strength.

"Sir, the weight of responsibilities and the clutter of things may distract us from God himself. When they are removed, we are free to be centered anew in our Lord in a way not formerly possible."

"John, you are giving me some very hard words."

"I know not why you are here. Fear not, milor—er, Cyprian, sir. God has not deserted you. Rather, the days ahead will be your richest, for He ever leads us onward. St. Paul knew the rigors of stonings and beatings and imprisonment, yet he wrote to the Christians in Corinth, 'Thanks be unto God, which always causeth us to triumph in Christ, and maketh manifest the savour of his knowledge by us in every place.'

"You are God's steward. As you know, it is required of a steward that he be faithful, not wealthy. God never deserts His stewards."

"Never?"

"Never!"

Thirty-three

The travel coach rumbled along slowly, stretching the London journey into two days. Riding beside it, Cyprian gave his thoughts free rein. He had not been to Town since attending George III's wedding and coronation well over a year before. Then he rode across the North Downs, using the old Roman way. Strange, then, to see Marianne in her new position at the festivities, troubled, but still sweet and attractive. Certainly attractive to Tony, who should return soon since the Paris Peace negotiations were concluded.

He had last traveled this road six years ago, bringing Angelea down from Town to Hillview. That trip was accomplished in the happy aura of renewed relationship and dreams of saving Omsbridge from Uxton. He viewed the future as an enthusiastic youth, with similar results. Dreams splintered on rocky reality. Cyprian smiled, thinking of one dream realized: the birth of his son John, the joy of his life. The boy's eager, inquiring mind, brave spirit, and zest for exploration were a continual source of amazement and pleasure. And John loved Lincoln as Cyprian loved Omsbridge.

Thoughts of Omsbridge brought a pain, only slightly dulled by time. Severely as he felt the loss, he was surprised how depressed Angelea became. At first he put it to breeding, but she remained despondent even after John's birth. Anxious for another son, her spirits improved with her next pregnancy. But, after a long, exhausting labor, Priscilla's birth was a disappointment. When the doctor informed her she must not bear another child, she went into a life-threatening decline. These last few months he thought he detected improvement. Although she objected to making this trip, he hoped social events in Town would stimulate her interests.

On the whole, Lincolnshire turned out surprisingly well. While one merchantman investment was lost at sea, and rain at harvest time impaired the second year's rents, all his debts were now discharged. By strict management, Eldridge had created a significant reserve against the time Omsbridge became available. This might be soon if rumors of Uxton's high gambling debts were true.

As a result of building up the small place, Cyprian discovered important changes in himself and a surprising degree of contentment. The disasters actually strengthened his relationship to God and deepened his understanding of the power of prayer. That power seemed to alter him more than manipulate events for his benefit. In this, as in all things, Angelea exhibited only polite, tolerant interest when he spoke of it. He longed for the time when she would share this vital part of his life. Perhaps, as John Michaelson said, Lincolnshire was a better place for him to grow.

John Michaelson. Society ignored the insignificant little man. But repeatedly he brought timely words of encouragement and guidance. Several in his employ responded dramatically to the man's preaching, creating a pleasant lightness of spirit in his household. Some months past, he learned an angry mob had dragged Michaelson to the gaol where he died from fever. Cyprian grieved his loss. Had he only known, he might have gained his release or at least had him held in a place free of the disease.

Seeing the Dog and Crown, he realized they were on the edge of Town. Time he joined the children and Angelea in the coach.

Afternoon sunlight cast a splendid radiance over the crowded streets. Cyprian could not wish a finer day for showing his son the glories of their capital. As the carriage wove through London traffic, Cyprian directed John's attention to the magnificent buildings they passed. The boy clung to the window edge, leaning out to see ahead. With a stream of unbroken words, he dutifully informed his parents of strange hawkers and marvelous horses.

Cyprian caught Angelea's eye and smiled. Her pleasant, weary response was dampening. Since Priscilla's birth she was obedient, dutiful, agreeable, but lacked her delightful sparks of passion. Perhaps here, the site of their reunion, they could restore their early happiness.

Priscilla sagged against her mother, sleeping deeply. Fortunately a small dose of laudanum finally ended her travel sickness. This adorable child, with her thick black ringlets, was doubly precious since there could be no others.

"There's Centaur!" John shouted in excitement. "No, it isn't, but it looked like him." John pulled his head inside to look anxiously up at his father. "You will let me ride him when we are home again, Papa?"

Cyprian tousled his hair and looked out the far window to see the horse attracting John's attention. "Yes. I always keep my promises. You and I will ride him together the day after we return. It will be quite some time before you may ride such a large horse alone. Ah yes, that is a fine animal, but see, he lacks Centaur's white blaze on his left hind leg."

With a shout, John pointed to a showy bay ahead, just as Cyprian identified the rider of the first horse. Lord Uxton was doffing his tricorn to ladies in a passing carriage. For a moment the profiles of Cyprian's son and his enemy were alined. Stunned, he saw an unmistakable likeness. *My son,* he thought, *my heir . . . not my own!*

Angelea asked in alarm, "Is something wrong?" She leaned forward to see what Cyprian was staring at, letting Priscilla slide onto the seat.

"Merely Lord Uxton," Cyprian replied, amazed at his calm voice.

"Uxton? Oh, there he is. He has aged. Rather paunchy, don't you think? Well, perhaps we won't have to meet him. I suppose we must be civil, but I shall give him a flat set down if he encroaches. He has no sense of propriety."

Priscilla's mouth had fallen open and she was snoring loudly. Angelea gently pushed up her little chin, silencing the unpleasant noise and said brightly, "Not much farther. Oh, there is Helen!" She waved frantically. "Good, she saw me and will very likely call tomorrow morning. Such an adorable bonnet! We must go shopping. I feel an absolute dowd. Fashions take forever to reach Sussex.

"Cyprian, I think I shall tumble straight into bed, I am so utterly weary. I shall order a tray sent to my room. And lots of *hot* water. I shall soak in the hip bath, and then"—her voice lightened with anticipation—"then later, after we have rested, let us sup before the fire upstairs. How cozy that will be, don't you think?"

Cyprian nodded absently, his mind assailed with memories of her seductive advances after the Melford's ball, enticing, exciting him. Never had he doubted John was his own. John, the delight of his heart, heir to all he possessed.

Dazed, he stepped down before his house and went through the rituals of arrival.

Fleeing the hounds of anguish and bitterness snapping at his heels, Cyprian strode rapidly to the near corner of the square. When he glanced back, he saw a movement at Angelea's window. She might well wonder where he was going. So be it. He could no longer abide under the same roof with her and her child. Indifferent to his direction, he rushed from his betrayer's presence.

It was apparent now. That night he had opened his heart, responding to her skillful lures. Foolishly eager, he believed her tale of innocence, feeling guilt at having wronged her.

Uxton! Why him? That gauled beyond endurance. His enemy possessed the Hall. Even if he regained it, Uxton's son would inherit. So Uxton won at last. What could he do? Deny the child? John's bright, trusting face came to mind. No, he could never deny the boy he loved. How cruel that he should love his enemy's son!

Oh, God! he called out silently, *how can this be? What have I done that I should be punished this way? Why? Why? Why?*

Blindly, he hurried past St. Stephen's Chapel, into the narrow, crooked streets of Westminster. Deaf to the shouts and cries of the street people, oblivious to those brushing past him, he strove to sort out his thoughts. Pondering actions he could take, he slowed his pace. Tell Angelea her deception was revealed for what it was. . . . Banish her from his life. . . . No more would he honor her as his wife. The splendor and purity he had once associated with her was really more akin to the mud spattering his boots.

But John held her in great affection, as did Priscilla. Unquestionably, she was his daughter. Her tiny face mirrored him even as William and Jenny. The children would not understand. Telling them the truth would injure them and destroy his relationship with John. Beloved boy, a son not his own.

"Michaelson, would you were here to advise me," he murmured. "Twice before you helped me through difficult periods. But now you are dead. Where can I turn? Who is there to understand my pain, my grief? God is silent, and so remote."

He skirted a puddle, lumpy with dark forms of nondescript refuse. Where was he? Two and three storied buildings on the west side leaned against each other, blocking out the sunlight and creating an early twilight. Their overhanging structures came within a few yards of like ones on the east side. The jagged strip of sky between them was bright blue mixed with graying clouds. Puzzled, he stopped. Lost—lost in London . . . lost in the world . . . lost in the universe. . . .

Michaelson first came to him with the welcome news that God loved him. He believed it. But now? After years of a reformed life, he faced a horrible joke. Where was God in this? Had He deserted His confused son? Neither future nor past held meaning. His efforts were a futile chasing after wind. Perhaps there was no God—only men's vain imaginings. Or, perhaps Rev. Pettigrew was right, that God created the world

192

and its inhabitants and went off to concern himself with other important business. He left men and women alone to work through their tangled lives as best they could with the resources He gave them.

Dejected, standing in the muck, he hunched himself against the chilling air, and focused his gaze on the street before him.

Ahead he saw a small gray stone church, identifiable by its unimpressive, stubby steeple. Surveying the slum district, he felt conspicuous in his fine coat. Struck with the realization that no one knew where he was, he decided to take refuge inside the building where he could deal with his thoughts safe from foot pads. As he mounted the stairs he made out the name partially hidden by vines: "St. Jude's in the . . ." He had heard that name before. Where?

The vacant sanctuary was lit by the dimming late afternoon sunlight through the small west windows. Cyprian slumped in the front pew, staring at the dark oak cross hanging against the stark, whitewashed wall.

"Why?" he demanded. "Why did You let this happen? I've tried to follow You these last years. You know I've tried." Although Marianne left his household several years before, he remembered her clearly. *She* would not have put him in this position. "I've lived the virtuous life I once ridiculed. And it cost me. You know what it cost. Oh, God, why?

"You did me a cruel turn!" he exclaimed, pounding his right fist against the back of the pew before him. "Sending Angelea to me when she was breeding with Uxton's child!"

Leaning forward, he covered his face with his hands. Anger, pain, humiliation, and battered pride tore at him with goads like demons from hell.

After some time a touch on his shoulder startled him. He heard a calm voice saying, "I am the vicar of St. Jude's. May I be of assistance?"

Looking up, Cyprian saw a tall man standing beside him, his black garb so blended into the evening's shadows that his face seemed nearly disembodied. The candle he held illumined fair hair and a slightly humped nose. His compassionate gaze touched Cyprian's aching heart so gently as to be embarrassing. "Forgive me, is there a service here?" He started to rise, ashamed at being discovered in his weakness.

"No." The vicar sat beside him. "I came because of your distress."

"It is nothing. You would not understand." He spread his hands in a gesture of futility. "I do not know how to express it."

"I, too, have known deep anguish of soul, friend."

Cyprian shook his head. "Not like this, Vicar. If my enemy were here, I would kill him!" He clenched his fists, then opened his hands and clasped them together violently. "With these very hands I would crush the life out of him—with pleasure! Much pleasure. Can you understand that?"

It was several moments before the vicar answered with tight restraint.

"Yes. I have felt a passionate desire to slay a man. In fact, several."

Astonished, Cyprian peered at him. "Who are you? I . . . do I know you?"

"Dr. William Knight?"

"Knight? Knight?" He reflected a moment until he recalled the long-forgotten encounter in vivid detail. "The Dancing Skillet. You were in Sussex some years past when Betsy, a servant girl, fell from a window and—and died."

"Sussex? I had been living at Tyne-at-the-Crossroads." He was silent, as if searching through his memories. "Yes, I was there. A tragic event."

"Yes. Tragic. Did you attend Oxford?"

"I took my degree from Christchurch. Later I was a tutor at Hertford."

"And you were known as the 'Black Knight'?"

He raised an eyebrow. "Some called me that."

"While I was up at Lincoln I heard of you. They said no one defeated you with sword or tongue." Cyprian took a deep breath. "Perhaps you would understand. My enemy has stolen my son."

"Do you mean taken him?"

"No. My son—my heir—is not mine, but his. Do you understand?"

"I believe so. You just learned this?"

"This afternoon."

"Are you certain? Is there no possibility of error?"

"If you saw them you would know. He is the *image* of Uxton. It always grieved me that John did not favor me. *Now* I understand. My blood does not flow in his veins. Uxton! How he must mock me. His son, heir to all I possess—as he threatened long ago. Bad enough that he seduced my wife. But my son not mine!"

Dr. Knight listened quietly.

"We often competed at Eton and Lincoln. I always beat him. At racing, with women, at cards, anything. He hated me! One day he said, 'Someday I'll have my own from you. *My* son will have your precious Omsbridge.' And it's true. It's true! Even if I regain my estates, they will be his son's!" Anguish burst deep inside. "Is God taking vengeance on me for my sins? I thought them forgiven."

"If you truly repented, they are forgiven."

"I'd not long been God's child, and I was reading in the Gospel of John where our Lord promised His followers if they asked anything of God the Father in His name, He would do it for them. And I asked. I asked God for a miracle, to send Angelea back to me. Within the hour I received word from a friend to meet him in Town. I came. I saw her here and we were reconciled. It was the most astounding answer to my prayer."

"He promises to give us the desires of our heart. Often we are not aware of our true requests."

"What do you mean?" Cyprian recalled hearing Marianne's light laugh just before his prayer. "Oh. Perhaps it was because of the children's new governess, the vicar's niece. But, you would not understand about that."

"Milord, I am fully aware of the charms of a dimpled smile or a well-turned ankle," the vicar said drily. "You forget, the Lord God created us as we are. There is little we may tell Him about ourselves that would shock or disturb Him."

"In my life, I seduced many women. Marianne was the sweetest, most tempting woman I had seen in many a month. But I did not touch her. I could not. I was no longer the same man."

The vicar nodded.

"An heir. I needed an heir for the estate, and if Angelea returned to me, then—"

"In due time you might have such an heir. And you did."

"But he is my *enemy's* son!"

After several moments of silence, Dr. Knight said, "Tell me of your son's birth. Were you there?"

"Oh yes, I was there," Cyprian said bitterly, "eager for the birth of my heir, as were all my people."

"When did you first see him?"

"Minutes after his birth. Angelea held him at her side when I went to her. I knelt by her bed and she gave me this most precious little bundle. I took him so carefully, the first time I'd held a babe. He frowned at me as if to ask my name. I kissed his forehead proudly. Angelea said, 'You have your son, Cyprian,' and it was all I could do not to frighten him with a shout of joy. But, she had spoken a lie."

"Mrs. Knight and I have three children, two boys and a girl. I felt as you when I held our first child. The wonder of it . . . A moment that stands alone. And, since then, have you spent time with him?"

"Nurse claimed I was an unnatural father, for daily I talked and played with him. When he was but six months old I began taking him about the property, explaining it to him. I knew he could not understand, but I wanted it in his blood as in mine." With a grimace he added, "He has the wrong blood."

"You named him John?" Dr. Knight persisted.

"Edmund for his grandfather and John because it means 'beloved.' I prefer calling him John. I thought when he is older he would like to know its meaning." He paused, then exclaimed, "I have been robbed! I love him deeply, and he is not even mine!"

"How old is he?"

"Five. Tall for his age, and quick in understanding."

"And has he learned to ride? Does he love the land?"

"Yes. He has his own pony. He has a good seat and a brave heart, a little braver than his skill, but his instincts are good. And he likes the special places, the glades where squirrels hide their nuts, the fairy ring under the old beech, and the ancient lookout tower, and the mysteries of the forest. Like all the children, he loves the land."

"You have others?"

"Three. John's sister Priscilla, and"—Cyprian shifted uncomfortably—"William and Jenny, my-my . . . But *John* is also—another's. My enemy's son!"

"Think, is he not truly *your* son? *You* held him when he was but minutes old. *You* molded him. *You* trained him. He is *yours*."

"Even though his blood is tainted?" Cyprian asked in surprise.

"God entrusted you with this child, and you treasured His gift. You need not let another rob you."

Cyprian considered these words hopefully. "A gift from God?"

"I should say so. A life for you to nurture and direct." After a pause, the vicar asked, "And what of your wife?"

"Angelea? What do you mean?"

"You must forgive her."

Cyprian leaned back against the pew, closed his eyes, and shook his head. With a sigh he said, "Vicar, you ask too much. She deceived me. She made me think *I* had wronged *her*."

"Had you?" the vicar interrupted.

Startled, Cyprian looked over at his interrogator. He nodded. "Yes. Yes, I wronged her. I believed her guilty when she was innocent. I think she was innocent, then. But she might not have been. When I took her back, I loved her, cherished her. In return she . . . she gave me kindness and deceived me with . . . *her* offspring."

"You said John has a sister?"

"Yes. Priscilla."

"And is she your child?"

"Oh yes. She has my look about her."

"So she gave you more than kindness and young John."

Cyprian looked over at the vicar in surprise. "Yes, she did that. She was happy and excited before Priscilla's birth. Not like with John's. Then I had to cheer her up. I thought she was anxious over giving birth for the first time. Having survived the experience, I thought she anticipated the second with more composure. Ironically, that one nearly cost her life. The doctor insisted on no account must she bear another child. We were both bitterly disappointed.

"One day I discovered her weeping uncontrollably. As I tried to calm her she said, 'And it was all just for a girl. I so wanted a son for you.' I tried telling her John was quite enough, but that did not console her. There has remained a wall between us all these years, blank and solid. I could not destroy it. Now I understand.''

"Yes. Mrs. Knight and I passed through rending times. We had to give up our pride and open our hearts to each other. God made our life together whole again. Doubtless, your wife suffered greatly, living a lie, fearing your discovery of the truth. . . . She needs your forgiveness.''

"Vicar, she did the unforgivable. You ask the impossible.''

To Cyprian's surprise the vicar agreed. "True. I do. The Christian life is impossible. It cuts across our instincts. Only the indwelling Holy Spirit makes it possible.''

Cyprian struggled with his meaning. It sounded very like something John Michaelson would say.

"You mentioned repenting of your sins and becoming God's child.''

"Yes. Yes. I was on the point of shooting myself. A man of God forestalled me, telling me of God's love. He was a Methodist preacher, John Michaelson. It was then I left my old way of living.''

"Indeed?'' The vicar nodded. "My wife heard John Wesley preach some years past. The experience changed her life. When you became God's child, the Holy Spirit came to live in you. He produces Christ's life in you, giving you power to live what is impossible—a Christian life.''

"I have endeavored to live a godly life.''

"You do well. In a recent book, William Law wrote, 'True Christianity is nothing but the continued dependence upon God through Christ for all life, light, and virtue . . .' And, 'Nothing but God in man can live a godly life in man.' The Spirit is in us. We must permit Him to live Christ's life in us. As Law pointed out, 'God must be all in all in us here, or we cannot be His hereafter.' ''

Staring into the darkness, Cyprian tried to absorb his words. "You are right. I cannot do this of myself.''

"Are you familiar with the prophet Hosea?''

Cyprian hazarded a guess. "In the Old Testament?''

"Yes. His wife bore children not his, and left him to become a whore. God commanded Hosea to love her.''

"He cannot have done! What did Hosea do?''

"He bought her out of prostitution, established her in his house, demanded her faithfulness and pledged his to her.''

Cyprian sat in stunned silence. At last he murmured, "He did that? He truly did that?''

"He did.''

For several minutes Cyprian stared into the darkness, trying to take in the enormity of Hosea's action. "God required that of him?"

"So Scripture records. And, you know our Lord's words when the rulers brought a woman taken in the act of adultery."

Cyprian nodded.

"He told her accusers, 'He that is without sin among you, let him first cast a stone against her.' "

"I am not without sin."

"None of us are. With Peter, our Lord set the standard for forgiving at seventy times seven. He even forgave His executioners while hanging on the cross.

"You say it is impossible. I, too, struggled along this thorny way. But, with God's grace and the power of the Holy Spirit, the impossible is possible." After a moment's pause he added, "It is even possible to forgive your enemy."

"Forgive Uxton! Never! Never! He seduced my wife and . . ." His voice faded as memory challenged his right to complain. "You ask too much," he finished weakly.

"*I* am not asking this," Dr. Knight responded. "Whenever we pray the prayer, we say, 'Forgive us our debts, as we forgive our debtors.' After teaching this to His disciples, Matthew quotes our Lord saying, 'If ye forgive men their trespasses, your heavenly Father will also forgive you. But if ye forgive not men their trespasses, neither will your Father forgive your trespasses.' It is a command for us to obey."

"That is a hard saying, Vicar."

"A very hard saying. Forgiveness is difficult labor worthy of a Christian, one who follows Christ's teaching and example."

"But—but John Michaelson said we are not saved by works," Cyprian objected lamely.

"True. As the church says, 'The only instrument of salvation is faith.' But, having experienced His salvation, we do God's works as His children, demonstrating His love to all mankind—even our enemies. Even Uxton."

"I must do God's work as I once did the devil's."

"Exactly."

"Impossible!"

Dr. Knight grasped Cyprian's arm, saying, "Never think the Christian life is easy. The costs are high. God promised a fight, not ease. He gave us armor and assured us that He is with us *when* not *if* we go through deep waters or fire. Remember, it took our Lord to the cross! We have no cause to expect an easier path!"

Thirty-four

As Cyprian handed Dagon his tricorn and gloves, he inquired after Angelea.

"Lady Omsbridge retired about an hour ago," was the reply.

"Thank you." He shrugged his shoulders wearily as Dagon assisted in removing his heavy coat.

"Mrs. Banks prepared a lamb pastie. Will you take it in the library?"

"Yes. That will be fine." He felt no hunger, but refusal would be unappreciative.

Fire and candlelight filled the library with a welcoming glow. Spent from his difficult talk with Dr. Knight, Cyprian dropped into a deep chair and examined the tips of his muddy boots. Knight. He chafed against what that vicar said.

Dagon entered carrying a silver tray with the pastie and wine.

"I fear I shall be in your black books if my boots are not removed— but, I am too tired to mount the stairs. Please send Feldman with my slippers."

"Certainly, milord."

Dutifully, Cyprian took a bite of pastie and sipped the wine. He sighed, shifted his body to a more comfortable position and closed his eyes. What should he do?

Years ago, in this very room, he and Tony described the ideal women they would woo and win. He thought Angelea his, but she cruelly deceived him. Dr. Knight said he must tell Angelea he forgave her. Words easily said. But how? The vicar also said she doubtless suffered greatly, fearing discovery. With reason. The child so clearly resembled Uxton that her secret was bound to be revealed. No wonder she was reluctant to come up to London. It was a marvel that she came. Out of desire to see her former lover? Not likely. The disdain she expressed on seeing him was genuine.

Of all men, why must she take Uxton as her lover? The thought of him touching her, of her welcoming his advances was intolerable! Forgiving that monster was too much to ask!

Feldman entered, distracting Cyprian from his thoughts.

As he tugged off the offending boots, Feldman asked, "Shall I inform Dagon you are not at home to callers?"

"Please. I am weary beyond measure."

After Feldman left, Cyprian dispatched the contents of the tray methodically, unaware of its taste. Angelea. How could he forgive her? Finally he concluded she may have been unfaithful with Uxton, but surely their relationship was too brief to say she took the man as her lover.

Physically refreshed by rest and food, Cyprian climbed slowly to his room. He paused before her door. Perhaps Uxton forced himself on her against her will. If so, why had she not told him? But then, she had no cause to think he would believe her.

On impulse, Cyprian removed a candle from a nearby sconce and continued up to the nursery.

First he stood beside Priscilla's bed, studying her sweet face. Black ringlets strayed out of her nightcap, curling over a rosy cheek. Her lips were parted as she breathed deeply and steadily. By chin, eyebrow, the tilt of her nose, she could be the incarnation of his great aunt Jane's childhood portrait hanging in the gallery.

Then Cyprian turned to John's bed. The boy was partially twisted in his bedding. One arm was flung over his head. The other hugged a small stuffed horse to his breast. As he studied the child's face, John's eyes opened wide and he looked about anxiously. His frown melted into a smile and he sat up, reaching toward his father.

"I told Prissy you'd come to see us," he whispered. "But she fell asleep while we waited."

Cyprian gave the boy a quick hug, lit John's bedside candle and extinguished his own. The moment he sat on John's bed, the boy scrambled onto his lap and began a whispered account of what he had done since arriving. He frequently interrupted his narrative urging they do certain things on the morrow.

Cyprian tucked a quilt around the boy while listening to the flow of words. He tightened his arms about John, defying anyone to break his hold.

John finished his recital, looked up at Cyprian in his customary direct way, and asked, "We will do that in the morning, won't we?"

Startled, Cyprian stared into John's earnest eyes, seeing Uxton's challenge.

"We will, won't we?" John persisted. "It's important, you know."

"Yes, John. But tomorrow I must go to the City on business. When I return, I will take you and Prissy for a walk in the park, or for a ride. Then we will decide what we three will do, what we will do with Mother, and what you and I, alone, will do. We will be here several days. Everything need not be accomplished tomorrow."

John frowned. "Are you angry with me for staying awake to see you? Nurse said I must go to sleep, but I could not."

"No, I'm not angry. Why do you ask?"

"You called me 'John.' "

"That is your name."

"But you always call me 'my boy' except when you are angry. If you are very angry you say 'Edmund John.' "

"Oh, I see." Firmly, Cyprian blocked Uxton's image from his mind and ran his index finger down John's nose, around his mouth to the point of his chin. "No. I am not angry with you . . . my boy. We will walk in the park tomorrow."

"Or ride," John amended as Cyprian laid him down. "What if Nurse takes us to the park before you come back?"

"I shall find you wherever you are." Cyprian kissed John's forehead, relit his candle, and descended to his room. Such a sensitive lad. He must be careful not to destroy his trust.

After Feldman left him in his banyon, Cyprian strode restlessly around his room. He stared at the fire, drew back the curtains to gaze at the dim shapes of the darkened city, and inspected the oriental design in the rug. None provided inspiration for resolving his dilemma with Angelea.

At least he understood why their relationship was so cool. Did he want that to change now? He thought of their early days of marriage. Her warmth and childish delight had pleased him greatly. Yet, even then, she became wary when he talked of their future family and his plans for his heir.

Following her miscarriage, she seemed as eager as he to have a son. It took all his resolve to exercise the restraint the doctor ordered until she was fully recovered. Actually, he welcomed the Resina trip, anticipating their reunion after her convalescence was completed. But he found Uxton at her side. She claimed it was an innocent event, successfully twisted by Uxton to separate them. Uxton's plans had succeeded far too long.

She looked like a blue and golden angel at the Melfords' ball. Her surprising eagerness for him so answered his own needs that he welcomed her readily. But she must have been aware of her pregnancy even then.

On their trip to Omsbridge, the idyllic nature of their reunion was marred by Sir Matthew's inability to raise the mortgage on Omsbridge and Angelea's feeling poorly. He later ascribed that to early pregnancy. Not so early as he thought. She surprised him pleasantly by graciously accepting William and Jenny and his sense of responsibility toward them. Perhaps she thought this evidence of his own sins would make him kinder in dealing with her, when he learned the truth. Certainly in condemning her, he condemned himself. His past behavior deprived him of self-righteous indignation. He was not without sin.

But, she deluded him for five years, building an irreproachable barrier of affectionate graciousness. Although she rarely complained, and was not overly demanding, he felt his prized treasure had been replaced by an imitation.

Wearily, Cyprian descended for breakfast. Finding the food on the sideboard offensive, he glumly sipped a cup of chocolate. Dagon informed him that Lady Omsbridge was in the garden selecting flowers for the house. Several hours remained before he was expected in the City. With a sigh, he left the table. Certainly he could deal with business better if this situation was resolved.

He walked slowly into the garden, praying, "Lord God, guide me. Give me Your words and Your grace to forgive. This is beyond me." If God provided the prophet Hosea strength to do the impossible, perhaps He would do as much for his unhappy son, Cyprian.

Then he saw Angelea, a man at her side as once before. On the instant he whirled about, striding toward the house, his anger flaring. But, halfway back, he turned, reversing his steps. From a vantage point on the path he saw the man, holding a wicker basket, bend and retrieve something from the ground.

Martin, Cyprian thought. *It's only young Martin.* Gradually, his fingers unclenched and the sick feeling dissipated.

───── Thirty-five ─────

With excessive deliberation, Angelea dropped a red rosebud into Tom's basket and studied those higher on the trellis. Certainly this was better than facing Cyprian in the house. But how long could she delay? Perhaps if business took much of his time, she might avoid him by busying herself with household affairs, shopping, and paying social calls.

During her sleepless night, hurt over his abrupt departure and absence from their supper matured into anger, and resolved into anxiety. Had he penetrated her secret, that deception that became a barrier, isolating her? Only a desperate hope that returning to the site of their reconciliation would revive their troubled relationship had lured her back to Town. A disastrous mistake. Never should she have left the safety of Lincoln, or permitted John to come.

Yet, as he grew older, her depressing sadness also grew, compounded by increasing terror. Any day she might be discovered and cast out. Even the early days at Omsbridge, which she expected would be delightful, were dulled by the pall of her guilt. In Lincolnshire she felt stifled, unable to live freely. Her one encouragement was seeing the light of anticipation restored to Cyprian's eyes after she agreed to come to London with him. He laughed more, as he used to, and his step was more energetic.

But coming to Town did not allow escape from her bonds forged by fears of discovery. This house heightened her constant awareness of betraying the man who plainly loved her. Here she deliberately used his affection to avoid social disgrace. Success kept her from being the loving wife she wished to be, and blocked her responses to his many fond advances. Knowing her apparent indifference hurt him increased the weight of her guilt.

How she regretted giving in to Uxton's amorous advances! The brief respite from her intense loneliness and frustration over Cyprian's rejection was as nothing compared to the years of anxiety she spent trying to conceal her action. At the time, it was an impulsive attempt to fill the void in her life. His subsequent treatment shoved her into total despair. Although Cyprian rescued her, she discovered an immense gulf between them. She did not know how to bridge that gulf without admitting her guilt, and she knew he was unable to understand it or to deal with it.

Snipping a half-opened bloom, she thought she hardly knew how to behave with Cyprian since she had learned of his religious turn. Before, she might have admitted her error, fighting his inevitable, bitter scorn with his own past. Now, she feared certain judgment, knowing full well she deserved it. At times she found herself envious of the strength he exhibited in Lincolnshire when he sustained major crop disasters. She longed to possess this ability to rise above circumstances and face her own fears. Even more, she yearned for freedom from that sense of wrong, draining the joy out of her life.

A step on the graveled path recalled her to her surroundings. She must compliment Engels on the perfect condition of the garden. "You have tended these bushes well, the roses are—" Her voice died on recognizing Cyprian. The shears slipped from her fingers and she felt her heart make an uncomfortable thud.

"I—I thought you were Engels," she murmured, glancing off to one side. Suddenly, she gasped with sharp pain, and dropped the offending rose to suck her bleeding finger.

Cyprian gently took her hand and pressed his handkerchief to the small wound. "Come, let us go to the arbor bench," he said, tucking her injured hand under his arm.

"But the flowers must be placed in water immediately," she objected anxiously.

"Of course," he said promptly. "How thoughtless. Martin, please take the basket to the kitchen and have the flowers placed in water immediately."

"Yes, milord." The man bowed and departed.

Cyprian raised his voice. "Engels!"

A man in brown jerkin appeared at the end of the path. "Yes, milord?"

"I noticed the hedge in front of the house is in urgent need of trimming. You will need Martin's assistance."

"Yes, milord." The man hurried down the path.

Cyprian's forefinger tilted Angelea's chin upward until she met his gaze involuntarily. He smiled and said, "No need to worry about the flowers. Now we may have some time to ourselves in this beautiful place."

"As you wish, milord," she answered with meek resignation.

They strolled along the graveled walk in silence. As they turned the corner into the wisteria arbor, he commented, "You seem agitated, my dear. Is anything wrong?"

"No, no, not at all. It is pleasant to be here," she answered, studying the freshly raked path ahead. "It is a remarkably fine day."

"Yes. You bring the sunshine with you. I trust you slept well."

"Very well, thank you."

"I regret my return was delayed until after you retired."

In spite of the tightness in her throat, she shrugged and said, "It does not signify."

He led her to the bench under a wisteria vine, thick with fragrant, purple blooms.

Nervously she asked, "Will you want me very long? John and Priscilla expect me to take them for a carriage ride this morning."

"They are in good hands and will not lack attention from their nurse." He paused, then commanded, "Angelea, look at me."

She obeyed apprehensively. "You . . . are . . . displeased?"

"Very."

"Oh." Tears blurred her vision and she felt taken with sudden chill despite the sun's warmth.

"The time of deception is over. We must deal together in truth."

With her free hand, Angelea wiped her wet cheeks. In panic, she vainly tried to think of a means of escape or a way of preventing his speaking. Her mind was blank.

"It does signify that I was not here to sup with you as you asked. The shadows beneath your lovely eyes tell me you are troubled and did not sleep. I am displeased that you do not confide in me."

"Oh . . ." Helpless to delay her fate, she turned her attention to the ground and sniffed, dabbing at her nose with his handkerchief.

"Angelea, I feel a wall between us. It must be removed."

"It may not be wise," she protested. "Some walls protect and shelter, like those around a home."

"For these past five years, I have felt a—a blight on our happiness."

Would he never stop? Unable to stop her trembling, in desperation she tried diverting his attention. "Our happiness was blighted nearly two years earlier."

"True. But this concerns John."

She tensed. "John? How is that possible? He was not even born."

"But he was conceived. As I remember, he was an eight-month baby."

She stared at him, her lips quivering. Beads of moisture dotted her forehead. She had difficulty framing words with her stiff lips. "Are you suggesting that I . . . that he. . . ?"

They sat as if molded of porcelain. Then he sighed. "I am not suggesting. Tell me how it came about. I must know."

Tears flowed down her cheeks. "How c-can you talk like this?" she whispered.

"I am sorry to distress you so."

Recognizing the implacable firmness in his voice, she bowed her head in resignation, steeling herself against the inevitable.

He waited, as if gathering courage for a fearsome risk. "I know John is not my son."

His words vibrated through her mind, nearly obliterating his voice. Her worst fears became shattering reality.

"I have no intention of disowning him or you," he added, "but I must know what happened." He removed his handkerchief from her clenched fingers and patted her face dry.

Mutely, Angelea awaited the scathing denouncement of her proud husband.

He took a deep breath. "Let me hazard a guess. You were hurt and lonely when I shunned you, not believing you, not even permitting you an opportunity for defense, and Uxton made himself agreeable."

"You know?" she exclaimed, looking up in amazement. She expected to see his features flushed and distorted with rage. They were not. Actually, his skin seemed paler than usual.

"Uxton has been my enemy since boyhood. I know him well. Too well."

Between sobs, she said, "That awful day, when you left here, he returned in the evening but I refused to see him. I went to the Willows, then Hillview, hoping to meet you there. But you did not come." Her words came tumbling out, released from their long captivity. "He called and apologized for the trouble his presence had caused. He inferred you were consoling yourself with—with some attractive . . . guests."

He frowned. "Wild, young bucks. None were women."

"I did not return to Town for a year, you know." The more she talked, the greater her sense of relief. "When I did, I saw him occasionally at social events, usually at a distance. Then, we met at the beginning of that last Season. He was kind. And you were not here. And I was miserable and so lonely! He sent flowers and called. He professed true affection for me, long lasting, since we had first met, before I was married. Finally, out of loneliness, I gave way. I know I should not have done, but—but I was so—so unhappy and—and . . . I wanted so to be loved. I have always been loved. Oh, Cyprian, can you forgive me? Is it possible to forgive the unforgivable?" She raised her hands to him, pleading for understanding, then dropped them to her lap, quailing before his stern expression.

After a period of silence, in a surprisingly tender tone he asked, "And when you told him you were to have his child?"

"He—he l-laughed, and—and . . ." Astonished, she felt his arms about her, holding her tightly. She pressed her face against his shoulder, sobbing. He stroked her back comfortingly.

"And he dropped you promptly."

She nodded, her yes muffled by his coat.

"And when you saw me, you decided to seduce me and solve your problem."

Again she nodded, then pulled back to add, "But it was not like *that*. I had longed for you since you left me here. My happiest days were with you at Omsbridge, before you went to Resina. I wanted so to return to that time." She drew a sobbing breath. "But it was all wrong. We had to leave Omsbridge. And John was born in Lincolnshire. And I watched him grow, looking more and more like—like that man. I feared any day you would see the likeness.

"I thought our next son would make it right. But it was only Priscilla, and the doctor said I must on no account bear another child. I despaired of life. You married me to gain a son, an heir. And I failed you. I couldn't bear it for you to discover the truth. You would hate me and send me away again and . . . I would die," she ended in a whisper.

She felt his lips brush the crown of her head; then he rested his cheek on her hair, rocking her. "My dearest Angelea, I forgive you." His unbelievable words soothed her ravaged soul like a healing ointment. "Have no fear, my love," he continued. "You are more important to me than an heir, and infinitely more precious than anything I own. I'll never willingly part with you."

Thirty-six

*C*yprian strode into the park, seeking the children and their nurse. Business and afternoon traffic had delayed his return from the City beyond expectation. Finally he saw Priscilla and her nurse, conversing with a woman appearing to be another nurse. John was not to be seen.

Anxiously he looked about for the lad. He saw him talking to a man holding a black Arabian much like Centaur. As Cyprian drew near, the man gestured as if offering the boy a ride. John began digging a hole with his right toe behind his left heel. Cyprian knew he was struggling with his fascination for beautiful horses, his desire to feel that powerful animal under him, and his shyness of strangers.

The man turned slightly, and Cyprian knew him for Lord Uxton. Icy rage halted his forward movement. That man with his son! How dare he? Cyprian wanted to call him out.

The vicar seemed to whisper in his ear, "Our Lord requires us to forgive those who wrong us even as He forgave those crucifying Him. It is not a choice. It is required."

"It is too much," Cyprian argued in his heart. "I cannot do this. Not for him."

Michaelson's words came in answer, "God gives grace and strength to do His will. Act in obedience and you can do the impossible."

He resumed walking, slowed by his internal conflict, observing John's indecision as he approached. Would his love of beautiful horses win him over?

The crunch of Cyprian's footsteps caught John's attention. Instantly he ran to grab his father's knees. Cyprian caught him up in his arms and received a strangling hug. "What have I here?" Cyprian asked lightly. "A monkey? A squirrel?"

John shook his head.

"Then what do I have?"

"Your own boy, John," he whispered.

Dr. Knight's words leapt from his memory. "God entrusted you with this child, and you treasured His gift. You need not let another rob you."

Uxton was truly the merest montebank. He would not permit such a person to defraud him further.

"Hello, Omsbridge," Uxton said with a nod. "I was just showing the boy my mount. He took a liking to him." His malicious, triumphant tone belied the almost pleasant smile curving his lips.

Clasping the boy in his arms, Cyprian sensed John as his beloved son on a deeper level than Uxton could imagine. For a moment Cyprian felt he glimpsed himself as he was before Michaelson found him. Cynicism, pride, darkness, and death marked Uxton's shallow life as it once marked his own. For all his conquests, no beautiful woman stood at Uxton's side to share his life. No child gave him adoring love like John's. Despite his elegant pose, his spirit was poverty-stricken.

By contrast, Cyprian perceived his own growth during these past years. While still far from perfect, he was vastly different from the self-centered man he had been.

Squinting into the late afternoon light, feeling a loving commitment to John, he said, "A fine piece of horseflesh. We both appreciate good horses." Staring meaningfully at Uxton, he added, "*My son* and I understand each other perfectly."